HOPE IS NOT A PLAN

HOPE IS NOT A PLAN

The War in Iraq from Inside the Green Zone

Edited by Thomas Mowle

Foreword by Larry Diamond

PRAEGER SECURITY INTERNATIONAL
Westport, Connecticut • London

Library of Congress Cataloging-in-Publication Data

Hope is not a plan : the war in Iraq from inside the Green Zone / edited by Thomas Mowle ; foreword by Larry Diamond.
    p. cm.
  Includes bibliographical references and index.
  ISBN 978–0–275–99445–7 (alk. paper)
1. Iraq War, 2003- 2. Iraq—Politics and government—2003- 3. United States—Politics and government—2001- I. Mowle, Thomas S. II. Title: War in Iraq from inside the Green Zone.
DS79.76.H67   2007
956.7044'3—dc22   2007000065

British Library Cataloguing in Publication Data is available.

Library of Congress Catalog Card Number: 2007000065
ISBN-13: 978–0–275–99445–7
ISBN-10: 0–275–99445–7

First published in 2007

Praeger Security International, 88 Post Road West, Westport, CT 06881
An imprint of Greenwood Publishing Group, Inc.
www.praeger.com

Printed in the United States of America

The paper used in this book complies with the
Permanent Paper Standard issued by the National
Information Standards Organization (Z39.48–1984).

10 9 8 7 6 5 4 3 2 1

To The People of Iraq,
Who deserve peace and freedom

CONTENTS

Contents

FOREWORD

Larry Diamond

This book was submitted for publication in the fall of 2006 as the tragedy of America's postwar engagement in Iraq was deepening. Neither an increase in American troops (to 145,000) nor an intensive security initiative to stabilize Baghdad appeared capable of containing the mounting bloodshed and sectarian strife. At least 14,000 Iraqis died in the first six months of 2006 (over 3,000 in June alone). With Iraqis being killed at an annual rate of some 30,000 per year, the country was slipping into a state of civil war. Dozens of bodies turned up each day, often bearing signs of unspeakable torture and mutilation. People disappeared from roadblocks and homes, never to be seen again. Terror so gripped Baghdad and some other urban areas that people huddled in fear in their homes to avoid murder or kidnapping. An estimated half million to a million Iraqis fled the country. The police became riddled with corruption and sectarian vengeance, heavily penetrated by the very militias they were supposed to contain. Between September 2004 and October 2006, according to official American military statistics, about 4,000 Iraqi policemen were killed and more than 8,000 wounded. By September 2006, the Sunni-based insurgency had intensified, along with American casualties, despite the killing of the leader of al-Qaeda in Iraq, Abu Musab al-Zarqawi, three months earlier. Meanwhile, the Iraqi government that took office following the December 2005 national elections remained crippled by corruption, weak leadership, and paralyzing political and sectarian divisions. Any hope of "victory" had long since evaporated. The only question that remained was whether the United States could find some way to bolster or pressure the competing Iraq political forces to act more effectively before the situation completely collapsed.

How did the United States find itself in such a disastrous situation?

Historians will spend much of the next generation of military and strategic scholarship trying to answer this question. In doing so, they will find this volume of considerable value. *Hope Is Not a Plan* is not the first book to chronicle the shocking failures of planning, preparation, and strategy on the part of the United States in Iraq. Titles like *Squandered Victory, Fiasco,* and *State of Denial* already attest to these in considerable detail.[1] This book is unique, however, in that it contains the forthright accounts of military officers who volunteered to serve in Iraq in various planning and operational capacities during 2004 and 2005 (with the book focusing principally on the transitional year following the transfer of power from the Coalition Provisional Authority on 28 June 2004). In this sense, it represents the first systematic and detailed public account, from within the military and based on direct operational experience, of three seminal types of failings, as summarized by Thomas S. Mowle in Chapter 1: "absence of robust strategic planning, ignorance of the ground truth, and lack of integration across lines of operation." In fact, if one looks for a concise anatomy of the American failure in Iraq, Mowle's dry but devastating conclusion may serve as well as any: "If you fight a war without solid intelligence, an adequate and robust plan for victory, and a well-integrated effort, problems will compound until one is left with no options that offer much hope for success." And indeed, problems have compounded (or in Secretary of Defense Donald Rumsfeld's immortal words, "stuff" has "happened") for three-and-a-half years of "post-war" war, until all that America is left with is a disintegrating hope that staying the course will (by some unknown future date) bring victory.

The authors of this book give us facts, insights, and analyses that will prove invaluable for understanding what went wrong in Iraq. Some of them have already been noted in print but are dissected with particular authority by officers who observed what was happening from inside the American mission in Baghdad. As I saw myself in Baghdad at the beginning of 2004, as a senior advisor on governance to the Coalition Provisional Authority, so the authors depict a country still trapped one year later in a vicious circle of instability. Security required some degree of government legitimacy to rally public commitment to the new order. Legitimacy required some degree of government effectiveness in delivering security and economic reconstruction. But the economy, and crucially, its physical infrastructure, could not be revived without some significant improvement in security. Security also required the implementation of a plan to disarm the militias. But that required a political settlement, and economic resources to offer jobs and incentives. Yet one reason why a political settlement could not be reached was the deepening violence due to militia action (and penetration of the police). In the absence of a viable plan (backed by adequate knowledge and resources) to change these dynamics, the vicious circles just kept circling and intensifying. The United States kept pressing the form of democracy without the understanding, savvy, and capacity to achieve much of the substance.

Ultimately, after failing to eliminate or contain one of the country's most profoundly antidemocratic actors—the radical Shia Arab Moqtada al-Sadr and his Mahdi Army—the Americans had to stand by and watch while he was wooed and welcomed into the electoral process (with a significant share of government posts).

Among other things, we see in this book how the field of political stalemate and crisis was sowed in the summer of 2005 by the American insistence that Iraqis finish the constitution drafting by August 15 (a deadline that could have been extended for six months), even though it meant marginalizing the Sunni Arabs, and thus driving them deeper into resistance. This, in turn, must be traced back to the Sunni Arab boycott of the January 2005 election and the subsequent decision to proceed with constitutional drafting despite the virtual absence (for the crucial early period) of Sunni Arab participation. That development, Mowle writes, may well be "seen as a preventable tragedy greater than disbanding the Iraqi army, the blanket de-Ba'athification order, and the looting of Iraqi infrastructure," which all took place in the first few weeks of the American occupation.

As for the resistance, we had little understanding of who they were and what motivated (and divided) them. During the time of these officers' service in Iraq, the United States did gain a more acute sense of the scope and intensity of the insurgency, however, as a result not only of the rising levels of violence in the country but also of the penetration of the supposedly impenetrable Green Zone by insurgent agents, including suicide bombers. Understanding was hardly facilitated by the relentless rotation of military and civilian personnel, not just in and out of the country but, as Mowle recounts, even between offices, "to the point where it could become difficult to know where to find people except in the dining facility."

Over and over, we see a depressing lack of coordination and integration, as in the isolation of the command responsible for training the new Iraqi security forces, and the disarticulation between the political effort to draw in the Sunni Arabs and the military efforts to crush their resistance. We are offered candid glimpses of the tension between civilian and military cultures, aggravated by the blithe indifference of some American civilian officials who had not quite yet grasped that they were serving in a war zone. We observe up close what might be termed the bureaucratic fog of war, a disorienting lack of communication between different functional sectors, each trained to stay "in their lane," leaving the overall mission caught in inertia and unable to absorb historical lessons. One reason why, Nathan Freier and Donald G. Rose suggest, in an analysis that compels serious policy reflection, is the absence of "an integrated interagency mechanism" capable of coordinating all aspects of the civilian and military effort and directing them toward a common set of objectives with "unity, discipline, and precision." Today, as they note, neither the American military nor the

American diplomatic service is capable of playing this overall managerial role in stability operations. My own view is that neither can be capable of doing so. We need a new and separate cabinet department for the purpose of leading and managing post-conflict reconstruction, with permanent expertise and significant civilian reserves that can be deployed into post-conflict situations on short notice.

Most of all, the authors show the pervasive evidence of the poverty of planning at every level. Sometimes the consequences were quite specific, as when forty-nine Iraqi soldiers were killed heading home on leave in October 2004 because (as William C. Thomas writes) "no one had identified an appropriate set of force protection procedures for these troops, leaving them vulnerable to insurgent attacks." The same scenario was repeated over and over in insurgent attacks on Iraqi police stations, training sites, and troops in transit. But these only reflected (and cumulated into) a failure of planning on a much grander levels. As Tomislav Z. Ruby writes, the coalition military commanders and civilian leaders, along with their Iraqi counterparts, "did not have a written, agreed-upon common objective"—in other words, they lacked any shared sense of the desired end state. And, Ruby does not hesitate to stress, "committing resources against an unattainable end state is a waste of lives and money." In the absence of clear objectives, the mission crept and drifted. The Americans identified specific numbers of trained and equipped Iraqi troops they sought, but not a more substantive vision of their desired capabilities. They set dates for elections to be held and constitutions written, but not realistic plans for the agreements that needed to be forged in order at least to stabilize the country. Thus, repeatedly, formal milestones were achieved, and even hailed as turning points, but with no discernible impact on the ground reality of deepening turmoil.

No doubt, these failures stemmed in part from the fact that the civilian and military "planners" lacked knowledge of the political, social, and military realities in Iraq, the "ground truth." Thus they missed the growing sense of popular frustration and despair, the deep political drivers of an increasingly formidable nationalist and religious resistance to a perceived American occupation of Iraq, and the parallel dynamics of an emerging civil war.

Significantly, the authors do not spare their own military leaders and institutions from the criticism that also falls, inescapably, on the civilian political leadership. Indeed, the authors are at times withering in their portrait of a military culture more reliant on high technology than common sense, disinclined to question assumptions, unable to define objectives or assess what they were really achieving, and obsessed with process over outcomes—to the point where general officers were personally setting the color scale on the templates for the omnipresent PowerPoint slides. In fact, Thomas observes, "the command's activities were driven by PowerPoint briefings and desired timelines rather than a well thought out roadmap."

One of the major lessons to be drawn from this book, again succinctly expressed by Mowle (in Chapter 6) is that "war is a political exercise as well as a military one." The postwar war to defeat the resistance and stabilize Iraq never went well in part because the Americans never got the politics right. And that owed in large measure to the failures of understanding, planning, and co-ordination that this book so forcefully documents. These were, at root, grand failures on the part of the highest civilian officials of the Bush Administration who I believe (perhaps in contrast to the authors) deliberately deceived the American public in order to maintain support for a failing war effort in Iraq.

Yet they were also failures of the American military leadership, all the more perplexing and distressing because of the U.S. military's heavy institutional emphasis on "lessons learned." Despite that broad concern, Thomas writes, "many officers are unfamiliar with the literature on past attempts at security force development," or for that matter, on counterinsurgency more generally. More provocatively, Thomas questions whether American military officers were not compromised by some of the same organizational incentives to please superior officers and thereby strive for success that, during the previous American debacle in Vietnam, drained them of the necessary will to question and disagree.

Six years before the American invasion of Iraq, one of the U.S. Army's bright-est rising stars, (then) Major H. R. McMaster, published a devastating historical account of how the senior American military leadership had abandoned their professional responsibility by going along with the deliberate lies of President Lyndon Johnson and Defense Secretary Robert McNamara, while failing to ques-tion or press for clarification of their civilian commanders' vague, and hence unachievable, objectives. McMaster's historical account (which earned him a Ph.D. at the University of North Carolina and two years of teaching history at West Point) was a searing indictment of the top military commanders. "The Joint Chiefs of Staff became accomplices in the president's deception and focused on a tactical task, killing the enemy." The American military commander in Vietnam, General William Westmoreland, in focusing merely on "attrition" in South Vietnam, lacked a real strategy. "The result was military activity that did not aim to achieve a clearly defined objective."[2] In Vietnam then, as in Iraq 40 years later, the generals were overpowered by a brilliant and fatally arrogant secretary of defense who believed we were in a new political and techno-logical era of warfare that privileged technology and management and that "had made traditional military experience and thinking not only irrelevant, but often dangerous for contemporary policy."[3] Then, as in Iraq today (and for similar political calculations), "The Chiefs did not request the number of troops they believed necessary to impose a military solution."[4] In Vietnam, as in Iraq, "The failings were many and reinforcing: arrogance, weakness, lying in the pur-suit of self-interest, and above all, the abdication of responsibility to the Ameri-can people."[5]

Ironically, the very same author of this brilliant and scathing analysis achieved one of the few real successes of counterinsurgency in postwar Iraq, when he commanded the 3rd Armored Cavalry Regiment in its campaign during 2005–06 to take back Tall Afar from insurgent domination. Colonel H.R. McMaster had a plan, not only for combat but also for post-combat operations, and a bold, multidimensional strategy for executing it.[6] He also had sufficient troops relative to population to deploy his soldiers and keep them living throughout the city. One cannot but wonder what might have come of the American engagement in Iraq if the American military brass had internalized McMaster's lessons from Vietnam and emulated his approach on the ground in Iraq. Instead, the United States became bogged down again in another foreign military venture, with no plan, no strategy for either victory or exit, not enough resources, and arguably this time with much higher stakes for its national security.

If the United States is to remain a great power, it simply cannot make this mistake a third time. If it is to avoid it, the lessons in this book, and in many others, must be studied and heeded.

Notes

1. Larry Diamond, *Squandered Victory: The American Occupation and the Bungled Effort to Bring Democracy to Iraq* (New York: Times Books, 2005); Thomas E. Ricks, *Fiasco: The American Military Adventure in Iraq* (New York: Penguin, 2006); Bob Woodward, *State of Denial: Bush at War, Part III* (New York: Simon & Schuster, 2006).

2. H.R. McMaster, *Dereliction of Duty: Lyndon Johnson, Robert McNamara, the Joint Chiefs of Staff, and the Lies that Led to Vietnam* (New York: HarperCollins, 1997), p. 333.

3. Ibid., p. 326.

4. Ibid., p. 333.

5. Ibid., p. 334.

6. Ricks, *Fiasco*, pp. 419–24.

PREFACE

This book developed from the authors' experiences in Iraq between the summer of 2004 and the summer of 2005. Our stories are different, and I would not presume to speak for my colleagues, but I suspect that we have similar reasons for going to Iraq. Whatever our opinion about the wisdom of the war itself, we shared a common commitment to national service. If the commanders in Iraq believed there was a need for officers with our skills, then that is where we should be. For myself, at least, I felt that anything other than trying to answer the call would be a betrayal of my oath of office and an embarrassment to my credibility as a social scientist. So very quickly, there I was, along with two colleagues, Lieutenant Colonel Neal Rappaport and Lieutenant Colonel Mike Davis, watching smoke billow from the fuel farm at Baghdad International Airport and wondering just when our ride to the Green Zone was going to show up.

Over the next several months, the other authors arrived, and we all eventually came home safely. We all felt we served honorably, living up to the values of excellence, service, and integrity. Yet we also felt that somewhere along the way, the war was not making much progress. I would be asked if things were better or worse than the press reported, and I would answer "yes." Was Iraq on a long difficult road to a successful peace, or was it sinking into a deeper war? We still do not know, of course. But it seemed to us—to Ruby and me, initially, and to the others who joined this project—that there was a story to tell here. Not an expose of problems in the Green Zone, but a sober description of what happened, what worked, and what did not. Most everyone who was in Iraq thinks they have a story to tell. We hope you find ours illuminating.

The story that emerges here is one of difficult decisions, missed opportunities, tangled lanes of responsibility, and lack of awareness of conditions in Iraq. This is a thickly detailed, practical, nontheoretical discussion. We were participant-observers, embedded in both military culture and the war itself. That may expose us to charges of bias, but we believe such claims will not stand up to scrutiny—and are more than balanced by the depth of knowledge we can bring to the subject. We did not fly in for a few days or interview some people after the fact, nor do we have careers or reputations that we are trying to protect. None of us have answers for Iraq—not fully on what happened, not on a bold plan for victory, and not on who is to blame for failures or to acclaim for successes. Nevertheless, we see lessons that can be drawn from this, lessons that may no longer be applicable to Iraq, but lessons for future wars.

We need to emphasize that the views expressed in this book are those of the authors and do not necessarily reflect the official policy or position of the U.S. Government, Department of Defense, or any of its subordinate organizations.

Parts of Chapter 5 were presented in a different form at the International Studies Association Conference, San Diego, in March 2006.

Parts of Chapter 6 were presented in a different form at a conference on The New Iraq, Yildiz Technical University, Istanbul, in March 2005.

The authors would like to thank many people with whom they were stationed in the Green Zone. First and foremost, special thanks to the Chief of the Strategy section, Colonel William Hix, who introduced most of us to the rigors of "combat" social science. Special thanks are also owed to Neal Rappaport, who would have been an integral part of this book had he not been deployed—again—to Kabul, Afghanistan, where it became impossible for him to complete the valuable story he had to tell. We cannot possibly list everyone else who helped us understand Iraq, but at the risk of offending those left off, we would like to thank Tom Duffy, Henry Enscher, Dave Filer, Tammy Fitzgerald, Shauna Hauser, Jerry Howard, Ray Kiefer, Mike Lewis, Laura Poitras, Stan Smith, Stuart Symington, Bernie Thompson, Tom Warrick, and Jim Xinos. Their insights and suggestions, and those of many others, were crucial to the development of the authors' understanding of Iraqi politics.

Kalev Sepp would especially like to thank people he interviewed in preparing his chapter: Ambassador David C. Gompert, CPA; Dr. Eric Haseltine, National Security Agency; Major General Paul D. Eaton, U.S. Army (ret.), CMATT; Brigadier General John Custer, CENTCOM; Brigadier General Barbara Fast, CJTF-7; Mr. J. W. Adamczyk, MPRI; Colonel John F. Agoglia, CENTCOM; Colonel Gil Baldwin, U.K.; Mr. Douglas Brand, U.K.; Chief Inspector Steve Burfitt, U.K.; Colonel James H. Coffman, Jr., ASD/SOLIC; Lieutenant Colonel Jeremy Green, U.K.; Lieutenant Colonel Michael D. Greer, CPA; Mr. Robert Hunt, U.K.; Major Jamie Laughrey, CENTCOM; Master Sergeant Ronald R. Mann, SOCCENT; Colonel Roger Marshal, U.K.; Mr. Ed McVaney, CPA; Major Mark Mitchell, SOCCENT; Dr. Olga Oliker, RAND; Mr. R.C. Porter, DOD; Lieutenant Colonel Scott Reynolds, DOD; Lieutenant Colonel Stephen

Sabarese, SOCCENT; Chief Warrant Officer 3; Steven L. Schmidt, SOCCENT; Colonel Jim Slavin, USAIC; Colonel Carolyn Stewart, CENTCOM; Constable Calvin Tonks, U.K.; and collective interviews with staff sections in CJTF-7, CENTCOM Headquarters, and the Tampa Police Department; and other officials not named here.

Finally, the authors would like to thank Juan Cole, Damon Coletta, Pat James, and Sandy Storrie for their comments on drafts of some of these chapters. Of course, all remaining errors of fact, interpretation, and analysis are the sole responsibility of the authors.

ABBREVIATIONS

ADM	Assyrian Democratic Movement
AFRS	Automatic fingerprint recognition system
ASAS	All-source analysis system
BIAP	Baghdad International Airport
CAG	Commander's Action Group
CENTCOM	Central Command
CJTF-7	Combined Joint Task Force 7
CMATT	Coalition Military Assistance Training Team
COA	Course of action
CPA	Coalition Provisional Authority
CPATT	Coalition Police Advisory Training Team
DIME	Diplomatic, informational, military, and economic
DoD	[U.S.] Department of Defense
DVD	Digital video disk
EOD	Explosive ordinance demolition
EU	European Union
GC	Governing Council
GRD	Gulf Region Division
GVN	government of Vietnam
HUMINT	Human intelligence
ICDC	Iraqi Civil Defense Corps
ICP	Iraqi Communist Party
IDC	Iraqi De-Ba'athification Council
IECI	Independent Electoral Commission of Iraq
IED	Improvised explosive device
IIG	Iraqi Interim Government
IIP	Iraqi Islamic Party
INA	Iraqi National Accord
INC	Iraqi National Congress

IRI	International Republican Institute
IRMO	Iraqi Reconstruction Management Office
ISF	Iraqi security forces
ITF	Iraqi Turkomen Front
ITG	Iraqi Transitional Government
JFC	Joint force commander
KA	Kurdistan Alliance
KDP	Kurdistan Democratic Party
KIU	Kurdistan Islamic Union
LTG	Lieutenant General
METL	Mission Essential Task List
MNC-I	Multinational Corps–Iraq
MND-SE	Multinational Division–Southeast
MNF-I	Multinational Force–Iraq
MNSTC-I	Multinational Security Transition Command–Iraq
MoD	[Iraqi] Ministry of Defense
MoI	[Iraqi] Ministry of Interior
MUC	Muslim Ulema Council
NATO	North Atlantic Treaty Organization
NCA	National Command Authority
NGO	Nongovernmental organization
NIA	New Iraqi Army
NSC	National Security Council
NSS02	National Security Strategy of 2002
OMS	Office of Moqtada al-Sadr
PCO	Project and Contracting Office
PUK	Patriotic Union of Kurdistan
SCI	Special Compartmented Information
SCIRI	Supreme Council for the Islamic Revolution in Iraq
SPA	Strategy, Plans, and Assessment
SSTR	Stability, security, transition, and reconstruction
TAL	Transitional Administrative Law
TNA	Transitional National Assembly
UIA	United Iraqi Alliance
UN	United Nations
UNSC	United Nations Security Council
UNSCR	United Nations Security Council Resolution
U.S.	United States
USAID	United States Agency for International Development
USG	U.S. Government
WMD	Weapons of mass destruction

CHAPTER 1

INTRODUCTION: THE GREEN ZONE IN 2004–05

Thomas S. Mowle

The war in Iraq was never hopeless. On the contrary, it was overflowing with hope.

American leaders hoped for a swift and easy military victory over Saddam Hussein. That hope was attained, as American forces stormed through Baghdad on 5 April 2003, only eighteen days after the invasion began.

But the American government hoped for a greater victory. American leaders hoped that the Iraqi population would welcome their forces as liberators and that the rest of the world would quickly see the wisdom of having disarmed Iraq from its WMD (weapons of mass destruction). They hoped that Iraq would become "peaceful, united, stable, and secure, well integrated into the international community, and a full partner in the global war on terrorism."[1] Beyond that, they hoped Iraq would be "democratic... an engine for regional economic growth, and proving the fruits of democratic governance to the region."[2] That is victory, as defined by the U.S. Government. These latter hopes have not been attained at this writing, and they almost certainly will not be attained at the publication of this book; it is difficult to find much basis for hope that in the long run, the outcome of the Iraq war may look better than it does in 2006.

The primary remaining basis of hope in Iraq is not in anything the United States does now but in the Iraqi people themselves. Most of them have historically rejected fanaticism and violence; they want a free state if they can only find a way to devise it, and many of their leaders have risked their lives in dedication to a political solution. Perhaps one must hope for a good result to the Iraq war, because the people of Iraq deserve it and because the alternative—an even bloodier civil conflict likely to draw in neighboring states and opportunistic forces adamantly opposed to liberal values—is almost too horrifying to accept as likely. One can hope that Iraqis recoil finally from that horror and find a way to reconcile. But that hope does not yield a plan for achieving success.

If you hope to find such a plan in this book, you will be disappointed. Enough plans emerged during 2006, culminating in the report of the Iraq Study Group on 6 December; there is no need to add to these. At one end of the spectrum, President George W. Bush insisted, "We're not leaving, so long as I'm the President."[3] At the other end, a variety of voices called for immediate U.S. withdrawal, most notably Senator Russell Feingold and Representative John Murtha, who said, "Iraq cannot be won militarily. It's time to re-deploy our troops from Iraq," adding, "Our military is considered occupiers and the U.S. does not have the popular support of the Iraqi people."[4] In between were calls for partitioning Iraq and rumors that a reestablishment of authoritarian rule in Iraq might be acceptable. All of these plans are either not plans at all or involve a substantial retreat from American victory conditions. It will be up to the President and the new Democratic majority in Congress to determine the best course of action for the United States, in consultation with the sovereign government of Iraq.

Instead, our goal in this book is to illuminate how American actions, most particularly the lack of cross-functional strategic planning, insufficient understanding of the situation, and insufficient cross-functional control over command and execution, contributed to the problems facing the United States in Iraq after the invasion. It does this to explain and also to warn. If the United States—or any other country—again seeks to occupy another country and install a stable, democratic government, its leaders may learn from this book. War is a difficult enough enterprise, and rebuilding afterward even more so. If you fight a war without solid intelligence, an adequate and robust plan for victory, and a well-integrated effort, problems will compound until one is left with no options that offer much hope for success.

Given this focus on American actions during the war, the authors do not examine the question of whether or not the military overthrow of Saddam Hussein was an appropriate way to deal with the problems posed by his regime. The authors themselves differ on the answer to that question, but all nevertheless volunteered to carry out their military duties in Baghdad. That is the nature of civil–military relations, especially for junior officers who aim to best carry out national policies, not determine them. Furthermore, we reject two of the charges raised about the war—that it was an exercise in imperialism, and that it was based on "lies" by the President.

The charge of imperialism is the easiest to rebut. The war and occupation would have been much simpler if the United States had simply set a pliable Iraqi in power—perhaps Iyad Allawi or Ahmed Chalabi—given him money and weapons, and let him run the country and provide oil contracts to American corporations. The United States has taken similar actions in the past, to its short-term benefit (and long-term detriment). Indeed, if democracy is impossible in Iraq, as some war critics allege, then imposing a strongman may have been the more reasonable solution. It is to American credit that it included democracy as a goal. If the United States were bent on controlling Iraqi oil, then the first oil drilling contracts negotiated by generally pro-American Kurdistan would not have gone to companies from Canada, Norway, Switzerland, and (amazingly) Turkey, of which only Norway supported the war.[5] If the United States sought to control Iraqi politics, its leaders would have been more pro-American. Ibrahim al-Ja'afari was clearly not the first choice of the United States in 2005 to be Transitional Prime Minster of Iraq, any more than Nouri al-Maliki was the first choice for constitutional Prime Minister in 2006. Yet they took office. In addition, the general public does not recognize the extent to which the preferences of Iraqi leaders limited and channeled American military actions, as soon as sovereignty was transferred on 28 June 2004.

The question of "lies" by the President is more complex. The United States had no hard evidence that Iraq was developing WMD, and its attempts to build that case publicly—yellowcake from Niger, machined aluminum rods, and so forth—have turned out to be clumsy exaggerations at best. Yet the circumstantial evidence was extremely plausible and widely accepted. Saddam had used chemical weapons on the Kurds in the 1980s. After the Gulf War, his chemical and biological weapons programs were found to be far more advanced than expected—and further projects were revealed in 1995. Under President Bill Clinton, the United States bombed Iraq throughout the 1990s, including a four-day operation in 1998 that began while the UNSC (United Nations Security Council) was still debating the latest report from its chief inspector, Richard Butler.

Saddam Hussein acted like he had secret weapons programs—perhaps he even believed that he did—and he fooled everyone. In the meantime, the sanctions regime was eroding to the point that the early diplomacy of the Bush Administration involved developing "smart sanctions" that might be more politically effective.[6] After UNSCR (United Nations Security Council Resolution) 1441 was passed in November 2002, inspections resumed but could not at this point convince anyone of Iraqi compliance—especially since it now seems clear that there were no weapons to find. At the time of the invasion, the U.S. Government had reason to believe that Saddam had secret weapons programs and that the increasingly leaky sanctions regime would be unlikely to prevent them from being completed. This belief supported the narrative of those advocating the overthrow of Saddam Hussein as an easy path to a more democratic Iraq and a more peaceful and pro-American regime, but a belief is not made less reasonable by the uses to which it is put. If in fact the President or his close advisors "lied," shame on them, but that question belongs to other books.[7]

More generally, we are not writing this book to cast blame. It may seem otherwise at times, simply because one cannot critique the operational effort and point out mistakes without at least implying that certain individuals made mistakes. But if we were to cast blame, then we would need to allocate some of the fault to ourselves. Not in the self-serving sense that we did not succeed in having our policies adopted by our superiors, but in the real sense that we also sometimes contributed to the problems we describe here. The question of Iraqi militias is particularly and personally relevant. It was easy in August 2004 to see what was wrong with the transition and reintegration plan; in the rush of events, it was less easy to then see what lessons could be applied from the knowledge at hand.[8] Furthermore, many of what now seem to be "mistakes" are more ambiguous and are seen as errors only because events have not worked out. Some of these "mistakes" resulted from hard choices, where the better course of action was not clear. Even today, in some cases, it is not certain that choosing a different course would have produced better results. Other such "mistakes" resulted from missed opportunities, opportunities that may not even have been recognized at the time. The common thread, however, was a tendency to select the most hopeful, most optimistic strategy rather than one that was more cautious. Planning must include strategically considering the future and incorporating robust fallback options.

Most especially, the authors are not casting blame on the soldiers and Marines engaged in tactical engagements. While the authors served in the middle of the war zone, eating and sometimes traveling with the actual war-fighters, we came under only relatively infrequent indirect fire and never fired our own weapons with hostile intent. While the soldiers' story belongs to other books,[9] it appears that as in most recent wars, the American and coalition fighting men and women almost always accomplished their tactical missions with skill and precision. The exceptions are well known but are not part of this book because for the most part they occurred or were revealed later in the war. The prisoner abuse at Abu Ghraib prison reinforced the difficulty of winning any allegiance from Sunni Arabs in 2004–05—though this also is not part of this book because it occurred before its time frame and was not part of American strategy. To be sure, each crime committed by a soldier undermines the war effort, which adds to the moral imperative to treat civilians and prisoners humanely. But such crimes have had little real impact on the course of the war—without them, the situation in Iraq would be no different.

Just as this book is not set at the battlefield level, it also does not describe the making of American strategy. Instead, it is set at the operational level, between the strategic and tactical levels. The military headquarters translates broad strategy prescriptions, set in Washington, into plans that will be executed at the tactical level in the field. It also integrates tactical results from the field and feeds the information back to Washington, shaping overall strategy.

This anthology is one of very few books on Iraq written at this operational level, which actually provides the best overall view of the campaign.[10]

Inside the Green Zone

The authors are particularly qualified to write on this topic because they all served at Headquarters, MNF-I (Multinational Force–Iraq), in Baghdad's Green Zone, between mid-2004 and mid-2005. The Green Zone was an unusual place, approximately four square miles on the west side of the Tigris River in the heart of Baghdad. Its centerpiece, holding the Ambassador, much of the MNF-I headquarters, the Iraqi Reconstruction Management Office, and many other offices, was the Republican Palace, a tribute to questionable taste and shoddy construction. The palace had three wings. The center, the original part of the building, was two stories of rectangles around courtyards—the strategy office was pleased to have a rooftop patio overlooking one of these swaths of concrete where troops could gather for hails and farewells in the evening breeze. This wing was crowed by a green dome with a ladder spiraling to the top. The Ambassador's office was in this area, as was the command operations center, not to mention a small movie theater, the single secure conference room, and the liaison to the Iraqi Olympic Committee.

The south wing held the main dining facility, a vast room whose tables overflowed into hallways decorated with pictures of the World Trade Center towers and quotations from the Koran. Beyond the dining facility was the South Ballroom, notable for its murals of Scud missiles thrusting into the sky and of a Jerusalem scrubbed of Jews. This wing, which seemed to go on indefinitely, included most of the financial offices and the Senior Advisors to various Iraqi ministries—senior civilians and mid-level officers assigned as mentors to Iraqi government agencies. Here the oil for food scandal was investigated, evidence was assessed for Saddam Hussein's trial, and haircuts were available until murders and death threats convinced the barbers to stop coming to work.

The north wing housed most of the major Embassy offices—political, political–military, and economics, as well as for a time the links to the North Atlantic Treaty Organization and the UN (United Nations), and the military training command. All of these surrounded the North Ballroom, probably the most attractive of the large rooms in the palace until it was filled with cubicles to house a variety of military offices, including the civil affairs units involved with election planning. The north wing also housed a makeshift chapel where Christian services, and the occasional memorial, were held in a converted foyer under blocks inscribed with the ninety-nine revealed names of Allah. It was somewhat surreal to stand at the lectern, reading an Old Testament passage about war with a pistol strapped in a thigh holster, the occasional explosion echoing in the distance, and as the days grew shorter, Islamic sundown prayers audible over a low partition.

Lest any of the above be seen as revealing the location of important offices, offices tended to move with no warning. This, along with the difficulty of electronic communication, harmed the ability of personnel to interact with each other. The Embassy and military offices were not on the same phone network or computer network. While every Embassy employee had at least one cell phone, tied either to an Iraqi network or to an extension of a Long Island area code (telephonically, the Green Zone was part of the United States), very few military officers below the rank of colonel held one. The best way to contact someone was to walk to his or her office and look around. It was good for exercise but bad for decision making and coordination.

Any concerns about keeping the location of offices quiet would also be mitigated by the fact that local Iraqis—usually Shia Arabs from Sadr City—handled construction in the Embassy as well as its janitorial services. One would try, with difficulty, to stop discussion of the day's intelligence before the crews came within earshot. Other Iraqis would spend time in the ceiling, laying cables, and one presumes nothing else. It was generally assumed that most of what we did was known to the insurgents—as they demonstrated by shelling the Halloween party on 28 October, fifteen minutes after it began. More troubling was the disappearance of rifles from the strategy office. They reappeared several days later, but mid-October, with the bombing of the Green Zone Café and the marketplace, was a nervous time. Many in the palace were convinced that the insurgents would try a spectacular attack on the Embassy as the American elections approached. Opinions differed as to whether they would do so to try to defeat President Bush, or to ensure his reelection.

By mid-2004, this was no longer the decrepit palace described by L. Paul Bremer upon his arrival, or even by Larry Diamond upon his.[11] Utilities generally worked; in 120-degree heat this was a blessing. The palace was surrounded by several forty-man (or -woman) tents for transient personnel and newcomers. Most people were housed in expansive trailer parks with names like "The Palms" and "Poolside Estates." Most trailers were approximately 15 × 8-foot shipping containers, holding two people—room enough for two single beds, two wardrobes, a small refrigerator, and a German combination television/DVD player that was not hooked up to cable and would not play American or Iraqi format DVDs. Two trailers would be connected by a short hallway with a small bathroom shared by four people—except when the water failed (a frequent and odiferous event) or the electricity went out. Communal showers served in those cases, usually.

The palace area included a large pool with a grassy picnic area, a well-equipped gymnasium, and a short walk away—past the heliport—a military exchange store and Ghazi's market, known to some, disrespectfully, as the hajjimart. Iraqis lived in the Green Zone as well, many of them squatters who occupied villas or high-rises when Saddam's loyalists fled. It seemed bad public relations to force these thousands of people out, but it seemed bad security to leave them in place. They were well-armed enough to celebrate Iraqi soccer victories in the Olympics with bursts of automatic weapons, pretty to look at but nerve wracking when you heard a bullet ping off the tent poles. These Iraqis operated the merchants' alley and cafes even after they were attacked, and also sold very inexpensive DVDs of newly released movies. The Green Zone also included many other army bases, each with its own neighborhood of trailers and with a dining facility that seemed better than our own. Several embassies were located in the Green Zone, as were many Iraqi ministries. The Iraqi government met in the Convention Center, about a mile and a half from the palace, and several top Iraqi officials lived in the Green Zone—and some rarely left.

This was our home for two to six months, a sandy, palm-covered expanse of barriers, heat, and armed men and women. The rules were different for everyone. Only the military and security contractors were armed; Embassy personnel only reluctantly wore even body armor and almost never wore their Kevlar helmets. American and Australian military could not drink; others could and did. With private security personnel making a rumored $1,000 per day—tax free (!)— high-stakes poker among armed and intoxicated players seemed only a few steps away from Deadwood, South Dakota. But for all that, there was only one incident we can recall of violence among those assigned to the Green Zone, and that is rumored to have involved a fight over a woman. The Green Zone was its own community, surrounded on land by Sunni Arabs who sympathized with insurgents who fired mortars at us, and across the river from Shia Arabs who fired rockets as well. Our link to the outside was *Stars and Stripes*, the internet—which worked well—and Route Irish to BIAP (Baghdad International Airport). BIAP's grounds were stretched to include the incongruously named Camp Victory where the rest of MNF-I was located. Transit was dangerous, at first in armored or unarmored sport utility vehicles, then in heavily fortified "Rhino Buses," and then only by helicopter after the buses were disabled by an improvised explosive device.

The Importance of 2004–05

We focus our attention on the reign of the IIG (Iraqi Interim Government). Most books on Iraq discuss the decision to go to war, the military campaign, and the first year of American occupation.[12] The substance of this book begins in August 2004, on the day of the National Council that selected the IIG that ruled the country after sovereignty was turned over by Ambassador Bremer on 28 June 2004. It ends in May 2005 with the selection of the Iraqi Transitional Government from the TNA (Transitional National Assembly) that had been elected on 30 January 2005. The nine-month life of the IIG held the potential of a new beginning for Iraq. Gone was Bremer's CPA (Coalition Provisional

Authority), which had exercised all the powers of government in Iraq; in was Ambassador John D. Negroponte. Gone was Lieutenant General Ricardo Sanchez and CJTF-7 (Combined Joint Task Force 7); in was General George W. Casey and the MNF-I. With the passage of UNSCR 1546 in June 2004, even the exclusion of the UN was partially broken. American troops no longer occupied Iraq; they were there at the invitation of a recognized Iraqi government. International legitimacy was given to the process of democratization, a timetable that would carry Iraq through the writing of its own constitution to replace the CPA's TAL (Transitional Administrative Law). Despite the summer-long upswing in violence, beginning with the battles in Fallujah and throughout the South in April, there seemed a new basis for hope in Iraq.

This life span of the IIG corresponds to the authors' unique experiences as scholar-practitioners. Most of the authors hold social science doctorates, and most were not in Iraq as part of an official deployment rotation (thus our informal nickname, "Doctors without Orders"). On 22 July 2004, Major General Steve "Burner" Sargent, head of the Strategic Political–Military division in MNF-I headquarters, asked the Air Force Academy Superintendent for some "strategic thinkers" to help with the war effort. Mowle and two colleagues responded immediately, and within two weeks were on their way. Mowle was a political scientist and acquisition officer; the others were a historian and an economist. In September, they were joined in what had now become the Strategy, Plans, and Assessment Division by Ruby, a political scientist and intelligence officer from the Air War College. Sepp, a historian and retired army special forces officer, came over from the Naval Postgraduate School in October at the request of Colonel Bill Hix, head of strategy. Other officers also arrived in a similar fashion—a psychologist, a mathematician, and other political scientists. Sepp, Ruby, and Mowle left Baghdad in December; Mowle was replaced by Rose, a political scientist and intelligence officer from the Air Force Academy, who stayed until his retirement in May 2005. Thomas, a political scientist and missileer, is an exception to the trend; an academic doctor *with* orders to the Multinational Security Transition Command–Iraq. He was in Iraq from October 2004 to February 2005. Rose was then joined by Freier, an artillery officer and strategic analyst from the Army War College (also *with* orders), the only active duty army officer among this group, who remained in Baghdad until July 2005. These six officers provide unique insight into strategy and planning in Iraq during this period.

However, the IIG period is relevant for more than its overlap with the authors' presence in Iraq—had a different span been sought, different authors would have been found. Decisions and policies during the IIG period set the future of Iraq, and the options for the United States, on a very narrow course. In July 2004, all important segments of Iraqi society accepted the basic plan of holding elections by the end of January 2005. The Sunni Arab insurgents were not as strong as they would become, and the segments led by Abu Musab al-Zarqawi were alienating many Iraqis as they targeted civilians, including children. Moqtada al-Sadr had an armed following, but it was still relatively small; by October, he would have been forced to retreat from Najaf by Grand Ayatollah Ali al-Sistani and then to sue for peace with the Americans in Baghdad itself. Sunni Arab, Shia Arab, Kurd, and cross-sectarian groups all were prepared to contest the upcoming elections.

This hopeful moment, when a shining path to victory could be perceived, did not last. One problem was that the Sunni Arabs, with the main force of the American effort falling on them as it had throughout the war, boycotted the elections. As a result, given that Iraq's electoral law provided for proportional representation based on a single national district, the Sunni Arabs were grievously underrepresented in the TNA. The Shia Arabs and Kurds were free to allocate government positions as they wished. While they gave the Sunni Arabs some posts, they excluded the trans-sectarian Arab groups represented by Allawi and Ghazi al-Yawr. The Shia Arabs and Kurds also gave the Sunni Arabs some representation on the committee to draft a new constitution but, not needing their consensus, overrode Sunni Arab redlines and devised a constitution that suited themselves. Most significantly, the new constitution provided for a very weak central government, with the existing Kurd region and possible Shia Arab regions controlling their own security and oil. Sunni Arabs would be left with little and little prospect of winning through democracy. The Sunni Arabs were unable to block the ratification of the constitution—coming only 12 percent short in Ninewa, the third province they needed, with Anbar and Salah ad-Din overwhelmingly rejecting it. Some Sunni Arabs trusted promises that the constitution would be open for revision after the next election. Little has been heard of these promises, a year later, other than Shia Arab and Kurd proclamations that they would not accept significant changes in the constitution. Sunni Arabs have little reason to trust their government or democracy.

The second problem was the slow development of ISF (Iraqi security forces) under the IIG. Most obviously, this meant coalition forces continued to accept primary responsibility for Iraqi security long after provinces were supposed to have been turned over to Iraqi forces. The high profile of the Americans contributed to higher American casualties, a continued belief among Sunni Arabs that their country was still occupied, and war-weariness in the United States and Europe. More subtly, the lack of professional Iraqi security created a vacuum that would be filled by Kurd and Shia Arab militias. These militias had survived in the absence of a realistic plan to address them, and different groups believed they needed them as insurance against a hostile state. With Iraq controlled by the militias' masters, the IIG's successors abandoned transition and reintegration and allowed members of the Shia Arab Badr Organization and al-Sadr's Mahdi Army to join the Iraqi Police. Sunni Arabs found themselves under attack by their own state, and were driven even closer to the insurgents, for protection. Knowing they could not win democratically, and fearing the consequence of living as a minority, civil war seemed like the best hope for the Sunni Arabs. By mid-2006, both Arab factions were escalating reprisals and ethnic cleansing, while the Kurds used its *peshmerga* to establish control over Kirkuk and its oil.

By the end of the period covered by this book, summer 2005, American leverage in Iraq was severely reduced. Negroponte's successor, Zalmay Khalilzad, adopted a much more active form of diplomacy. While Negroponte was content to allow the Iraqis to make their own decisions, however long it took, Khalilzad tried to intervene in the constitutional negotiations. There was little he could do, however, since he had no votes in the committee; he simply ended up with his fingerprints on the murder weapon of Iraq's united future. As a Sunni himself, Khalilzad's efforts were interpreted as hostility by some Shia Arabs. Sunni Arabs would have been won over only by success. While it may not have mattered in the end, to Khalilzad's activism goes the final great miscalculation of this period. The TAL said the Constitution was to be finished by 15 August, a schedule that assumed the January elections would not have been held only one day before the deadline and that the new government would be seated in less than the three months it took. There were provisions for extending the deadline by up to six months, but Khalilzad, backed by Washington, pressed the Iraqis to finish it on schedule. With no time for compromise, the Shia Arabs and Kurds did the only thing they could: outvote the Sunni Arabs and write their own constitution.

Plan of the Book

Mowle's chapter 2 sets the stage for the IIG period. It explains the constraints that MNF-I inherited from the CPA and CJTF-7. It traces four key decisions which reduced the options present in 2004. The first was going to war without UN approval. This undermined the legitimacy of the war from the beginning and deprived the United States of valuable expertise and additional forces. The second was the decision to invade and occupy with a relatively small force. This decision was based on the belief that Iraqis would welcome the United States and that nationalist members of the Iraqi Army would help to maintain order. The third was the decision to formally disband the Iraqi Army and ban most members of the Ba'ath Party from public life. These people would become the early leaders and supporters of the insurgency and could not be reconciled with the coalition. Finally, faced with two military problems in April 2004— the loss of control of Fallujah and an uprising led by al-Sadr throughout the South—the coalition took only incomplete action against both. Fallujah was left to be refought during Ramadan shortly before the elections; al-Sadr escaped to continue fighting on his own terms for several more months and to maintain his legend.

Ruby's chapter 3 then provides a more philosophical background to the war. It discusses five considerations that planners take into account. Perhaps the most vital of these is the importance of establishing the ground truth, distinct from people's beliefs about current conditions. Perceptions and beliefs are important in that people act on them, but commanders must understand reality. Other considerations include the need for a clear written set of objectives, including the political constraints on the operation. The victory conditions for this war were vague and subjective, with no way of distinguishing which factors were most important to national leadership. Political limits on actions were also shifting and varied from country to country. Ruby also describes how the "pathologies of the staff" weaken the effort to coordinate within the military, within the different American agencies in the Green Zone, within the coalition, and with the Iraqi government itself. Finally, planners should understand from the beginning how they will measure success. As it turned out, the mission's goals and desired outcomes were not articulated until 2004, and even then they were not clear. The campaign plan did not systematically consider the political constraints on Iraqi operations—what American, coalition, and Iraqi governments would demand, accept, or reject from the occupation force. The campaign plan also suffered from a lack of knowledge—the "ground truth" that includes understanding the culture and motivations of Iraqis, as well as the economic realities they faced. The campaign plan also assumed a smoother integration of different American agencies, not taking into account certain pathologies that developed and could have been anticipated. Finally, the campaign plan did not include adequate means of assessing progress, which are critical to evaluating and adjusting political and military operations.

Sepp's chapter 4 addresses the coalition's attempt to develop intelligence within Iraq. Strategic thinking demands that you understand your opponent as well as you know yourself. Yet American intelligence was lacking, and the Iraqis were not able to provide it either. Like Ruby and Mowle, Sepp goes back to the early stages of the occupation, describing how the coalition tried to develop Iraqi intelligence capabilities. These efforts were less than fully successful. In his view, the coalition did not fully understand the key role that intelligence played in a counterinsurgency effort and thus did not do enough to overcome the lack of trust between different Iraqi groups and the coalition forces. As a consequence, the coalition did not have enough information to assess its progress and develop better plans.

Thomas' chapter 5 addresses the coalition's work at training ISF. The occupation could only succeed in the long term if it helped develop Iraqi forces that can ensure their own country's security. There were serious problems with this effort, however, starting with the lack of mission planning and the absence of coherent guidance from the overall military command. The training command tended to work in isolation from the rest of the coalition effort and from the Iraqi government as well. Its plans were little more than schedules or goals, briefings based on numbers rather than capabilities. The greatest problem with military training was the lack of appreciation that the coalition was creating security forces from nothing, rather than maintaining or improving a force in place.

Mowle's chapter 6 begins with the strategic review of the campaign plan in the fall of 2004, which tried to determine which strategic points were most vital to success. The review concluded that the political track drove the security and economic tracks and that at this point, it was almost pointless to try to win Iraqi acceptance of the occupation force. Only the political path to constitutional rule could win Iraqi acceptance of a legitimate government, so coalition efforts should focus on facilitating the three elections of 2005. The chapter then discusses how those elections came about, and the coalition effort to anticipate their outcome and what it could mean for the future of the resistance. Long-term success in Iraq could only result from the inclusion of all Iraq subcultures. This meant engaging with the Sunni Arabs, to ensure they would participate in the elections. Engagement suffered from a difficulty in finding interlocutors, and it was undermined by the military's consistent preference for kinetic actions seen in the second invasion of Fallujah and the raid on the Abu Hanifa mosque, operations that contributed to the Sunni Arabs' boycott of the elections.[13] This boycott, and the resulting underrepresentation of the Sunni Arabs in Iraqi politics in 2005, made Iraqi democratization very difficult.

Freier and Rose's chapter 7 takes the narrative into 2005. The 30 January TNA elections did not end or even reduce the violence. Nevertheless, they created a new situation that gave MNF-I a fresh start on addressing Iraq. This opportunity, like the one of summer 2004's transfer of sovereignty, was missed. The focus of the military headquarters turned to items that would be addressed in conjunction with a new Iraqi government, but the process of actually forming that government was allowed to drift. By the time a government was formed in May 2005, a new crisis emerged: the drafting of the constitution. Any momentum gained from successful elections was lost. A new training focus reflected the reality that the stability of Iraq was to become more a function of the Iraqis themselves, rather than the actions of the coalition. During this period, the lack of a clear strategy for success and above all the failure of different elements of the coalition to coordinate their efforts dissipated any momentum that could have been achieved from the January 2005 elections.

Chapter 8, the conclusion, is a joint effort by Freier, Ruby, and Mowle. This chapter summarizes the book's findings and presents common lessons learned from across these different areas: lack of cross-functional strategic planning, insufficient understanding of the situation, and insufficient cross-functional control over command and execution. This chapter and the book conclude by taking a broader look at how the United States can operate to restore a country whose civil authority has collapsed. There is no reason to believe that Iraq is the last time it will face such a situation. The United States may directly induce the collapse of other states, or, more likely, some such states may collapse on their own. If these states are in strategically important regions, or contain important resources or dangerous weapons, the United States will likely be drawn into attempts to restore the state. The lessons of this book are vital for ensuring that these future exercises of national power are less costly.

CHAPTER 2

PRELUDE: STRATEGY, OPTIMISM, AND HARD CHOICES

Thomas S. Mowle

On 25 May 2006, a journalist concluded a White House press conference by asking U.S. President George W. Bush and British Prime Minister Tony Blair, "You spoke about missteps and mistakes in Iraq. . . . Which missteps and mistakes of your own you most regret?" Bush critiqued some of his blunt language about terrorists and said, "I think the biggest mistake that's happened so far, at least from our country's involvement in Iraq is Abu Ghraib."[1] This answer expressed regret for a terrible event that was merely tactical, not strategic. The prisoner abuse at Abu Ghraib had more of an impact in the West than among Iraqis, who expected prisoners to be abused, especially at Saddam Hussein's old prison. Truly serious mistakes are those of policy, not simply those of individual tactical actions. Certainly, if the United States had had a policy directing the abuse and torture of prisoners, that could qualify as a national mistake. If this abuse was only the actions of a few undertrained and overworked servicemen, then it may only be a symptom of a larger mistake, a lack of sufficient qualified personnel in Iraq.

Blair's answer was more sophisticated and to the point. He said, "I think that probably in retrospect – though at the time it was very difficult to argue this – we could have done the de-Ba'athification in a more differentiated way than we did."[2] CPA (Coalition Provisional Authority) Order 1, the de-Ba'athification of Iraqi Society, was a conscious and calculated decision by L. Paul Bremer's office, demanded by the DoD (Department of Defense). One could argue that this decision contributed to the alienation of the Sunni Arab population of Iraq and made effective government more difficult—although, as Blair implies, there were also strong reasons in favor of de-Ba'athification at the time. By itself, perhaps de-Ba'athification might not have been a problem, but it was compounded by counterinsurgent tactics, constitutional ratification rules, and the electoral law.

Blair went on to add,

> I think it's easy to go back over mistakes that we may have made, but the biggest reason why Iraq has been difficult is the determination of our opponents to defeat us. And I don't think we should be surprised at that.... You know, they can't afford to have these countries turned round.[3]

Perhaps we should not be surprised, although coalition planning does not seem to have taken the opposition into account. The first mistake in Iraq may well have been our lack of a robust strategy. Strategy is a poorly understood concept.[4] Often, a strategy seems to simply be understood as a big, or long-range, version of a plan. Strategic thinking involves contingencies and trade-offs. Strategy includes recognizing that your actions are intertwined with those of your opponents and partners. It also includes understanding the interaction between your own goals and those of your opponents. It is shaping your opponent's options and preferences, understanding how your opponent might react to what you do, and being prepared for the unexpected. For many alleged mistakes in Iraq, one can point out how the opposite COA (course of action) was no better—or could not have been seen as better at the time. The mistake was in not anticipating the possible problems, so the coalition would be more ready to react to or mitigate the negative consequences when things did not go as planned, or in not devising better ways to address the problem.

A good strategy is a robust one. Without strategic thinking, hope becomes the plan. This is not to say that your plan is to hope everything works out, but rather that you have no fallback plan and no method for shaping the result. Without strategic thinking, you are not able to anticipate the consequences of your actions—you hope they will be beneficial, but you have no real basis for your expectations. At the highest level of policy, democratizing Iraq, in the end it is not enough to observe that large majorities of the Iraqi people favored democracy (although without knowing what it meant). It also mattered that more Iraqis over time came to oppose U.S. goals because they opposed the occupation, and that they came to believe that their opposition could be successful. While Blair did not think this should have surprised the coalition, he and it did not have a strategy for addressing a concerted opposition. We did not understand the opposition, terming them "dead-enders."[5] In a sense, we did not have a full strategy, only a set of plans.

Many factors conspired to dampen strategic thinking. Once decisions were being made in Baghdad, the pace and intensity of the work made strategic thinking difficult. Bremer's references in his book to "Baghdad time" illustrate this: one quickly lost track of time, even the passage of days within a single day.[6] It was frequent to hear "remember when X happened?" and have the answer be "yes, it was this morning." In the Green Zone Headquarters, there was always a hot issue to address immediately, either from the opposition or the chain of command. There were concerns for personal safety that are unusual for a head-quarters, which would usually be located well behind enemy lines rather than in the heart of an unsecured capital surrounded by mortars and rockets. The rapid and irregular turnover of personnel—in principle, a year for reservists and state department, six months for regular army, four months for air force—did not help, although one also could find oneself after a few months getting closed off to fresh ideas. Perhaps more troubling was the rapid movement of people between offices, and of offices between rooms and buildings, to the point where it could become difficult to even know where to find people except in the dining facility.

An even greater hindrance to strategic thinking was an inability to see the big picture. Insufficient intelligence contributed to this, but insufficient sharing of information caused as much damage. There was considerable mutual distrust between the MNF-I (Multinational Force–Iraq) and the Embassy—military officers would at times be urged not to share our ideas with the [expletive] state department, while some state department officials adopted a policy of refusing to comment on MNF-I initiatives. The lack of strategic thinking was by no means limited to the military. Some (not all, of course) state department officers would become visibly upset if asked to hypothesize how something might turn out—their job, as they saw it, was to report on what was happening, not consider the future.

There was one exception to this, the Future of Iraq project, which has become mythic for the Defense Department's refusal to use it. The project was headed up by Tom Warrick and included seventeen working groups of Iraqi exiles and international experts, each of which met for a day and a half, with limited follow-up.[7] The DoD, however, rejected the document and those associated with it.[8] The most important consequences of Warrick's blackballing was that it enhanced the disconnect between State and Defense, a disconnect that had not been closed by 2004, when Warrick would periodically rotate through the Embassy. The project itself is not nearly as useful, however, as one would expect from its reputation.[9] It describes issues but does not describe what to do, and it is nearly silent on some issues, for example, militia disarmament, that would have been useful to think about.[10] On the question of amnesty and the Ba'ath Party, the project advocates the abolition of the Ba'ath Party itself and eventual estab-lishment of a truth and reconciliation commission modeled after South Africa but does not specify the level of crimes that would become ineligible for amnesty nor what to do with individual Ba'ath Party members. It suggests revocation of Ba'ath Party privileges and building "a monument for the regime's victims...in every Iraqi city," along with "a national museum of the regime's inhumane practices."[11] This same working group recommended that transitional government in Iraq be run by independent figures, unassociated with any party (and thus lacking any base of support), who would be ineligible for election in the future to avoid "conflict of interest."[12] On the other hand, the working group did recommend an immediate curfew after Baghdad was captured to prevent looting from getting out of control.[13]

The heart of the American difficulty with strategic thinking may have been best captured by Brigadier Nigel Aylwin-Foster of the British Army. He noted that in the U.S. Army, "planning tended to be...focused on process rather than end effect." While "laudable" traits in themselves, "self-belief and resilient optimism are...unhelpful if it discourages junior commanders from reporting unwelcome news up the chain of command." As a result "Commander over-optimism...could sometimes compound the disinclination to adapt plans, since it raised undue confidence in higher headquarters that existing plans were on track."[14] Aylwin-Foster agrees with John Nagl's comments that the U.S. Army seems to be a case where "a strong organizational culture can prohibit learning the lessons of the present and can even prevent the organization's acknowledging that its current policies are anything other than completely successful."[15] These views are congruent with the authors' experiences in Iraq, where the British officers were notably more concerned about having backup contingencies for failure. Americans are more likely to express faith in success and agree with Gene Krantz of Apollo 13 fame: "failure is not an option." None of this means that Americans cannot think strategically, just that it is not rewarded. It seems that Americans are more likely be criticized for doing nothing rather than the wrong thing—this seemed to be the gist of the popular reaction to the Bush Administration after Hurricane Katrina in fall 2005. Strategy involves thinking hard before acting, and realizing that sometimes doing nothing is the best thing to do, even though doing nothing makes for a dull performance report.

This chapter illustrates the lack of robust strategic thinking by reviewing well-known situations where strategic thinking might have resulted in different decisions—though not necessarily decisions that would be recognized as better. Strategizing involves paying more attention to long-range consequences, to nuance and balance, but it does not yield a certain outcome. Strategy involves hedging your bets, being aware of the alternative outcomes, and trying above all not to paint yourself into a corner without options. Each of these situations has been discussed in other works,[16] but they are reexamined here both to provide a more complete picture of the war in this book and also to discuss the importance of strategy.

The first of these situations is the American inability to obtain a UN (United Nations) resolution that authorized its invasion. By March 2003, the United States had to either go to war without UNSC authorization or publicly back down. A more clever strategy might have avoided that problem, or perhaps only delayed the dilemma, or led the United States to break its promises. The second, perhaps best-known, situation was the American inability to quickly stop the looting of Baghdad after Saddam Hussein was driven from the city. Because the

United States assumed a large occupation force would not be needed, there were no reserve forces in Iraq to deter or stop looting. A more strategic outlook on post-combat requirements would have led to a more conservative troop deployment, which may or may not have actually defused the resistance; a massive show of force might also have increased resentment. The third situation was the removal of the Iraqi military and members of the Ba'ath Party. Bremer's choice early in his tenure was between retaining or eliminating those institutions; either choice would alienate part of Iraqi society. A different choice could have been better but also could have created entirely different problems. Finally, the fourth situation is the security crisis of April 2004. By this time, the CPA was reacting to uprisings in Fallujah and by al-Sadr's Mahdi Army. The invasion of Fallujah could have been handled differently, and al-Sadr could have been arrested early, but again this might have led to other problems. This chapter presents an introduction to the first year of the war in Iraq that considers the strategic options that the United States faced and could have chosen. It provides the history needed to appreciate the events and themes described in subsequent chapters and introduces topics addressed in later topics, including campaign planning, assessment, weighing the political–military focus, and training the ISF (Iraqi security forces).

Going to War Without the UN

If we take the decision to go to war in Iraq as a given, then the first question facing the United States was whether or not it would fight under authorization from the UNSC. UN authorization would be difficult to achieve and operationally would probably not contribute very much to the military invasion itself besides debate and tangled lines of command. On 6 March 2003, Bush made the American policy clear, stating, "when it comes to our security, if we need to act, we will act. And we really don't need United Nations approval to do so."[17] In a purely military sense, he was correct. The invasion itself would be easier and quicker without the UN, while its approval would only matter if the war went badly.

The American strategic decision was to dispense with formal UN approval and act on its own authority. Doing so left the United States open to charges of unilateralism—a term that refers less to the number of countries participating, and more to whether or not an established multilateral institution [in a pinch, as in Kosovo, the NATO (North Atlantic Treaty Organization) would suffice] deliberated and sanctioned the war. A UNSC resolution authorizing the American-led coalition invasion would have offered some material benefit as well. In the absence of such a resolution, other countries were less likely to provide support for the mission, and it was easier for critics of the war to call it illegal. A UNSC resolution would have decreased (not eliminated) public opposition around the world and more importantly given other leaders political cover to support the war. Turkey would have been more likely to have allowed a northern front in the invasion, which might have allowed more Ba'athists to be captured early in the war rather than go on to give expertise to the resistance. Other Islamic states, or India, may have been more willing to contribute forces to the invasion or occupation. The occupation also would have been more acceptable to more (not all) of the Iraqi people, because it would have been more than a crusade by western Christian countries. A UNSC resolution was most useful as a backup in case the operation became more complicated than expected—and might also have helped avoid those complications.[18]

Bush's statement about not needing "United Nations approval" for war had legal consequences as well as practical. Under international law, there are three legal reasons for going to war: a response to a direct attack, preemption, and UNSC authorization. Iraq had not attacked the United States, but the principle of preemption could justify the war and bypass the need to convince France, Russia, and China. Preemptive war is based on the accepted notion that one need not accept the first blow before retaliating—one may strike first upon clear evidence that an attack is on the way. Had the United States recognized Japanese aircraft on their way to Pearl Harbor, the United States could have tried to shoot them down before they arrived. Preemption is distinct from preventive war, a war begun because you believe that a country will attack you at some point in the future and you want to strike that country before it builds up its strength. Preventive war is considered illegal.

The United States put a lot of thought into arguing that a war on Iraq could be considered preemptive. In its NSS02 (National Security Strategy of 2002), it argued "We must adapt the concept of imminent threat to the capabilities and objectives of today's adversaries."[19] The old notions of preemption no longer applied. Preemption normally involved situations where you see the other country's attack coming and strike first. In an age of nuclear weapons and international terrorism, there would likely be no warning of an impending attack. Furthermore, traditional notions of cautious preemption carried the risk that you might end up absorbing a first strike for fear of launching an unjustified war. With WMD (weapons of mass destruction), that first strike might be too severe to be borne. The official assessment by the City of New York, for example, measured its own direct physical losses from 9/11—an attack on two buildings by unarmed aircraft—as over $21 billion; with indirect losses and lost lives, the cost to the City was over $80 billion.[20] A strategy of waiting implies that the only defense one needs is deterrence—the promise of unacceptable retaliation for an attack. The NSS02 rejected this strategy, arguing,

> deterrence based only upon the threat of retaliation is less likely to work against leaders
> of rogue states more willing to take risks, gambling with the lives of their people, and

the wealth of their nations. . . Traditional concepts of deterrence will not work against a terrorist enemy whose avowed tactics are wanton destruction and the targeting of innocents; whose so-called soldiers seek martyrdom in death and whose most potent protection is statelessness.[21]

While the logic of NSS02 is sound, it still must be applied on a case-by-case basis. If, after the invasion, the United States had discovered a well-developed nuclear weapons program, and extensive evidence of operational collaboration between Saddam Hussein's government and terrorist groups that targeted the United States, the war would have been perceived as justified (and the French would have been vilified for their obstructionism). When no such weapons were found, it was easy for other countries and the Iraqi population to claim the war was unwarranted on the basis of preemption and was simply a preventive war based on imperialist motives.

One might point out, correctly, that everyone from Bill Clinton to French President Jacques Chirac also believed that Iraq had a secret program. The problem with that argument is that none of them invaded Iraq on that basis. If one is going to use preemption as justification for war, one must be certain or be willing to accept the consequences in how others portray your intentions. There does not seem to have been much strategic thinking regarding "what if no WMD are found?" In fairness, there may not have been any fallback possible after an unauthorized preemptive invasion without evidence. That made UNSC authorization all that much more valuable. In any case, Vice President Dick Cheney had signaled the American belief with his speech on 26 August 2002, when he detailed the history of Saddam's defiance of UNSC resolutions and his past success in building WMD despite restrictions, and concluded, "there is no doubt that Saddam Hussein now has weapons of mass destruction. There is no doubt he is amassing them to use against our friends, against our allies, and against us."[22]

In essence, the United States was beginning to argue that this confrontation was a continuation of the 1990–91 war. It built on this to reach the November 2002 UNSCR 1441, in which the UNSC found that Iraq was "in material breach of its obligations" under resolutions dating back to 1991 and offered Iraq "a final opportunity to comply with its disarmament obligations." In this new round of inspections, "false statements or omissions in the declarations submitted by Iraq. . . and failure by Iraq at any time to comply with, and cooperate fully in the implementation of, this resolution shall constitute a further material breach of Iraq's obligations." The UNSCR concluded by reminding Iraq that "the Council has repeatedly warned Iraq that it will face serious consequences as a result of its continued violations of its obligations."[23] The United States argued that this was enough. In addition to stating that he did not need UN authorization for war, Bush also stated in the same press conference, "I want the United Nations to be effective. It's important for it to be a robust, capable body. It's important for its words to mean what they say."[24] Other states, most notably the United Kingdom, preferred an explicit authorization for war, but Chirac closed out that option by announcing on 10 March 2003 that France would veto any authorization.

Thus by March 2003, it seemed impossible to quickly obtain a UNSCR that explicitly authorized the use of force. France wanted to continue the inspections that had begun a few months before, in which Hans Blix reported more co-operation than before from Iraq but still some obstruction of his efforts. Chirac was more isolated, however, than is sometimes recalled. Russia and China also opposed the war, and most rotating members of the Security Council preferred not to be forced to choose between defying the United States and their own domestic opinion for a futile vote. Within the EU (European Union), however, on 30 January eight member and candidate states signed a letter, later endorsed by other candidate states, which largely agreed that UNSCR 1441 must be enforced, or else "the Security Council will lose its credibility and world peace will suffer as a result."[25] They insisted that Iraq "give[] up its weapons of mass destruction."[26] Their letter was followed by a European Council position that "Inspections cannot continue indefinitely in the absence of full Iraqi coopera-tion. . . . Iraq has a final opportunity to resolve the crisis peacefully. The Iraqi regime alone will be responsible for the consequences if it continues to flout the will of the international community."[27]

France could defy European pressure because the United States had commit-ted itself to action by deploying troops to Kuwait throughout 2002 and at an increasing rate in early 2003.[28] This deployment was, of course, perfectly legal and made a lot of sense in terms of preparing the United States for possible war in Iraq. However, it left the United States in a position where it had to act or back down; the United States did not want to leave those troops in place indefinitely and in particular preferred not to launch a war during the summer. Since the United States was unlikely to back down, France could assume that the war would occur and it could reap the benefits of principled opposition. If Iraq had WMD, the invasion would eliminate the danger, and France would suffer little lasting penalty for having wanted only to wait longer for inspections. If Iraq had no WMD, France would appear vindicated and gain moral advantage over the United States in the UN and EU.[29] The key to their opposition was being able to call the U.S. deployment a sign of aggressive intent.

Instead, the United States could have won UNSC endorsement of the deployment as a sign of the "serious consequences" that awaited Iraq if it did not comply with the UN. This endorsement was not needed but would have made the United States appear to have more concern for international law. It would have suggested that the United States was only going to act with UN endorsement. The pressure then would have been on France to authorize the invasion—neither Russia nor China was likely to stand alone in opposition, and French support might have allowed a NATO resolution of support, which was used to justify the Kosovo War in 1999. Another round of inspections might have been needed, but France probably would have voted for a UN resolution by fall 2003. Strategic diplomacy, understanding French interests, could have won international support for the war. That support would have made the invasion and occupation easier. This would have required, however, consideration of the possibility that neither easy success nor the discovery of active WMD programs would justify the war after the fact, something some Senators of both parties recognized.[30]

Seeking a UNSCR, even at the cost of several months' delay, would have brought some collateral benefits. Most notably, it would have allowed the United States to build up a larger invasion force, which would have been useful as discussed in the next section. It also would have led to UN involvement in the reconstruction of Iraq—an issue this chapter lacks space to discuss. It also entailed some risks, however. One could not be sure that France would ever agree, and delay increased the danger to the United States, in the minds of those who believed Iraqi WMD programs posed an imminent threat. UNSC authorization would have ended Saddam Hussein's apparent confidence that the United States was bluffing, and so some of the catastrophic consequences, including torching the oil fields, might have happened after all. UN oversight also might have made it more difficult to successfully prosecute the war to its conclusion. Nevertheless, the conservative choice—the more robust strategy—would have been to more strongly pursue UN authorization, rather than to play into French hands by committing forces so early.

The Size of the Occupation Force

Concurrent with the question of UN authorization was the question of the size of the force to use. Coalition forces defeated the Iraqi military in a few weeks. On 5 April, Saddam Hussein issued a good-bye to his followers near the Abu Hanifa mosque in the Adhamiyah district of Baghdad and vanished until his December capture. The conventional combat phase of the war was nearly over and could be celebrated as a "mission accomplished" by Bush on 1 May. This did not bring peace to Iraq, however. In the aftermath of the American occupation, Iraqis began looting the city, destroying public utilities and the bureaucratic infrastructure, and taking weapons stockpiles that would eventually be used against the occupying force. For weeks, American forces stood by while taking very little action. Secretary of Defense Donald Rumsfeld noted that the disorder was "part of the price of getting from a repressed regime to freedom," and "freedom's untidy, and free people are free to make mistakes and commit crimes and do bad things."[31] Finally, in May, Bremer—replacing Jay Garner as the leader of the American occupation government—ordered a change in the troops' mission.[32]

The damage was done, however. The looting of Baghdad contributed to a sense of lawlessness in Iraq, a sense that people would need to protect themselves. It undermined confidence in American forces. If the United States was incapable of preventing the looting, then in the views of unhappy Iraqis, it would have difficulty addressing a more focused resistance movement. If the United States was capable of preventing the looting, then again in the view of some Iraqis, it must be complicit in it. Either the United States had ill intentions or was unable to act on its good intentions. Either way, there was reason for Iraqis to consider supporting resistance. The looting also changed the baseline for economic reconstruction. The American air campaign had been designed to minimize damage, having learned from past experience that it would have to rebuild what it destroyed. Ideally, economic reconstruction would improve Iraqi conditions, winning goodwill among the citizens. Instead, reconstruction had to aim at restoring even the poor level of services provided before the invasion.

In this case, it is clear that the alternative strategies were considered and rejected by national leadership. Using a larger force carried with it problems similar to seeking UNSC authorization—at some point, Saddam Hussein would conclude that war was imminent. The conservatism implied by a robust invasion force also interfered with Rumsfeld's program of transforming the military into a lighter and more responsive force. As early as 2001, the military plan for an invasion of Iraq called for a force of up to 500,000; Secretary of Defense Donald Rumsfeld countered with a marker of 125,000.[33] Over the next year and a half, military planners presented trimmed force requirements, and Rumsfeld continued to press them lower.[34] Repeatedly, military planning passed over requirements for occupation forces and administration.[35] This pressure ended after 25 February 2003, when General Eric Shinseki, army chief of staff, was asked by Senator Carl Levin, "Could you give us some idea as to the magnitude of the Army's force requirement for an occupation of Iraq following a successful completion of the war?...A range?" Shinseki, deferring to the "combatant commander's exact requirements" for details, replied

> What's been mobilized to this point, something on the order of several hundred thousand soldiers, are probably...a figure that would be required. We're talking about post-hostilities control over a piece of geography that's fairly significant with the kinds of ethnic tensions that could lead to other problems. And so, it takes significant ground force presence to maintain safe and secure environment to ensure that the people are fed, that water is distributed, all the normal responsibilities that go along with administering a situation like this.[36]

The reaction to this public dissent from Shinseki's bosses' position was swift and decisive. Two days later, Rumsfeld told the press

The answer to the question that was posed to [Shinseki] is not knowable...What is, I think, reasonably certain is the idea that it would take several hundred thousand U.S. forces I think is far from the mark...The reality is that we already have a number of countries that have offered to participate with their forces in stabilization activities, in the event force has to be used. Second, it's not logical to me that it would take as many forces to win the war – following the conflict as it would to win the war.[37]

Around the same time, Deputy Secretary of Defense Paul Wolfowitz broke away from his prepared text to the House Budget committee to echo Rumsfeld.

There has been a good deal of comment—some of it quite outlandish—about what our postwar requirements might be in Iraq....I am reluctant to try to predict anything about what the cost of a possible conflict in Iraq would be...But some of the higher-end predictions that we have been hearing recently, such as the notion that it will take several hundred thousand U.S. troops to provide stability in post-Saddam Iraq, are wildly off the mark.[38]

Wolfowitz went on to explain "it is hard to conceive that it would take more forces to provide stability in a post-Saddam Iraq than it would take to conduct the war itself and to secure the surrender of Saddam's security forces and his army—hard to imagine."[39] Still echoing Rumsfeld, he said, "whatever numbers are required...there is simply no reason to assume that the United States will or should supply all of those forces...I would expect that even countries like France will have a strong interest in assisting Iraq's reconstruction...."[40] Wolfowitz added, "Moreover, the Iraqis themselves can provide a good deal of whatever manpower is necessary. We are training free Iraqi forces to perform functions of that kind, including command of Iraqi units, once those units have been purged of their Ba'athist leadership."[41]

This statement of Wolfowitz is fairly well known. He continued his diversion from his prepared text, however, to indict the very concept of strategic planning.

The fourth and most fundamental point is that...we simply cannot predict...We have no idea what kind of ethnic strife might appear in the future, although as I have noted, it has not been the history of Iraq's past...On the other side, we can't be sure that the Iraqi people will welcome us as liberators, although based on what Iraqi-Americans told me in Detroit a week ago, many of them, most of them with families in Iraq, I am reasonably certain that they will greet us as liberators, and that will help us to keep requirements down...In short, we don't know what the requirements will be. But we can say with reasonable confidence that the notion of hundreds of thousands of American troops is way off the mark... Fundamentally, we have no idea what is needed unless and until we get there on the ground.[42]

Wolfowitz, of course, is absolutely correct about the difficulty of prediction "especially about the future," as he twice cited the New York Yankees catcher, and Mets and Yankees manager, Yogi Berra. The question for strategic planning, of course, is whether one assumes things will go as well as one hopes—in which case the smaller force is quicker and less expensive—or builds in a larger force as a hedge against things going badly. The latter course is more robust, although it might make things take longer and be more expensive.

Wolfowitz wrapped up this diversion from his prepared remarks to point out that there were risks and costs in not acting:

> our preliminary estimate is that it has cost us slightly over $30 billion to maintain the containment of Saddam Hussein for the last 12 years. And it has cost us far more than money, because as I think many of you know, it is that American presence in the holy land of Saudi Arabia and the sustained American bombing of Iraq as part of that containment policy that have been Osama bin Laden's principal recruiting device, even more than the other grievances he cites. I can't imagine anyone here wanting to spend another $30 billion to be there for another 12 years to continue helping recruit terrorists.[43]

The decision on troop sizing might be more defensible if Shinseki had been speaking truly off the cuff. His argument, however, was based on historical analogy—one Wolfowitz rejected in his testimony to the House committee. Shinseki was not alone in this opinion. Bremer says that before he left for Iraq he sent Rumsfeld a RAND study that recommended 500,000 troops to meet the historical requirements for taking order; he got no response.[44] Other worries about looting, including those brought by Iraqi exile leaders, were dismissed.[45] Ironically, if Shinseki's advice had been followed, it might now be seen as a case of overkill. With 500,000 troops keeping order, looting may never have become serious, Iraqi citizens may never have become disillusioned with the American occupation, and some of the resistance may have been deterred. Instead, American military leaders seem to have been deterred by Shinseki's example from asking for more troops.

Post-invasion planning was based on the most optimistic expectations. This may partly be accounted for by Rumsfeld's preoccupation with defense transformation, reforming the military into a lighter force. A large troop commitment to Iraq would undermine that goal—and one can only be happy that he was correct that a smaller, lighter invasion force would suffice for the war. Post-invasion planning also gave credence to the claims of Iraqi exiles, most notably Ahmed Chalabi, who claimed that Iraqis would welcome the Americans (and himself) with flowers and open arms.[46] If this was true, if Iraqis would regard themselves as liberated rather than occupied, then one could hope that a large occupation force was unneeded. Furthermore, it was anticipated that Iraqi units would defect to support the occupation and could be used to supplement American forces.[47] The strategic plan did not consider the possibility that things would not work out as planned—as hoped.

Draining the Ba'ath and Disbanding the Army

The questions became more difficult once Bremer arrived in Baghdad. In addition to the looting, Bremer was confronted with the question of what to do about the remnants of the political and military infrastructure of Saddam Hussein's regime. His first two CPA orders, removing Ba'athists from civil society and disbanding the Iraqi military, have been widely criticized. Some decision, however, was required—not disbanding the institutions meant leaving them in place, which might not have been a better COA.

The strategic implication of Bremer's actions is that both orders disproportionately affected the Sunni Arabs, the portion of the Iraqi population that was inherently most hostile to the American occupation. Disbanding the Iraqi military left thousands of veterans unemployed, more likely to join the resistance; the coalition has ever since been trying to reconstitute ISF.[48] De-Ba'athification, cited by Blair as the greatest mistake of the war, also took thousands of Sunni Arabs out of legal employment and emptied the Iraqi bureaucracy of experienced personnel. While CPA Orders 1 and 2 both had serious negative effects on the war, they must nevertheless be evaluated in context with the strategic situation at the time.

Bremer has argued that he did not disband the Iraqi army, it had disbanded itself. Rather than surrendering to coalition forces, it melted away. Thus his choice was not between maintaining the army or eliminating it but between accepting its disappearance or trying to piece it back together. There are compelling reasons for making the choice he did. The Iraqi army, while a source of national pride in the country's wars of the previous decades, was also a symbol of Saddam Hussein's oppression. Kurd leaders knew that the Iraqi army had conducted genocide against their people in the 1980s. Shia Arabs knew that the Iraqi army had brutally put down their rebellion after the Gulf War in 1991. Both groups told Bremer that reconstituting the army would be seen as another betrayal, a sign that they would not be safe under the new leadership in Iraq.[49] Bremer needed the support of those groups; given that the army no longer physically existed, it was easier to ratify that fact. Disbanding the army also laid the legal foundation for creating new national military institutions.

The Ba'ath Party, on the other hand, continued to exist after Saddam's overthrow. The Ba'ath Party, ruling both Iraq and Syria, was the primary source of government employment; in a socialist state, such government jobs dominate the economy. Ba'ath membership is comparable to Communist Party membership in the old Soviet Union and Eastern Europe, or even Nazi Party membership under Hitler. Not everyone who joined the party was complicit in its crimes—but its crimes were many and heinous. Like the army, the Ba'ath Party represented Saddam's oppression to the Kurds and Shia Arabs, and those groups' leaders wanted it eliminated if they were going to trust that politics would be different. As long as Ba'ath members remained in government, they would fear the return of the old days.

Bremer's choice therefore was difficult: if he kept the army and Ba'ath, he would alienate the 75 percent of the population who opposed those institutions. If he eliminated them, he would deepen the alienation of the other 25 percent of the population. He chose the latter, perhaps as the most economical, perhaps not recognizing that by doing so he was compounding the impact of the war on the Sunni Arabs. They had lost their national leadership, they had been more affected by both the war and the looting, and now they were losing their national institutions. As the war would continue, the resistance became centered among the Sunni Arabs. Strategic thinking even at this stage would have recognized the ultimate importance of that subcultural group for the success of Iraqi democracy. Ultimately, the support of the Sunni Arabs would be lost, as these blows would be compounded by large numbers of internments and the two invasions of Fallujah. They would boycott the elections in January 2005. This in turn led to their underrepresentation in the constitutional process and the approval of a constitution very disadvantageous to their interests.

In the end, Bremer eliminated both institutions. Members of the four highest of the six levels of Ba'ath Party membership were "removed from their positions and banned from future employment in the public sector. . . [and] shall be evaluated for criminal conduct or threat to the security of the Coalition."[50] Futhermore, "individuals holding positions in the top three layers of management in every national government ministry, affiliated corporations and other government institutions (e.g., universities and hospitals). . . [who were] full members of the Ba'ath Party shall be removed from their employment," regardless of their level of membership.[51] Initially only Bremer or his appointed official could grant exceptions to this policy,[52] but a few days later he created an IDC (Iraqi De-Ba'athification Council) which would advise Bremer on things like "a means of identifying and classifying Iraqi Baath [sic] Party officials and members" and "individuals who the Council considers should be exempt from" CPA Order 1.[53]

Pending the stand-up of the IDC, Bremer delegated authority to the military commander of coalition forces, who would establish Accreditation Review Committees to determine individuals' status. Guidance for exceptions included public renunciation of the party, level of membership, education and skill level, timing of leaving the party, and proof that membership was driven by economic need. The guidance also said to consider whether the party member "continues to command the support of his colleagues and respect of their [sic] subordinates," though it is not clear if this would increase or decrease chances for an exception.[54] By the end of 2003, the CPA turned de-Ba'athification over to the GC (Governing Council) and its Higher National De-Ba'athification Commission.[55] This commission would be retained under the Transitional Administrative Law, which served as Iraq's interim constitution until a new one was ratified on 15 October 2005.[56]

With respect to the military, all branches of the Iraqi armed forces and defense ministry were dissolved on 23 May 2003. In general, pensions would be maintained and termination payments made, except that "no payment, including a termination or pension payment, will be made to any person who is or was a Senior Party Member. Any person holding the rank under the former regime of Colonel or above, or its equivalent, will be deemed a Senior Party Member."[57] The Order went on to promise the creation "in the near future" of "a New Iraqi Corps" which "will be professional, non-political, militarily effective, and representative of all Iraqis."[58] This New Iraqi Army was created in August with former members of the four top levels of the Ba'ath Party prohibited from service and "the absence of affiliation with the security and political control organs of the former regime" considered a criterion for measuring "suitability for service."[59] Subsequent CPA Orders created a Facilities Protection Service and Iraqi Civil Defense Corps, separate from both the army and the police and subject to the same membership restrictions.[60] This proliferation of security services would by 2006 provide cover for militia killings and a general lack of central control over armed forces.

The choice, which Bremer says was directed by Undersecretary of Defense Douglas Feith,[61] need not have been so stark. Both issues could have been finessed in ways that would have lessened the impact. With the army vanished, a new army could have been built from its shell without gratuitously firing its old officers. This reformed army would have been as acceptable to other Iraqi groups as the one being created by the occupiers, but it would have been more acceptable to the Sunni Arabs. The Iraqi Army would thus have retained continuity with its past, rather than being the creation of the occupier. With the army retained, some of its members could have trickled back over time and been vetted for resumption of duties at that point. The army vanished in April; June was a bit early to assume that no parts of it would ever return. As for the Ba'ath Party, CPA Order 1 placed the burden of innocence on the party member. Party members could appeal to a commission and demonstrate that they were not guilty of crimes. Even had this commission not been turned over to Chalabi, a rabid anti-Ba'athist, this made restoration difficult and humiliating. The CPA could have lessened the impact on Sunni Arabs by placing the bar for automatic exclusion at a higher level of membership and by having members left in a probationary status while any crimes were investigated. Taken together, these steps might have reduced the antagonism of Sunni Arabs toward the occupation. It would have taken strategic thinking, however, anticipating the possibility of a broadly supported resistance, to appreciate the importance of Sunni Arab opinion. It is easier to disband the institutions if one does not expect resistance to develop.

Twin Uprisings and Militias

While there are many more decisions that can be discussed, the substantive portion of this chapter concludes with a discussion of the security crises that erupted in April 2004. The first year of occupation was more peaceful than what was to come. At the end of March, this ended as al-Sadr's Mahdi Army rebelled throughout southern Iraq. This would be the most geographically widespread violence in Iraq since the invasion, and it was put down only with difficulty. Al-Sadr's forces fought the coalition again in Najaf in August and in Baghdad in October before he agreed to end the violent campaign. His militia survived, however, and became an important part of the civil violence in Iraq, as his forces murdered Sunni Arabs in mixed areas and fought government forces (and other militias) in Shia Arab areas. The strategic issue with al-Sadr always was how strongly to move against him. Just as the coalition was trying to respond to the Shia Arab rebellion, four Blackwater contractors were captured in Fallujah, murdered, and hung from a bridge. The United States responded with an invasion of the city, which was cut short when the GC, a group of Iraqis selected by Bremer as advisors, rejected the action. Fallujah was turned over to a Sunni Arab brigade that promised to keep order. Security in Fallujah quickly became the worst in the country, and after two months of preparations, the city would be reinvaded at the end of Ramadan. This second invasion had a devastating impact on Sunni Arab participation in the elections; the first abortive invasion emboldened the resistance.

Bremer has said that the murders in Fallujah have been portrayed as requiring response, lest the United States be seen as "irresolute."[62] This logic in itself is not clear. Fallujah was no more dangerous after the killings than before, but its prominence in the media was greater. The gruesome display outraged Americans, though many equal atrocities have been committed since then with less response. It is not clear what ills would have resulted from ignoring the Blackwater deaths. Indeed, one could argue that the Fallujah invasion was a case of strategic overreaction. While the judgment is harsh to the loved ones of the murdered contractors, one does not ordinarily invade a city in reaction to the deaths of four civilians, no matter how horrible the circumstances. Having decided to invade the city, however, the CPA failed to secure GC support. Faced with threats of resignations by Sunni Arabs, including the thoroughly pro-American Adnan Pachachi, and expressions of solidarity even from Shia Arabs, the invasion was halted.[63] The Marines were not allowed to finish the battle, and the city was turned over to a local militia. This experiment in Iraqi control failed, as the First Fallujah

Brigade proved unable and unwilling to stop the resistance. This seemed to Iraqis like an American defeat—more so than if the United States had just deplored the deaths. American actions resulted in a loss of support among Sunni Arabs. In this case, however, it did not even increase its support among other groups. Al-Sadr took advantage of the invasion to appeal to Iraqi solidarity, and Shia Arabs were also outraged by the action.

Al-Sadr posed a more complex problem. The heir to a family of prominent clerics, many of them murdered by the Ba'athist government, al-Sadr himself had little clerical credibility. His charisma won him a strong following, especially among poor, young urban men. His calls for action contrasted with Grand Ayatollah Ali al-Sistani's advocacy of restraint. His militia became known as the war ended, but it was difficult to decide what to do about it. There were many small Iraqi factions, some of which have faded away. Al-Sadr seemed more dangerous than most because of his name and heritage and because he was implicated in the assassination of Grand Ayatollah Abdul Majid al-Khoei, a leading Shia Arab advocate of democracy, on 10 April 2003 at the Imam Ali Shrine in Najaf. His forces also rebelled briefly in Karbala and elsewhere, including Baghdad, in October 2003.[64]

While his potential for causing trouble was recognized early on, al-Sadr was able to retain the initiative because the CPA could not decide how to deal with him. While most Shia Arabs, particularly their spiritual leader, al-Sistani, opposed al-Sadr, arresting him risked provoking an uprising among his followers. Al-Sadr was repeatedly put on the back burner until March 2004. After a sermon in Kufa advocating violence, one of his newspapers was shut down, and arrest warrants for al-Khoei's murder were served on some of his followers. In response, al-Sadr's Mahdi Army rebelled throughout the Shia Arab south, Baghdad, and even as far as Kirkuk.[65] As with Fallujah, the CPA had great difficulty convincing the GC to accept strong action against al-Sadr. Gradually, the coalition forced his militia out of cities like Kut, Karbala, Hillah, and Nasariyah; by June, his forces left the Imam Ali Shrine in Najaf,[66] only to return in August.

It appears that it would have been better to arrest al-Sadr in fall 2003 when his movement was weaker. This, of course, is an easier assertion to make in retrospect. Since one could not know that al-Sadr's movement would become so powerful, one could not assume that dismantling it was a high priority— or a higher priority than civil affairs efforts or addressing the Sunni Arab portion of the resistance. Kinetic operations during counterinsurgency are often counterproductive, and if al-Sadr had been targeted earlier, it might have only provoked an uprising like that of April 2004 earlier. It also might have increased his appeal—since al-Sadr was more clearly the aggressor in taking over important shrines and mosques, his popularity was limited among more traditional Shia Arabs. An American or coalition initiative might have allowed him to increase his support earlier—and might have fractured the GC if it went badly.

Conclusions

It is difficult to say what Bremer "should have done" in spring 2004, though it is easy to criticize him. In general, if results are poor, the strategy is seen as poor; if results are good, the strategy is seen as good. By April 2004, or even October 2003, Bremer and the CJTF-7 had very few choices. The lack of UN cover had minimized the organization's potential involvement as a neutral arbiter and placed the United States as the governor of Iraq. Low troop levels had contributed to the destruction of Iraqi civil infrastructure and dispirited Iraqi supporters, emboldening both al-Sadr and the Fallujah resistance and easing their recruiting and tacit support. Loss of the Iraqi military and mid-level noncommitted
Ba'athists had increased support for the resistance and reduced potential support for the occupation. Bremer had two hard choices in April 2004, and it was difficult to know the best course of action—in part because the United States still lacked a comprehensive campaign plan, even at the military level.

For all this, however, the situation in summer 2004 was not irredeemable. The restoration of Iraqi sovereignty on 28 June 2004 indicated that the United States was serious about letting Iraqis rule themselves. The United Nations and every major Iraqi political faction had endorsed an 18-month schedule for the Iraqis to write their own constitution and elect their own leaders. Iraqis directed most of their violence at the coalition rather than at each other. If handled well, the next year would bring Iraqis to the verge of complete self-rule, and the coalition to the verge of transferring operational control to Iraqi security forces. That was the schedule, but as it turned out there was no real plan for making it happen.

CHAPTER 3

CAMPAIGN PLANNING: THE GROUND TRUTH

Tomislav Z. Ruby

When countries engage other countries in the international arena, there is no set of universally agreed-upon procedures that govern state actions—no checklist of considerations to discuss, actions to take, or even a set order to in which to make decisions. Militaries have doctrine to guide actions, but military force is only one instrument of power that states can use when engaging in international relations. The United States, for example, calculates what type of power to use in some circumstances and decides to play the diplomatic card, such as in recent confrontations with North Korea over nuclear weapons already in hand. In other cases, such as Iraq, the United States went directly to the military option even though there was disagreement over whether these weapons of mass destruction yet existed or were only in production. In the 1990s, the United States intervened in the former Yugoslavia to prevent ethnic cleansing and somewhat dubious claims of attempted genocide while standing by while true genocidal acts took place in Rwanda and other parts of Africa.

When deciding whether to undertake military operations, or what the strategy for such operations should look like, military and civilian planners alike must consider all the logical outcomes of their actions and put those outcomes in the context of the present-day international environment. They must also consider the long-term ramifications of those decisions for the United States and its allies alike. Failing to do so can easily make the situation for their country far worse in the future than the one they are dealing with in the present. By not making consistent decisions with respect to international crises or opportunities, other actors cannot model U.S. behavior and know how the United States will act. This uncertainty can cloud the international context and set the players on more dangerous paths than if consistent decisions were always made. Even the presence of the occasional brilliant individual is not enough. The American campaign in Iraq was damaged in its early stages because its leaders did not develop plans robust enough to survive setbacks. States can be more consistent, and successful, in their application of the various instruments of power if national leaders take their roles as decision makers more seriously. If they actively considered the forces that shape their decisions and the likely outcomes of their actions, there would be a more consistent, recognizable environment in which their country could act. If they instead rely on hope, then the results will not usually turn out the way they wish.

This chapter proposes a set of five normative issues that planners, both military and civilian, should deliberately consider with respect to military campaigns. First, they must know the stated mission. Second, they must know the bounds placed upon them by national leadership. Third, they must attempt to break through perceptions to know in detail the situation on the ground in the region they are considering operations. Fourth, they must consider the pathologies of the staff—both their own and the coalition they may be entering. Finally, they must consider how they will know when they have achieved their end state or desired objectives. In keeping with the theme of this book, the majority of supporting material will be drawn from the coalition's experience in Iraq. These five considerations may seem self evident on the surface; however, they were not well thought out prior to or during operations in Iraq. Furthermore, if these considerations are so basic and self evident, one could easily ask why countries so often find themselves in situations they did not plan for.

U.S. Joint Doctrine defines a campaign as a "series of related military operations aimed at accomplishing a strategic or operational objective within a given time and space."[1] But in today's international environment, that definition is probably too narrow in that campaign planning must include more than military operations. In fact, one major reason the United States struggles in its present operations in the war on terror—not just in Iraq, but in Afghanistan as well— is that its campaigns are seemingly planned solely as a series of military operations without taking into account how diplomacy, information, culture, and economics might impact the situation. Such campaigns require an integrated application of all the national instruments of power.

Part of the problem may be the nature of military planning. Planners are those men and women, both military and civilian, who develop options and present them to senior decision makers for action. They are not necessarily experts in the region or topic for which they plan. In the U.S. military, there is no career specialty for campaign planning; officers are made planners based on the position in which they serve at the time. Officers serving on a planning staff most often remain on those staffs for a period of two or three years before moving on to another assignment. Furthermore, there is no database within the U.S. military to ensure officers with specific knowledge or background in a region are called upon to plan operations in that area if the need arises.

This chapter's list is not in any way complete, but it is meant to be a departure point from which national leaders deliberate, decide, and act. They need to be sure that they understand these issues and provide guidance to those who plan. Likewise, the planners themselves, both civilian and military, must consider these issues well before options are presented to national leaders for decisions. In essence, planners must learn to be politically astute without being political. Naive planners who are not aware of the realities of the world within which they work are not prepared to argue for the plans that are right for their countries, even if their national leaders do not recognize the fact because they are too focused on short-term "solutions" without thinking about the long-term implications of those solutions. Many political leaders will take what they consider to be a pragmatic view of the international and domestic context and say that these considerations are easily dismissible. However, these same dismissals likely lead to the poor outcomes of decisions leaders make without deliberate consideration of the issues outlined herein.

What Is Your Stated Mission?

From the very beginning, even before a group of people is brought together to plan a campaign, the country must clearly articulate the results that are desired. That desired end state must be the single point of reference for all actions undertaken in diplomacy or military operations. The desired end state should be specific, so there is less room for interpretation and mistakes. Thus, it is important that the end state or objectives are not only clearly articulated but also written. National leaders conveying written orders and direction reduce the need for questions and the opportunity for misinterpretation.

In the case of the war in Iraq, the campaign's end state was not articulated in its final form until the campaign plan was approved by General George W. Casey in August 2004, fully seventeen months after the initiation of combat operations. Planning for combat operations had been under way for months prior to the commencement of the war. Yet the planning went on for those months without a written end state. As of this writing, one member of the Strategic Planning council, a small group of hand-selected mid-grade officers from the fours services which advised the Secretary of Defense on options from 2001 to 2003, says that the reason the Air Force representatives so strongly urged against invasion was because of the lack of a clear end state.[2]

This means that no matter how strong the leadership within the coalition, and no matter how precisely national leaders knew what they wanted, military commanders, intergovernmental planners, coalition partners, and Iraqis did not have a written, agreed-upon common objective. This was not an isolated incident. In the NATO air war against Yugoslavia in 1999, there also was not a written end state or objective given to military planners prior to the war. Instead, several different sets of objectives were given in speeches by various national leaders, and many only after hostilities were initiated.[3] Once an operation is begun, it is too late to ask where the coalition is going.

Some critics will argue that requesting this level of detailed instruction from national leadership is a dodge by the military in an area where they are the experts. They know what the civilian leadership wants and should do it. But this is not a dodge at all. The end state is a political decision which should be made by political leadership. The strategy by which to achieve that end state or objective is what the military leadership are experts in and should develop. But if the military was to determine end states and objectives, then the entire tradition of civilian control of the military would be undermined.[4] Military officers are taught to analyze national security and military strategic direction as well as appropriate guidance in alliance and coalition directions, including long- and short-term objectives for conflict termination. That springs from direction in Joint Doctrine for Campaign Planning which states in bold lettering: "When objectives are unclear or ambiguous, the combatant commander or subordinate joint force commander must seek clarification and convey the impact, both positive and negative, of continued ambiguity with the NCA [National Command Authority]."[5]

The end state must be the starting point of all planning and the ultimate goal of all the instruments of power. The end state must be attainable. Otherwise, it is merely a hope. And committing resources against an unattainable end state is a waste of lives and money. To that end, all actions in an operation must be deliberately and measurably tied to that end state. Perhaps the best way to ensure this happens is to establish an organization that is tailored in mission and scope with the single aim of attaining that end state.

Not every planning staff is, nor should be, the same. Just as the saying goes in the U.S. military that joint does not mean equal shares of the pie, but the right forces for the job, a planning staff and the headquarters of the coalition should not necessarily be based on a strict template. Templating may work to ensure a base cadre is available to form the core of the staff, but the template cannot ensure the expertise for all foreseeable situations. A tailored organization is appropriate because each situation that a country finds itself in comes with its own unique context. That context dictates that while all four of a country's instruments of power—diplomatic, informational, military, and economic—will play a role in resolving the conflict, only one can necessarily be the lead in a given segment of the operation at a given time. A tailored organization that melds military and civilian personnel, perhaps from multiple countries, and one that is focused on attaining a specific end, is more likely to stay on track than to drift off course to the end state.

Finally, when planning to use instruments of power abroad, planners must be ready for change. Ground truth changes during wars and during campaigns within wars for a myriad of reasons. Coalitions add and lose members. Internal dynamics within countries change. Old leaders lose influence, and new leaders arise. Sudden defeats or victories embolden one side or another. Unforeseen events take place, and equipment fails at higher rates than planned. For all these reasons, planners must be ready for change, even given a clearly articulated end state.

Measured change is the work of a mature staff. Well-deliberated, researched decisions may take longer to develop than snap decisions, but they will have the backing of reason and logic behind them. Anticipating alternative futures will save the staff and national leaders many headaches and perhaps many lives as well, since they should have plans in place for expected potentialities rather than being purely reactive and ceding the initiative either to the opponent or to chance.

What Are the Bounds Placed on You by Political Leadership?

The second major issue civilian and military planners must consider is the boundaries placed on them by national political leaders. Within this category of considerations, planners must remember that politicians think in terms of near-term political expediency, that they give broad, often unmeasurable directions, that various leaders have to concern themselves with varying local constituencies, and that they may ask planners to do something they are unable to effect.

The first thing that planners must take into account is that their national political leaders think in terms of near-term political expediency. There is much evidence that leaders from country to country consider the next election cycle more than they do long-term issues facing their countries.[6] What does this have to do with campaign planning? It means that while there may be a real or perceived national interest that drives a country to take particular actions, and although some leaders will be genuinely interested in the long-term good of their countries, many leaders will leave those operations to subordinates or their militaries if they have "more important" near-term political issues to consider, such as elections. National leaders may even try to influence planners to maximize their short-term political needs, rather than allowing them to develop the best long-term plan for the country.

American officers saw a classic example of this phenomenon during counter-insurgency operations in Iraq. In the autumn of 2004, the number of phone calls received on a daily basis in Baghdad by the multinational force headquarters from Washington dropped dramatically during the election campaign for the Presidency and congressional seats. Having become accustomed to spending hours answering questions from Washington about every detail reported on the news, the staff in Baghdad welcomed the opportunity to focus on operations and not answering calls from various actors in Washington demanding answers.

Nevertheless, in October 2004, the strategy division of the Multinational Force, Strategy, Plans, and Assessment Directorate explicitly took into account the impact on the Presidential election of the varying COAs (courses of action) being considered at the time. This was not to affect the outcome of the election but to try to foresee the potential long-term impacts of these decisions and the likely direction given to those courses based on which candidate would end up in office as President. The most serious of these, delaying the assault on Fallujah until after the election, helped push Sunni Arabs away from the election process.

However, it is not just elections that lead politicians to make certain decisions. National leaders may be willing to accept greater risk abroad to satisfy other domestic and international relationships. This is where some interesting social science work can be made to explain how these decisions are weighted by the politicians making them. For example, some European countries like the Netherlands and Poland and Bulgaria joined the multinational coalition despite mass popular opposition in those countries. In the short term, their leaders had varying domestic issues that weighed against their involvement abroad, yet all decided to act. In fact, according to one Bulgarian staff officer in Baghdad, Bulgaria spent over half its 2005 military budget to support operations in Iraq by its military forces deployed there.[7] Certainly, this was not out of any mass political movement in Bulgaria in support of Iraq but more likely because of hopes for long-term benefits to their relationship with the United States. However, other politicians, despite terrorist cells in their own countries, like Spain, Germany, and France, decided to pull their forces out of the operations or stay at home altogether.

Even after the 2004 U.S. election firmly placed President George W. Bush beyond the threat of personal defeat, talk in Washington turned from a protracted stay in Iraq to the possibility of bringing home the forces in early 2006. Why? Bush was not under any personal pressure to do so. There must be some other mix of variables that applies, and the most important thing for campaign planners to understand is that these realities exist and they must be ready for various national leaders to make various decisions that will stress the concept of unity of effort within a coalition. While some countries in the coalition may be between election cycles, other countries might be in the midst of national election campaigns, while still others might be contesting regional elections which portend future direction. Threats to pull out of a coalition by one country's candidates may stress the unity with which that country's officers plan and recommend action to coalition military leaders. While these election cycles are all natural and reoccurring political events, military planners must know the potential implications of these events on their operations and take them into account while planning.

The second point in this section is that national leaders often give broad, unmeasurable guidance for their planners. It is natural that national leaders want to show that they are doing something for their countries, but without wanting to open themselves to potential subsequent blame for outcomes that are not reached. Leaving the details to subordinates to hash out protects national leaders from making the tough decisions they rarely feel comfortable with and also seems to allow for the virtue of letting the "experts" handle the details. But these experts are generally not accountable to the people in a democracy and can take a country down a path for which the leaders are ultimately responsible and that they did not foresee.

Some recent examples of leaders giving broad, unmeasurable guidance come since the end of the Cold War. In 1992, President George Bush sent U.S. forces to Somalia in support of a UN (United Nations) resolution to "provide a secure environment in which to deliver relief supplies to break the famine and to establish conditions for a rapid transition to U.N. control."[8] But how did that operation rapidly turn to nation building and major combat operations? One reason is that there was not a clear and measurable end state that planners could mold operations to achieve. Likewise, in 1999 President Bill Clinton determined the United States would "demonstrate the seriousness of NATO's [the North Atlantic Treaty Organization's] opposition to [the Serb] aggression [against Kosovar Albanians] and [NATO's] support for peace" as the first objective of Operation Allied Force.[9] From a political standpoint, NATO leaders certainly wanted to show that they were doing something in the face of Yugoslav intransigence, and certainly it would be safe to list as an objective that they wanted to demonstrate resolve. But how that objective naturally leads to any measurable end state is beyond the ability of most planners around the world.

Likewise, when planners in Washington, D.C., went to the President via the Secretary of Defense to request specific guidance on direction and end states in the Global War on Terror, the President turned the question back to the planners and asked them to come up with objectives for the President.[10] Such a logic train would be dismissed as tautological by methodologists. But with politically astute planners, a national leader could be helped to form a strongly worded end state and objectives that achieve national interests and keep the mission focused throughout. That is exactly what happened in September 2001 when Pentagon officers got together, discussed what they thought the President and his advisors really meant, not just what they said, and offered a set of objectives for operations in Afghanistan, which the President promptly made his own.[11]

Once the objectives are clearly defined, campaign planners must consider whether or not they actually have the means to achieve those objectives and end states. Why would they be given objectives without the means to achieve them? For the same reason that political leaders think in terms of near-term political expediency. Planners must understand that force sizing is not always based on military requirement. Larger force sizes are often harder to sell domestically, especially if those larger force sizes seem to indicate that the mission will be more difficult than what the leadership told the public. In Somalia, Secretary of Defense Les Aspin denied the request of military commanders for heavier equipment to protect U.S. service members. Many believed this refusal was based on the understanding that beefing up the forces in Somalia would signal that the mission was harder than originally explained by the administration.[12] While the first Bush Administration got the United States into Somalia, it was clearly President Clinton's situation, and in the early days of his tenure, he likely did not want it to seem that the United States was staying in a very difficult military situation which needed reinforcing. While we cannot go back in time to prove whether the requested equipment and forces would have made the difference in the Blackhawk Down situation, the question remains today.

Likewise, prior to the commencement of the war in Iraq, Secretary of Defense Donald Rumsfeld and his office continually stated that required manpower for the operation would be far lower than stated by military officials if they relied on innovation, speed, and precision. But when the Army Chief of Staff, General Eric Shinseki, testified before Congress that the occupation force would require several hundred thousand troops, his replacement as Chief of Staff was announced fourteen months ahead of schedule, and he was cut out of all future planning discussions within the Department of Defense. Thus, planners must consider that while they may want more forces, or a certain mix of forces to do a particular job, the national decision makers might see the decision within a context beyond the military operations and may deny those requests.

In these cases, campaign planners must understand that there are often multiple possible strategies to attain a specific end. Some strategies will assume a greater risk with fewer forces, such as the operation to depose the Iraqi leadership. Those decisions on how much risk to accept in the overall conflict must be made by national political leadership. Thus planners must be careful not to select a strategy that will leave them unable to affect what is truly important to attaining the end state. They must consider the art of the possible and remember that the perfect plan is often the enemy of the plan that would be good enough to win. The perfect plan may not be executable because the plan may need more resources than it would be physically or politically expedient to provide.

Next, campaign planners must understand another aspect of varying pressures placed on political leaders from other countries in a coalition. Based on their domestic contexts, national political leaders will decide to bring home their forces at varying times during an operation. How they will fill critical gaps left when countries decide to bring home their forces? For example, the Netherlands decided to bring home their forces in Iraq after Iraqi elections in January 2005. Based on the Dutch understanding of the situation and their interpretation of the UN mandate, their leadership decided to bring home their forces at a point before many others in the coalition decided to leave Iraq.[13] Campaign planners were happy to have the Dutch commitment of a reinforced infantry battalion for conducting combat operations but had to plan for their backfill when the Dutch departed.

But planners, like the general public, must understand the contributions offered by even the smallest coalition partners. Some small states bring small contingents but with capabilities that are critical to the effort, such as special operations companies. Furthermore, some smaller contingents are proportionally much larger to the effort than even the Americans when the countries they come from are small to begin with. A small country that sends a battalion may send a third or even half its military and thus take on a greater risk according to the size for their population for a cause that may not provide them with the same benefit as it would for a larger state like the United States or Poland or the United Kingdom. But when any country decides it is time to bring their military forces or other civilian capabilities home, campaign planners must have foreseen the need for a backfill of those capabilities, or else the coalition leadership will have to accept the greater risk by not having those capabilities present. All commitments are valuable and must be integrated as best suits the capabilities offered and the needs of the coalition for those capabilities. In the grand comparison of capabilities, some commitments are truly feeble, but they sent an important message of international solidarity and legitimacy that is important for the rest of the coalition as well as for the Iraqi people.

What Is the Ground Truth?

Determining ground truth is one of the most difficult tasks of the campaign planner. The perception of ground truth changes based on a person's location, understanding of the context, and interest in the situation. An entire literature exists studying the distinction between reality and perception and how it impacts daily life.[14] It is a hard concept for some planners to understand, but people in one place may absolutely believe something to be true that people in another believe to be patently false. This concept should be differentiated from intelligence by the nature of the information. Intelligence is of value to a specific operation or a specific issue for a specific decision. Understanding the cultural and political issues and perceptions which frame a context in which campaign planning is conducted may affect specific operations, but they are grander and underpin the assumptions and going-in mindset of the planners and commanders. While intelligence is collected to answer specific questions, such as where arms caches are hidden or who commands a particular cell, the ground truth discussed in this section, such as how much electricity is available, forms the foundation for decisions ranging from logistical supplies to manpower to combat timing.

Americans are often unaware of how different perceptions and reality can be in different places even though examples abound to show this truth in the United States. Some Americans believe that the police set up people of certain demographics, while other people believe that authorities are always honest. Likewise, people in certain countries believe that Americans make political decisions around the world in an attempt to expand an empire, while others welcome U.S. aid and intervention.

Planners must take into account several factors dealing with ground truth. First, they must know what kind of conflict they are in. Second, they must consider the population demographics of the area they are trying to affect and whether or not there is an accepted ground truth. Next, campaign planners must consider whether or not what they propose has been tried before, and if so, has the context changed so as to make it a different course in fact. Finally, they must consider whether or not the coalition must be 100 percent successful in every action in order to succeed overall.

First, when considering the ground truth, the campaign planner must know what kind of conflict they are in or planning for. Is it a "conventional war", one in which two sides line up and see who is stronger? Is the planner considering how to plan for a humanitarian operation, or a stability operation after a cease-fire or a counterinsurgency? Each of these types of operation requires different assumptions, force mixtures, and capabilities. But throughout the new U.S. Doctrine for Joint Operations, the Chairman of the Joint Chiefs of Staff warns planners that they will likely have to consider the entire range of military operations in each conflict at the same time.[15] This is referred to as the three-block war. On one block of the city, there can be humanitarian relief operations with military forces assisting or supporting international NGOs (nongovernmental organizations) delivering relief supplies. On the next block over, the same unit of military force is conducting stability operations with a different set of rules of engagement. And on an adjacent block, they can be fighting house to house in a full-scale conventional conflict with yet a third set of rules of engagement.

So it is critical for planners to consider not only what kind of operation is called for at the outset of planning but also what is potentially envisioned as a natural consequence of operations once they are begun. Thus, it is critical to know and define the conflict up front. For example, are you planning to fight an insurgency or a resistance? Some will argue that the difference is semantic. But when considering the opponents' goal, the differences are fundamental. In an insurgency, the opposing forces are trying to overthrow the sovereign and replace it with another more to their liking. In a resistance, the opponents are merely trying to make the occupier leave the country. The resisters are not necessarily interested in running the country. They only want freedom of action without interference from the sovereign.

In Iraq, the multinational coalition has in fact been fighting a resistance, yet thinks it is fighting an insurgency, and thus is making fundamental choices and assumptions about the enemy that are not taking it toward its desired end state. Campaign planners must understand their situation and the perception of it as seen by those living in the region they are trying to affect. Likewise, they must know how the truth is seen by the adversary they are planning to defeat, for that perception of the situation is believed as truth by the adversary and affects the adversary's decisions.

The next issue of ground truth that planners must consider is how culture affects operations in the area of interest. In this case, it is extremely important for campaign planners to forget political correctness and to understand how culture affects perceptions, and the ground truth. National political leaders, and especially campaign planners, must understand that what may seem oxymoronic to Western observers or planners may be perfectly acceptable in another culture. And discussions about why a culture accepts certain things as truth may be germane to sociologists, but planners must not get carried away with why people in a region accept certain things as a truth. They must simply understand that they do and plan accordingly.

In Iraq, it was rarely if ever publicized that when multinational forces cleared a location that enemy forces held, nearly every time the coalition seized not only weapons but also stacks of pornography, drugs and drug paraphernalia, and liquor. These findings were often not seen as important to Western media, as if showing it would be a besmirchment of the entire Arab culture. But doing so might have gone a long way toward discrediting the enemy forces and casting them apart from local populations. On the other hand, after coalition forces cleared a protected site, such as a mosque, of enemy fighters who clearly were in violation of international law, and a U.S. soldier is shown walking across a prayer rug lighting a cigarette, the event is publicized internationally and coalition forces are set back in their attempt to win over the Iraqi population.

Campaign planners, both civilian and military, must take into account how these and other like actions and decisions will be perceived by a population that does not necessarily share a common Western understanding or context. The people in the target country are more interested in whether or not they can go safely to the market or if the lights come on when they turn a switch. Saddam encouraged the worst behaviors and severely eroded Iraqi civil society. The result was that people were afraid to turn in wrongdoers—they were fence-sitting politically. They were not sure that coalition forces would truly clean out the old regime, and if that old regime returned, the people did not want to pay for their actions yet again. This type of fear presents coalition forces with problems that they would not face in other regions with other histories or political cultures, and campaign planners must take that into account. Each cultural context in each type of planning situation necessitates planners understand the risks involved to their forces in particular and to the success of the operations in general and national political leaders have to make those risk decisions.

So how does culture impact operations? Let us consider some specific examples from Iraq in 2004. There was a large gap between the actual ground truth and the perceptions of the society at large and that impacted operations in several ways. First of all, the difference between the population's perception of Iraqi demographics and the statistical reality made for a difficult political dialogue between the main Iraqi actors. A true and methodologically sound census was never in Saddam's best interest. If certain sectors of the populace were shown to have a smaller population than publicly stated, then he might lose power, or be forced to crack down even harder to maintain it. Iraq held censuses in 1987 and 1997, but few in the West believed them reliable enough for the international community to consider valid.[16] So in 2004 when the coalition and international diplomatic missions began the task of preparing for the 2005 TNA (Transitional National Assembly) elections, there was no sound data on the size of the various Iraqi subcultures—the Kurds (mostly, but not all, Sunni), Sunni Arabs, Shia Arabs, Turkomen, Christians, Yazidi, and others. When all were asked what proportion of the population they held, the total number came out to be well over 100 percent.

Planners knew the Shia Arabs were the majority but not by what proportion. They knew that Sunni Arabs ruled the country as though they were the majority, and were concerned that their actual population would be underrepresented if the long-repressed Shia Arab community gained power. Kurds would now be given a formal seat at the table, and nobody knew what their actual population percentage was. So what does this mean for campaign planners? This is just one example of a truth they must try to ascertain prior to the conduct of operations. They must understand the cultural and social implications of what may happen when the expected perceptions do not necessarily match up with reality if the planners hope to see a desired end state achieved.

If it seems like coalition military forces are directing their primary effort on a small segment of the population, then regardless of whether the major threat is coming from that segment or not, that segment may think they are being unfairly singled out and may fight even harder. So the political leaders of the coalition, in consultation with whatever leaders there are in the target country, must do what they can to bring in all elements of the population to get them to agree to a political settlement. If that means accepting greater risk to coalition military forces in certain areas in order to bring particular factions along politically, then planners must accept those risks and plan accordingly.

A second area of perception not being in line with reality is in public safety and attacks against the population. In Iraq in 2004, the Iraqi population said they generally felt safer, even given the occupation and insurgency, than they would if the coalition departed Iraq. Furthermore, the Iraqi majorities said that they felt that insurgent attacks were an attempt to incite civil war and that the same attacks showed a need for coalition forces to remain in Iraq.[17]

But why are these statistics not known or publicized in Iraq or abroad? Two reasons, primarily. First of all, when people live under the threat of stray mortar

and rocket rounds hitting their neighborhoods, they may not be as interested in
the statistics on street crime. So telling them that they are safe when they do
not feel safe does not make it so. And those that differentiate between insurgent
attacks and nonwar-related murders miss the point that death is death to those
affected.

Second, reporting of enemy attacks in 2004 was largely done by incident and
often from a distance. Most Western journalists in Iraq stayed in one of several
hotels in a specific section of Baghdad, and they stayed in that one location,
reporting from the roof or from their balcony only on the attacks that they
saw. Many did not feel safe enough to leave, so they did not report on the
reconstruction efforts or the open markets full of fruits and vegetables.[18] They
only reported the attacks they could see from their hotels and thus the population in Iraq and in the West saw only attacks on the news and not any other side
of life in Iraq, certainly not those aspects that were improving. So what was
the ground truth, and how did it matter? The truth was that although attacks
on the coalition and civilians were increasing in number, other positive aspects
of reconstruction often went unreported. But staff officers could not merely
complain that the good work by the coalition was not reported. The truth was
that the attacks being reported were really occurring and were causing a disruption in the collective life of the Iraqi populace. That is the key for planners to
understand.

Unemployment was another area of clouded ground truth. Unemployment
and underemployment are major factors in planning a multifaceted campaign.
When more people are out of work and dissatisfied with their situations, then
it is possible that those people will cease supporting the coalition and may
support enemy forces. How to deal with the unemployed is a major issue for
planners. But knowing how many are unemployed is the first step in knowing
how to deal with the issue. Working with various agencies in the U.S. Embassy
in Baghdad, it was difficult to navigate the numbers and get to ground truth
when assessing progress on the campaign plan. In polling done for the coalition
in Autumn 2004, the Iraqi Central Statistics Office found that when adding
those who listed themselves as unemployed or private sector part-time employed,
the actual reported unemployment rate was right at 30 percent. However, the
same survey found the popular perception that unemployment was between 60
and 75 percent with nearly 60 percent of the sample claiming a family member
unemployed.[19]

This disparity is important for two reasons. First of all, figures given by the
State Department and the Iraqi Central Statistics Office may not take into
account underemployment, which is important because the official figures may
count people who are working but not earning enough to support themselves
and their families. Second, if the perception by the public is that there is no
hope, then it might not matter what the reality is. People in certain locations

may not be able or willing to move to areas where jobs are available, leaving certain regions without the prospect of jobs and thus vulnerable to enemy coercion.

Planners must take this into account before decisions on reconstruction are made. For example, one reconstruction project in Basra required a many thousands of oil barrels to be cleaned. Reconstruction managers initially considered giving the contract to a foreign firm with high-tech equipment to complete the job in a matter of several days. The money for the project would have gone outside Iraq, and the local population would not have seen any impact. Instead, coalition leadership decided to hire several hundred local Iraqis to clean the barrels manually. Since the barrels were not needed on a rush basis, it made sense to use the same amount of money to hire more men locally, thus giving them jobs and putting the money into the local economy. So this was seen as a positive outcome of planning foresight. However, when a job like that is finished, the coalition must be prepared to either offer other jobs to those workers or accept blame for putting them out of work.

In a final example of how ground truth and perceptions must be reconciled, the multinational coalition was fighting a losing battle with electricity and power production. According to polling by the Iraqi Research Institute, more than half the population said that they have more electricity now than they had under Saddam. Yet more than 70 percent of the population was "extremely disappointed" with the availability of power.[20] But even the coalition military officers specifically working the issue of power production for the multinational force could not consistently determine the amount of power generated on a daily basis. When they briefed Casey on a daily basis, they would tell him how many "hours of power" were delivered to Baghdad the previous day. But when repeatedly questioned by fellow planners developing COAs, they were unable to determine whether that meant that the entire city had that much power, whether that was how much was generated at a single station, or what the distribution of that power was throughout the city. Furthermore, if you flew over the city at night, you would see a city of lights, mainly powered by portable generators. So there was more power being used in many homes than generated by the power plants in many parts of the country.

Several factors made electrical power production and delivery problematic. First, the infrastructure was in terrible shape. Many power generation sites were targeted during Desert Storm and not repaired. Many others were not given any repair priority or maintenance under Saddam. The result was a power system that was not on any computerized grid, without any means to ensure full electrical coverage. Furthermore, what power was being generated was more equitably distributed around the country to locations that often had little to no power in years past, while some areas that had power all the time under Saddam, such as Baghdad, saw their share drop.

A complicating factor in this issue was that to distribute the power, all switching was done manually by individual operators or managers who decide when the power comes on and what lines it flows through. So when people in one southern city destroy a power line in the belief that doing so will keep "their" allotment of power local and not allow it to go elsewhere, coalition leaders and planners must understand that this is not necessarily an insurgent act and does not require military force to deal with it.

Furthermore, when electrical power is free and people do not understand how peak demand lowers availability, they expect electricity to always be available. Any aerial photograph of Baghdad taken by the summer of 2004 showed an explosion of satellite dishes on the roofs of houses. Furthermore, people bought air conditioners and refrigerators, items with high electricity drains, and expected the power to always be there. So although there was more power available in terms of total electricity produced, there was a far greater draw on that power and an expectation, given the polling results that showed people greatly dissatisfied even though more power was being produced, that it should be on all the time, despite the inability to restore and repair the infrastructure.

Finally, the Iraqis could not reconstruct this vital infrastructure by themselves. They did not have the equipment in country to repair and replace power turbines and sensitive electronic equipment. This meant that the money for this reconstruction would go outside of Iraq. Iraqis will ultimately see the benefit but not in the near term with jobs. Furthermore, the power plants are mostly outside the cities where the people cannot see the work being done. So does it matter that the ground truth was that there was more power available than under Saddam? Not if the population is overwhelmingly "extremely dissatisfied" with what is available and perceives that the coalition is not doing enough to get them power. That is what planners must take into account and try to overcome.

When considering ground truth, campaign planners must ask if there are any historical parallels that they can learn from. But they also must be careful to derive the proper inferences from past operations and not merely what seems obvious. For example, many pundits and historians warned against American military involvement in Afghanistan in 2001 based on failed British and Soviet military campaigns in that country. However, the U.S. objectives in Afghanistan were very different from British and Soviet objectives. Although all three sought to replace governments, the American-led coalition did not intend to occupy the entire country and to rule but to set up a popular government and support that government only until it was strong enough to control the country itself. Furthermore, technology was different, as was the enemy and his motivation. So the operations, although not guaranteed to be successful, were guaranteed to be sufficiently different so that the analogy was not valid.

On the other hand, in Iraq, there were several parallels between what the coalition was doing in 2003–04 and what the British did in the 1920s and 1930s, and what Saddam tried to do during his reign. The British never took a census to determine who the players were prior to their occupation, and they, like the coalition today, tried to conduct the operation with a smaller ground presence than what many thought were necessary. However, the American objectives and desired end state were different from those of the British in the 1920s.[21] The present coalition sought to establish a democratic state able to defend itself and function with limited support from abroad. This alone makes COAs different. While acknowledging certain parallels in the local social context between 80 years ago and the present, the different desired ends dictate that the context requires different strategies for success today than it did under a different objective in another era. Planners cannot simply look to history for a roadmap today.

One final issue to consider when dealing with the difference between ground truth and perception is the global information network. All operations today are able to be viewed in real time around the world. In times past, journalists went into the field on their own, took film footage of events, came out days or weeks later, sent the film back to producers on the other side of the world, and competed for news time with other actors in a thirty-minute nightly newscast. But today, satellite communications, multiple international 24-hour news channels, the Internet, and journalists embedded with the very military forces they are covering offer the global viewing audience virtually unlimited access to real-time combat operations.

So what does this mean for campaign planners? First of all, if national leaders count on support from their populations when they see their national forces performing bravely and morally under fire, then opposing forces can count on the same, even if what is taken as moral in the West is not by enemy forces. In Iraq, there have been many occasions when al-Jazeera, the Arabic all-news network based in Qatar, seems as well placed with opposing forces as BBC and CNN are to coalition forces. Al-Jazeera often showed the Arab world every misstep and norm violation by Western forces as much as Western media show those of enemy forces (more so, many would argue). The result is that it is harder to win over the local population when they are bombarded with negative images of coalition forces. Planners and national leaders cannot undo negative reporting or even blatant lies. The best they can do is ignore them and hope that the local population is savvy enough to realize absurdity when they see it. When Arabic news reported that American tanks were driving through Fallujah looking for old women to run over and that American bombs selectively killed only innocent women and children while leaving enemy fighters unscathed, coalition leaders decided that answering these absurd claims would lend more credence to them than ignoring them.[22] In the end, the Iraqi populace saw the claims as propaganda of the enemy forces.

Furthermore, instant news coverage affords national leaders to see the events as they happen and offer their advice or guidance every time they see something reported in the media instead of when told by their subordinates. In many ways, this is a very favorable consequence of media technology. There is greater transparency, and thus it is extremely unlikely that any wrongdoing or norm violation will go long before being discovered and addressed. On the other hand, when national leaders ask their military commanders to explain details of every event covered in the media, commanders spend less time commanding and more time on the telephone. Planners must take into account how the global information network impacts decision cycles and how perceptions, not ground truth, leads to decisions and plan accordingly so as not to become reactive once in an operation. They must decide from the beginning whether they must be 100 percent successful everywhere in order to achieve desired effects. If it is possible to reduce, if not eliminate, the difference between the ground truth and perception, then they may not have to fight military battles in all parts of the country.

What Are the Pathologies of the Staff?

In any operation, planners must consider the sociological and bureaucratic pathologies that organizations inherently encounter. When combining officers from various services with different service cultures, there will be friction and competition. When more than one department within the government, such as the diplomatic corps of the State Department and military, come together, those natural pathologies are magnified. When you include multiple countries and multiple international governmental and nongovernmental organizations, planners face unsteady waters and fierce storms to chart courses through to a desired end state. It would be overly simplistic to say that the Clausewitzian reminder of fog in war should be expected. It would be more akin to Sun Tsu's admonishment to know yourself and your enemy. In this case, in addition to the enemy, the campaign planner must know how his own culture and the cultures and expectations of the various organizational elements both support each other or cause conflict within the staff. This must be thought-out, expected, and avoided whenever possible.

When setting out to plan a coherent campaign, planners must take into account several sociological issues. First, they must acknowledge that they cannot make people talk to each other, even those who are supposed to work together. Second, not all leaders are cut from the same cloth. Third, there will be a tension between direction and coordination. And finally there is the fear of delivering bad news.

The first point is simple and straightforward, however, it does not make overcoming the issue easy. Simply put, when senior leaders, be they generals, or ambassadors would not act, make decisions, or publish directions, you cannot effectively coordinate vital options. Planners and staff officers must work hard to understand and work around the egos of all persons involved in decision making. But if the leaders decide they do not want to talk to each other, there is nothing their subordinates can do to make them coordinate.

The next point is that not all senior leaders are cut from the same cloth. This is true within any given country, but the effect is magnified when adding coalition members from other countries to the command and control decision process. In Iraq, the senior coalition staff was made up of officers from all U.S. services as well as from all countries in the coalition. The following are the author's personal observations from coordinating on the campaign progress review in the fall and winter of 2004. They are not meant to be broad generalizations of what happens in all situations but illustrations of the points made above.

The U.S. Army senior leadership in Iraq in 2004 was very focused on centers of gravity of the opposition, looking for the one silver bullet that could bring them down. Armies generally think linearly and in time-phased sequences because of the two-dimensional plane within which they operate. Their leadership did not seem to see the possibilities for simultaneous operations against non-traditional targets, yet they were willing to "make it happen" in the hopes that working longer hours and expending more energy will win the fight. The U.S. Air Force often seemed out of place on the coalition staff in that many Air Force officers had a difficult time accepting that this was an Army war in which air power would not play the dominant role. At one point Air Force planners attempted to impose rules on the Iraqis whereby the fledgling Iraqi Air Force would have times and locations where they fly dictated by the U.S. Air Force. Those that did try to explain the possibilities of nonlinear thinking to their Army counterparts were often dismissed as not understanding the war. The U.S. Navy had so few people in the headquarters that they did not have a major voice, yet those that were there did a fine job on the staff. And the Marines believed that any task could be accomplished with a Marine and enough supporting firepower. In many instances they were proved right.

The next largest contingent was British forces. Interestingly, though the British officers saw the same situation and had the same objectives and end states, their culture was such that they were willing to question any almost any notion brought forward by American leadership and were very willing to tell the emperor that he was naked. Interestingly, that same willingness seemed to disappear when the notions were put forward by their own leadership. Other countries appeared to send the very best officers they had forward. Australia sent Major General Jim Molan to fill the position as the director of operations on the coalition staff. His Australian staff contingent was extremely capable, intellectual, and focused on the outcome coordinating with others as if well-oiled cogs in a machine. Likewise with staff officers from all the other coalition countries.

Below the general officer ranks, staffs functioned very well. It was only at the highest levels of command that egos seemed to affect decision making. This is the key point about the sociology of the staff that planners must take into account. The variance between the backgrounds, abilities, education, and egos of senior leaders, military and civilian, is difficult for staff officers to navigate. They take direction from one boss, who may or may not be from their country and branch of service. They must then coordinate his position with officers that work for another person, again from another service or country. And they must take their boss's boss into account when recommending decisions.

Staff officers also must deal with leaders who are more keen on coordination versus those who provide direction. It was my experience that while most senior military generals provided direction, often in contradiction to other senior officers, the civilian diplomatic corps were more interested in coordination. Importantly, staff officers and campaign planners must know before an operation that they will be expected to bring senior decision-makers options that take into account the context of any given situation with potentially several subsequent options for branches or sequels depending on the outcome of initial decisions.

The final sociological issue planners must consider is the staff's fear of delivering bad news. But the fundamental truth that must always be considered in any operation is that the truth does not change based on the rank of the recipient. The general tendency on the staff in Baghdad was to avoid bringing bad news to the boss, especially the higher in rank "the boss" was. There is a natural tension when staff members complete their assigned task and the result is the news they believe their superior will not want to hear or will be disappointed with. For this reason, it was good to have people from other services or countries at the table who did not fear losing their chance of promotion or positions when delivering news their senior leaders might not want to hear. So for the purposes of transparency and accurate decision making, it is worth dealing with cultural and sociological differences if the result is greater movement of information and truth up the chain of command.

Sociological issues were not the only ones planners must consider. Bureaucratic politics comes into play even among military staffs. A recent theory of bureaucratic politics seemed to be thrown on its heads by the workings of the multinational coalition in Baghdad. The principal–agent model of bureaucracy normatively states that principals want to control their agents and that agents want to shirk control.[23] Control by agents is argued to best be done through "fire-alarm" oversight (such as congressional investigations after an incident occurs),[24] through deliberate discretion (wherein politicians give certain leeway to bureaucrats in a deliberate fashion),[25] and through motivational alignment (whereby superiors and subordinates deliberately work to align their motivations on an issue in order to prevent disagreements in an operation).[26] But when planning campaigns, officers must understand that it will not always be so, nor should it be so.

First of all, it is questionable whether or not national leaders actually want to exert control over agents once decisions are made. The more they control their subordinate military officers and diplomats, the more they themselves are held accountable for decisions and consequences. In cases such as Iraq, fire alarm oversight cannot be relied upon because once a "fire" ignites, it may be so big that it damages national credibility or interests for years to come, as was the case with the Abu Ghraib prisoner mistreatment scandal. And while national leaders may truly trust their subordinates and deliberately cede levels of discretion to them, military officers that were not confirmed by the Senate are not accountable to the people and should not be given decision authority over issues that have long-term international consequences for the country.

It seems that the best way to ensure principals control their agents is through alignment of motivations between national leaders and those assigned to carry out the missions.[27] Officers and diplomats that have differing agendas from national leadership endanger the end state and require more oversight than may be practical during war. In my observations on the coalition staff in Baghdad, I never saw senior leaders whose motivations differed from national leaders. I saw multiple cases in which they did not agree on how to act on those motivations and what news to give their leaders, but their motivations for attaining the end state were all in line.

On the other hand, the principal–agent model posits that agents want to shirk their direction. Experience showed this to be outright wrong. Staff officers and civilians overwhelmingly craved direction from above and the resources to carry out that direction. Part of the reason for this could be attributed to fear of failure and blame if operations went wrong, but generally it was because officers understood their role as agents whose job was to carry out direction from above and not determine policy.

Bureaucratic politics models aside, there were serious bureaucratic cultural issues which made coordination and attainment of the end state very difficult. The first was the culture of the U.S. State Department and its impact on coordination with the other elements of the coalition. British diplomat Andrew Rathmel said of the U.S. diplomatic mission to Baghdad that there was a "fundamental failure to understand that they were more than an embassy with a military element attached."[28] From the outset, there were limitations of what the military element of the coalition could and could not do.

Certain issues were the purview of the diplomatic corps and required decisions from that sector. Yet while individual Foreign Service officers provided outstanding work, the senior leadership of the American Embassy would not plan for the future. Their mantra was that they observed and reported but did not plan. It was like living a Star Trek episode in which the Enterprise crew struggled with the Prime Directive. Observe, but do not impact the evolution of a society. However, when one of the lines of operation in the campaign plan is assigned to the diplomatic element and that element does accept that assignment, there is a serious disconnect and potential to not achieve the desired end state.

The most contentious issue between the military and the American diplomatic element within the Baghdad Embassy was the seeming inability of the State Department personnel to acknowledge that there was an ongoing war. While military staff members wore body armor and helmets to and from their offices, many (but certainly not all) foreign service personnel lounged at the palace pool and indulged in parties with free-flowing alcohol. All the while, military personnel were under a general order prohibiting alcohol usage. Even after threat conditions were raised and specific alerts made, many State Department personnel continued to act as if they were back home. Two specific instances deserve mention: the bombing of the Green Zone Café, and the Halloween party at the Embassy pool.

The Green Zone Café was an eatery several blocks from the Embassy compound and a favorite of the diplomatic corps. The restaurant was put off limits to all coalition personnel when a bomb set to explode in the facility failed to detonate. The following week, another bomber succeeded in blowing up the restaurant, killing five people and wounding many others, including several Americans who disregarded the warning.[29] One State Department secretary seriously injured in the explosion said she went there despite the warning because she figured it only applied to the military officers. Such a disregard for the situation made it difficult for many military officers to deal with their civilian counterparts and for the civilians to take their military counterparts seriously when they did not think the threat was as real as it was.

The second situation involved a publicized party at the Embassy pool on Halloween. Military officers were told to stay away from the swimming pool facilities when the threat situation became such that opposition forces seemed to be specifically targeting Westerners at the pool within the Embassy compound.[30] However, many State Department personnel held a planned Halloween party, which was in fact targeted with mortar and rocket fire. When Embassy security was ordered to break up the party and get the people inside the building, many revelers told the security personnel that they had no authority to tell civilians what to do.

However, the bureaucratic issues were not only the purview of the civilian diplomatic corps. The American military found out that they did not know exactly who they needed for what specific jobs and how to get the right people in the right places. Because the Americans did not have a database from which to determine who they can call with what experience on for what tasks, they tended to bring in more and more people in the hopes that "the right" would be a sufficient subset of "the greater." Many generals on the staff circumvented the established personnel channels by cutting what were termed "drug deals" with friends and fellow officers back in the States to bring officers (including most of the authors of this book) over to the staff for temporary duty outside the official deployment channels. Thus, the personnel system had to fill requirements for people and could track who was on certain types of orders while others came and went inside the longer tours of those on deployment orders.

Furthermore, once the size of the staff grew, other issues came to the forefront. It became evident that it would be impossible to fight and manage a war in today's technological environment without network cards and toner for copiers and printers. When all correspondence is done through computer systems and those systems go down, nearly all work comes to a halt. And when all decisions require a PowerPoint briefing rather than a paper or verbal explanation, officers spend more time building briefing slides than they do researching a recommended decision.

Not all PowerPoint presentations are unnecessary, and they do help to visually explain a position. However, when general officers make it their job to personally set the color scale on slide templates, and when the headquarters staff issues a ninety-page directive detailing proper staff procedures and paper routing, then not only do coalition military partners wonder if the U.S. military takes their task seriously, so do the Iraqis. Many coalition officers were heard joking "How did the Americans ever make it to the moon" without PowerPoint and e-mail accounts. So it is important for campaign planners to establish organizations and staffs that can remain focused on the actual end state and not the process itself.

One final point to discuss about life within the Embassy complex was the near inability to communicate between the military arm and the diplomatic staff apart from face-to-face meetings. The Embassy personnel and MNF-I (Multinational Force–Iraq) staff were on completely different phone systems (which were different from the system the British Embassy was on), making it nearly impossible to call on the phone to coordinate or even to set up meetings. Furthermore, the two entities were on completely different computer networks. MNF-I officers had to send e-mails to diplomatic officers' State Department accounts because e-mails within the same building could not go through. In contrast to the security disregard, each State Department employee had at least one cell phone for use in emergencies or as primary communication, while in the MNF-I cell phones were restricted to general officers and selected colonels only.

The next organizational and bureaucratic hurdle to discuss was the difficulty of coordination between the coalition and the Iraqi state. While not a pathology of the MNF-I staff, the fact that the Iraqi state suffered several issues of disunity made it a factor for planners to take into consideration. First, the population is not homogenous. Beside the fact that there are Sunni, Shia, Kurd, Turkomen, and other identities, some based on religion and some on nationality, the greater consideration was tribal and clan affiliation. Coalition planners could not count on all Sunni or all Shia to act and think as a bloc because local tribal issues nearly always were more important than a greater identity. That made negotiations difficult because it is nearly impossible to reach a national consensus in any given issue.

Second, Iraq was in a very precarious international position. The West wanted Iraq to succeed for several reasons. After having expended resources and blood to overthrow Saddam, Western countries wanted to see their efforts bear fruit. Furthermore, there was a desire to see Iraq succeed and be strong enough to prevent terrorist elements from using Iraq as a base for attacks against Western interests. But not all of Iraq's neighbors shared that interest in Iraq's success. A democratic and stable Iraq would be seen as a nuisance to some autocratic leaders in the region. They might have been concerned that if they do not liberalize, their countries would be next to fall. Thus while not overtly sponsoring the opposition forces, some neighboring countries might have been doing all they could to stop cross-border movement of forces supporting the opposition.

Third, Iraq did not have a unified government in 2004. The TNA and Interim Prime Minister succeeded twenty-three nearly independent ministries in which ministers did not coordinate and discuss between each other or even with their deputies and staffs. It was extremely important for the diplomatic missions and the IRMO (Iraqi Reconstruction and Management Office) to mentor the new bureaucrats and teach them to function effectively under fire. It was also vital that they act in their own best interests and not be seen as puppets or stooges of Western states. Furthermore, nobody knew the extent to which any opposition forces had infiltrated the Iraqi government. These realities can lead to multiple different outcomes that must all be envisioned by planners and accounted for in recommendations to senior decision makers.

Finally, the UN must be taken into account in Iraq. Although it is not the key driver in this situation, neither is it a bit player. It was under the UN resolution that the Iraqi Interim Government was established, a timetable for elections was developed, and the mandate for coalition forces to operate in country was outlined. While the UN did not have great numbers of personnel on the ground in Baghdad, its influence as a legitimizer was important. However, neither could the coalition allow the UN or individual international diplomats to derail the transition to democracy. Campaign planners must foresee potential situations, such as the UN Secretary General's announcement that perhaps it would be best to postpone elections until a safer security environment was established, and plan to deal with them, always with an eye on the end state.

How Do You Know If You Are Winning?

The final area which campaign planners, both civilian and military, should consider is in assessing effects of their planned actions. This last area is potentially that hardest to do because no country is well equipped and organized to do that mission well today. First you have to know what to assess. Then you have to figure out how to assess it. Then you must determine who makes the judgment call.

In figuring out what to assess and how to assess it, it is imperative that planners, commanders, and national leaders understand the difference between measuring performance and measuring effects. Measures of performance can be considered as inputs. We measure performance fairly well. The problem is that performance is not the same as effects. For example, the coalition was regularly measuring amount of reconstruction dollars spent, number of weapons turned in during the buyback program, and number of Kevlar helmets handed out to local police. But these measurements did nothing to tell senior leaders how far the reconstruction projects were toward completion, how many fewer shots were being fired at coalition personnel, or how effective the Iraqi police were. These were the desired effects, but they are hard to measure and difficult to link to any specific action.

So why do we measure performance and not effects? First of all, it is easier to do. Measuring effects takes a lot of brain power to look for and to isolate the effects of any given action. Second, it may not be easy to measure. If a staff is interested in bringing down the number of foreign fighters in a given country, it is easy to tell the leadership how many border posts were built. But it is very difficult to count and then track the numbers of foreign fighters there are from month to month. Thus, sound inference must be made to assess effects. For example, if there is a decrease in the numbers of unclaimed bodies at local morgues, the staff might be able to infer that there is a decrease in the number of people killed without local clan members to claim them.

The danger in continuing to measure performance is that countries will fall into the trap of the "body count." Instead of telling national leaders how far along they are to achieving the end state, military commanders brief what they actually did, not what they achieved. At one point in mid-October 2004, General George Casey, the MNF-I commander, told his staff that he was tied of hearing how many anti-Iraqi forces we killed, or what percentage of a building was destroyed. He said he wanted to know how much of a town we controlled or if the enemy force was effective. This is the essence of the problem. What we decide to measure can determine if and when we declare the end state met. If protecting the force is the overall mission, then the best way to do that is by not going to where the threat is.

Countries have to be careful not to craft their measurements so as to avoid getting themselves in an endless cycle of mere numbers reporting instead of achieving their desired end state. A fundamental problem for the United States is that it is not presently organized, trained, and equipped to measure effects. It will require a change in the organizational culture of the U.S. military away from accepting inefficiency as long as there is overwhelming power. The future international context will likely not allow such thinking.

But once a decision is made to assess effects and the organization is established to do it, who should make the call? Should subordinate units be allowed to report on their own effectiveness? As we have seen in Iraq and throughout history there is a fear of delivering bad news. Assessing effects should reside at the general officer level and be done by persons on the staff outside the operational chain of command. In a coalition, this job should be given to an officer of a country that is not the majority force. For example, in Iraq, the person best suited to assess effects would have been a British general on the staff and not out in the combat chain of command. This person would have the authority of the commanding general to challenge the assessments made by subordinate units as to their progress toward achieving effects. That way you do not have units delivering good news when the situation is actually going poorly. This recommendation was made by some of the authors of this book in 2004 because of the inability of field units to accurately assess their own performance. The recommendation was accepted by Casey in early 2005.

Conclusion

These five broad points about campaign planning are purely normative in nature, but they are based on experience planning operations in multinational and civil–military environments from the Middle East, to the Pacific, to Europe, from large-scale wars to peacekeeping operations. The point with all of these anecdotes and recommendations is that every action planners determine should be taken and every action commanders take must deliberately and measurably lead a country or coalition toward a specific, articulated end state or objective.

Campaign planning is a difficult process. The international geopolitical context is not what it was when World War II was planned and conducted. Communications and knowledge are shared instantaneously and weapons, while more precise, are more lethal. Campaign planners must take into account various concepts and integrate thinking that links seemingly disparate topics toward the attainment of an end state. Perhaps more difficult is the proscription that in understanding these issues, campaign planners must learn to be politically astute without becoming political in order to attain the goals their national leaders set forth. Without doing so, the commanders, staff officers and the entire force are relying on a hope that the pieces will all fall together the right way the first time; that the staff works, that the phones are connected, that there is enough toner and network cards and paper, that people know their objectives and where they are supposed to be at what times. These are hopes that rarely see their fulfillment. With sound campaign planning considerations, however, operations stand a chance of seeing their objectives met.

CHAPTER 4

WE DIDN'T KNOW WHAT WE WERE GETTING INTO

Kalev I. Sepp

From the beginning of the new Iraq in 2003, first under the direction of the Office of Reconstruction and Humanitarian Assistance, then the CPA (Coalition Provisional Authority), and then elected Iraqi politicians, the survival of the new government of Iraq has been threatened by an insurgency. When a totalitarian regime collapses and civil control is lost, criminals move into the vacuum. In Iraq, insurrectionists, "resistors," and radical jihadists also found a permissive operating environment following the fall of Saddam Hussein. Insurgents and criminals thrive in conditions of instability and insecurity, often cooperating and sometimes functioning as one and the same.[1]

Exacerbating the situation is the country's unhelpful human terrain. As early as 2004, U.S. military officers called Iraq "a country at war with itself." Within its borders, there is often violent competition between its peoples, based on religion, economics, demography, or ethnicity, cast in terms of Shia Arab versus Sunni Arab, Kurd versus Arab, Baghdad versus Basra, urban versus rural, and tribe versus tribe. Iran is the country's most significant foreign enemy but is unlikely to invade with regular military forces while coalition units remain in Iraq. The government's response is a counterinsurgency, which is first and foremost an intelligence war. The major categories of intelligence operations are foreign, domestic, and military. These are not neatly divisible and are in fact closely interrelated.

Iraqi Military Intelligence

At the start of the coalition occupation, the future of Iraqi military intelligence was tied to the coalition effort to create a wholly new Iraqi armed force. Major General Paul Eaton, chief of the CMATT (Coalition Military Assistance

Training Team) in 2003–04, envisioned the mission of the NIA (New Iraqi Army) to be to defend the territory of Iraq with no internal security requirements. In the first year of building a force capable of this mission, the general decided to concentrate on what he called "the meat and potatoes"—the creation of tactical combat units, particularly twenty-seven infantry battalions. At the end of twelve months, he wanted to be able to relieve the coalition forces in Iraq of any external defense duties they might be performing. In Eaton's words, the goals of his CMATT were to "train the New Iraqi Army" and "give them terrain" to defend.[2]

The first Iraqi battalions were to operate in the zone then occupied by the U.S. 4th Infantry Division, an operational environment of small towns, highways and supply routes, and national borders. The second set of battalions would be assigned to the urban centers patrolled at the time by the U.S. 1st Armored Division. Initially, the Iraqi units were to be under the operational control of the commanding general of CJTF-7 (Combined Joint Task Force 7). In due course, the NIA would organize the twenty-seven battalions into nine brigades, grouped in turn into three "division equivalent" units, all under a single joint military headquarters responsible to the new Iraqi MoD (Ministry of Defense). In the distant future, the NIA would eventually expand to a force of eight to twelve divisions, of which at least half and as perhaps two-thirds would be equipped with tanks and armored vehicles.

Iraq was also to have a small navy, of five 30-meter patrol craft, purchased several years ago but held by the United Arab Emirates. This Iraqi Coastal Defense Force would be stationed in the port of Umm Qasr on the Persian Gulf.[3] The new Iraqi air force would have its initial home base at Baghdad International Airport. In addition to a C-130 cargo transport aircraft already on hand at the airport, Jordan was to provide sixteen UH-1 "Huey" helicopters and the flight training for its pilots. The basis for this choice of helicopter was made solely on price, as the current standard UH-60 "Blackhawks" are more capable but considerably more expensive. The CMATT held as a long-term goal that the Iraqi air force would have two to three air wings, able to conduct aerial intercept of intruding aircraft, and provide close air support for Iraqi ground forces.

The rationale for the establishment of an Iraqi army was defense against external threats. Internal threats were to be managed by the various police organizations, the border patrol, the ICDC (Iraqi Civil Defense Corps), and other elements belonging to different government agencies tasked with fixed-site protection, such as of oil pipelines and electrical power lines.[4] In contrast to the militia-like ICDC, which recruited its members locally and operated under local commanders with local responsibilities, the army was to be national in character. As a defensive force, the NIA was not to have any expeditionary capability and would have limited logistical support to ensure a limited range of operations.

In assessing how his training team had performed up through January 2004, Eaton said "We didn't know what we were getting into." He remembered that in mid-2003 there was no particular sense of urgency to create a new armed forces establishment for Iraq. Then on 15 November 2003, Ambassador L. Paul Bremer, head of the CPA, made that mission one of his top priorities. The CMATT faced several immediate challenges, including only having 50 percent of their authorized number of personnel and having to adjust the design and functions of their organization accordingly.[5] However, Eaton stated "Money is the biggest problem, and the bureaucracy associated with spending that money."[6]

The NIA faced serious equipment shortages due to battle losses and the devastating post-invasion looting, including basic items such as trucks, jeeps, uniforms, and even basic infantry weapons. In a country notoriously awash in small arms, noted Eaton, "We have to buy AK-47s from Bulgaria." The assault rifles that seemed so readily available were not in arms caches, but "hidden under beds," and not easily recovered. For their own use, the CMATT staff purchased Motorola radios and Hyundai trucks from commercial sources to gain some rudimentary means of communications and transportation to execute their mission.

By February 2004, the CMATT staff had formed one brigade headquarters and three battalion headquarters, with a fourth under development. They were also forming an administrative divisional headquarters, planned to later gain a warfighting capacity following the creation of a U.S.-style battle command training program for the NIA. The Jordanian Army was training the Iraqi staff officers in Jordan, while American, British, and Australian trainers in Iraq schooled the noncommissioned officers who would eventually be sent to Jordan to join their officers. Eventually, they would become the core of the leadership of the NIA and provide the cadre to train additional Iraqi military forces. The CMATT staff recruited seven hundred former "old" Iraqi army captains and lieutenants for the new tactical headquarters, employing a ten-day screening and vetting process utilizing in part Iraqi personnel database records from the Saddam era. The candidates also underwent a series of physical examinations and testing for personal fitness. The CMATT staff selected six hundred of the original seven hundred candidates and sent them to Jordan for their initial training.

Eaton acknowledged "Intelligence is the hardest specialty to train and teach. It cannot be taught in two weeks, or two months, or six months." In the second year of the process of building the NIA, the general intended to not add any more structure but to focus on improvement of the army's proficiency in its combat missions. His concept for tactical intelligence capability in the NIA was "exactly what you'd find in the U.S. Army." He expected that this standard could not be met for at least three years, but perhaps no less than five. Significantly, the CMATT staff discovered there was "zero intelligence equipment" left after the nationwide looting spree. They reported to Eaton, "The most sophisticated sensor in the New Iraqi Army is binoculars."

Because of Eaton's focus on formation of infantry units, his staff only directed military intelligence training for four officers from the first new battalions, and this was to be done by the Jordanian army. These officers in turn were expected to train their own intelligence staffs. As more battalions were established, the Jordanians and then the Iraqis themselves would train more intelligence officers, in the rank of captain or lieutenant, as necessary. In any regard, the CMATT could not have done the training itself, as there was only a single military intelligence officer assigned to Eaton's staff.

While it was expedient to allow the Jordanians to train Iraqi intelligence officers, it allowed those officers to drift yet further from United States contact and influence. In order to move toward viable intelligence sharing between the United States and the Iraqi individuals and organizations, it might have been useful to foster a degree of dependence and professional association on the part of the Iraqis toward their U.S. counterparts, in terms of education, processes, and equipment. Otherwise, the United States could find itself without contacts in the Iraqi intelligence community to provide any insight into their operations, let alone to monitor them for compliance with their own laws and international human rights accords.

When he departed Iraq in June 2004, Eaton placed the NIA in the charge of an Iraqi LTG (Lieutenant General). The CMATT was in turn replaced by the new Office of Defense Cooperation at the U.S. Embassy in Baghdad. Key questions about the future development of the Iraqi military intelligence were largely unanswered, especially how its organization and functions would be integrated into the larger Iraqi defense community. Was the Iraqi military intelligence corps to be shaped by the U.S. military, or would that responsibility be left primarily to the Iraqis themselves?

The division of "internal" and "external" security in defining military roles and their limits seems to be unsuitable to the situation in Iraq, where external threats—from Syria, Iran, Turkey, and stateless foreigners—manifest themselves as militant insurgents and instigators operating within the country's borders.[7] Local paramilitaries could also turn against the Baghdad government and be so well organized and heavily armed that they would be comparable in combat power with regular army units of similar size.

When these threats might prove themselves too much for police and neighborhood defense units to cope with, the national government would certainly turn to the country's traditional guarantor of homeland security and stability: the Iraqi armed forces. More than battalions of disciplined infantry, the government would expect and demand incisive and useful intelligence in order to make informed decisions about how to combat an insurgency. However, Iraqi military intelligence staffs trained and equipped on the model of the conventional

U.S. Army battalion and brigade would likely be as unprepared for this "most likely" mission as was the U.S. military itself when Baghdad fell in May 2003.

Iraqi Police Intelligence

As it reestablished Iraqi police departments and precincts throughout the country, the coalition made some attempt to concurrently develop a police intelligence capability. This effort was made problematic by the dysfunctional nature of the CPA and the deficient police organization of the deposed regime.

Chief Inspector Steve Burfitt of the U.K. police, the CPA's leading expert on police intelligence operations, discovered that under Saddam Hussein's rule no such function existed, not even to investigate organized crime.[8] The old regime employed police as "a reactive response force" with only a minor and informal intelligence and planning capacity. The previous government maintained a "crime information office" with a collection of fingerprints and some other records, but it lacked personnel with expertise in statistical analysis. The police archives held 350,000 sets of individual criminal records, from which 100,000 sets of fingerprints had been electronically documented on a Russian-designed software program, SONDER 7, installed by the Switch Company of Switzerland. This automatic fingerprint recognition system (AFRS in police terminology) survived the 2003 war but was a unique program that was not accessible outside the office where the hardware was installed.

To give purpose to police efforts, Burfitt sought to design an "intelligence-led policing concept" for Iraq. He wanted to eliminate the various "adversarial systems" that had been emplaced independently throughout the country and replace them with a single database system for low-level police operations. His preference for this database was the Canadian-designed "Niche Records Management System," which was then not available in Arabic.[9] Because the inspector found that almost all Iraqi police lacked personal computer skills, he envisioned that at the station level, paper would still be used for intelligence collection and reporting. The electronic system would begin at the municipality, where there would also be dedicated police intelligence officers and units—the lowest level for such personnel and organizations—to support the intelligence operation. There would be similar intelligence offices at the east and west division headquarters, at the national headquarters in Baghdad, and a separate "National Crime Intelligence Unit" subordinate to the main police command center. The CPA planned for the Iraqi Ministry of the Interior to oversee all police activity nationwide.[10]

Burfitt felt a critical aspect of the police intelligence organization was the separation of the activities of intelligence and policing within the police force itself. His intent was that any future Iraqi police intelligence organization not be like Saddam's *Mukhabarat*—that is, that the Interim National Intelligence Service be denied the power of arrest and detention. There was a degree of guarded optimism about the future of Iraqi law enforcement. The Iraqi Penal Code of 1969, amended in 1971 and still in effect, was closely based on the Scottish Law of Criminal Proceedings, a modern and progressive set of legal orders and regulations that is well regarded among jurists. This code could provide a solid grounding for the legality of Iraqi police intelligence operations.

In the CPA's Security Institutions Steering Group, Eerik Kross was also working on the police intelligence database issue, although apparently not in close coordination with Burfitt, and studying different security factors. The most significant of these was the need for a nationwide system of personal identification. For effective law enforcement, let alone the prosecution of a counterinsurgency campaign, a national I.D. card is essential. Such a system already existed, a result of the United Nations "Oil-for-Food" sanctions program that required every Iraqi adult to have an I.D. card in order to be eligible for individual aid.

Kross, an Estonian national experienced in post-Soviet government security reorganization, had found several extant databases. These included a criminal records database the Iraqis had been working on improving and expanding for about four years using an Oracle software program, the beginnings of a criminal statistics database, a partial vehicle licensing database, and a traffic violation database that had been in actual use for two years. Also, an Iraqi company named "Heat Software" had completed 85 percent of a two-year contract to collate the "Oil-for-Food" I.D. card system into a single national identification database. The 2003 war permanently interrupted this contract.

The CPA lacked the personnel and resources needed to oversee the rapid creation of a police intelligence service. The U.S. Department of Justice contracted the consultancies Dyncorp and SAIC to provide 150 civilian police trainers in Iraq by January 2004, but only fourteen arrived. The Iraqi police departments were seriously undermanned as well. In February 2004, Kross estimated that Baghdad required at least 17,000 police, but only 7,000 to 8,000 Iraqi police were on duty. (The estimate of 17,000 security personnel to maintain order in Baghdad is wholly inadequate to the population of the city. According to RAND Corporation's study of police-to-population ratios, the number of police and auxiliaries needed to control Baghdad's seven million people, given its wartime level of violence, is 140,000—eight times higher than Kross' estimate. It is possible, although uncertain, that Kross based his calculation on his earlier experience with creating new police forces in Eastern Europe, which were peaceful transitions.)

Kross assessed that the "biggest obstacles" to creation of a police intelligence database were (1) a shortage of money—only $12 million of $75 million requested had been received; (2) a lack of a project team with links to the Ministries of Justice, Trade, and the Interior, and especially a team leader with high-level project experience; and (3) the overfocus of the CPA on Baghdad, rather than the entire country. Kross also noted that his advisory section shared three vehicles from a motor pool with several other sections, and he protested at the time that he "can't get around" to visit the police units he was supposed to oversee.

Within the Iraqi law enforcement community, the development of a police intelligence capability was further hampered by what Kross described as long-standing internal friction. "Iraqi police don't trust the investigative judges," he said, "because they think the judges are all corrupt. The investigative judges don't trust the police because they think the police are incompetent." Support from several European police agencies, including those of Germany, France, the United Kingdom, Spain, and Poland, was expected to increase, and Kross anticipated that the Germans would provide the Iraqis training in police forensics, as well as granting them associated equipment. His basic tenet in his programs for developing Iraqi police intelligence functions was "This effort needs civilian police, not military police."

This ideal notion had already been obviated by the appointment of Lieutenant Colonel Jeremy Green of the British Army's Royal Military Police Corps as Provost Marshal of the United Kingdom's military sector in southern Iraq. A twenty-year veteran of the Royal Military Police, the Sandhurst graduate received much of his law enforcement training from British police agencies and schools, attended the National Police College in England, and worked in the Special Investigative Branch of the Military Police. Green had served in Canada and South Africa, and observed insurrections firsthand during assignments in Lebanon and Algeria. He evinced a firm comprehension of the problems facing the Iraqi police he was tasked to train, equip, and advise.

Green was most concerned about the "malign influence" of radical political and religious groups over the police. Foremost among these was the anti-Coalition Badr Corps—the armed wing of the Supreme Council of the Islamic Revolution in Iraq. Developing criminal intelligence on these groups required cultivating sources able to penetrate these outlaw organizations. He knew that the information then had to be collected at the provincial police department level and provided to a suitable police intelligence unit at the national level. In the absence of a functioning intelligence network linked by secure communications systems, British military personnel working directly inside Iraqi police stations provided the connectivity of information and intelligence to give a rudimentary utility to police operations.

The commanding general and senior staff of the MND-SE (Multinational Division–Southeast), headquartered in Basra, believed that the so-called "saturation patrolling" was actually counterproductive to the goal of gaining the confidence of the Iraqi population and establishing an environment of security and normalcy.[11] The multinational staff of MND-SE had found through interviews with Iraqis that high-profile Iraqi police patrols were perceived in a positive way by the public, while coalition military patrols were less appreciated. Using the same terminology as Burfitt used, Green saw the solution as "intelligence-led policing." Some of this effort could be accomplished by dedicated advisory work at the police station level, which with due progress over time would evolve from "mentoring, to monitoring, to strategic overwatch."

The necessary technical means to accelerate this process was a database, integrating computers, surveillance equipment, and encrypted communications means down to the police station. Green favored the British HOLMES software program to support police database operations, because it could also manage covert human intelligence sources. He also considered ordering a version of the CRIMES 2000 database system, released in 2003 after ten years of development. A customized British program, it included a crime database, a police library with all applicable technical manuals, templates for planning and investigations, and British military records on individual veterans dating back to World War II. However, Green estimated that even under optimal conditions, it would take four to five years—until 2008, at the earliest—to install such a system combining computers and software programs, and properly train the Iraqi police force to use it.[12]

U.S. Army Military Intelligence in Iraq

In July 2003, the commanding general of U.S. CJTF-7, LTG Ricardo Sanchez, replaced his J-2 intelligence chief with Brigadier General Barbara Fast, who had been serving as the deputy commander at the U.S. Army's intelligence school in Arizona. On her arrival at the headquarters adjacent to the Baghdad airport, she saw her goal as "taking a tactical organization, and making it capable of strategic and operational intelligence activity, with tactical reach." At the same time, she received a tasking that originated from the Secretary of Defense to "do a study on intelligence architecture" in the major headquarters in Iraq. She assessed that there were two options for arranging her staff: "combined, or most efficient."

To deal with the shortcomings she found, Fast elected to create three major staff groupings. The first was a coalition intelligence cell, focused on (1) forensics of improvised explosive devices, (2) religious groups, (3) tribes, (4) the national infrastructure, (5) coalition forces, (6) current operations, and (7) weapons. She deliberately set the level of classification for these functions below "Special Compartmented Information (SCI)," so the products and information could be shared with all the non-U.S. coalition forces. Separately, she established a "big main," an intelligence fusion cell manned by Americans, British, and Australians who, unlike the coalition intelligence cell, operated at the highly restricted SCI level.[13] The fusion cell dealt with targeting, counterterrorism, interrogation support, political–military matters, and the insurgency. By the beginning of 2004, a Joint Interagency Task Force was added inside the fusion cell to discern and target the financial support of the anticoalition insurgents. Fast also appointed Dr. Derek Harvey to lead a "Red Cell" to consider the "tough problems" facing the coalition from the perspective of the various anticoalition elements. Harvey was to submit the Red Cell's estimates to the other cells to include in their analysis. As she neared the end of her tour of duty at CJTF-7, Fast recognized that she needed to improve the linkage between the coalition and the intelligence fusion cells "to make it more unified."[14]

As the senior military intelligence officer in the coalition in Iraq, Fast considered ways to share intelligence with the new Iraqi government and its official and semiofficial agencies. Since there was no Iraqi MoD, she worked through the Ministry of the Interior in assessing how to manage intelligence personnel and equipment requirements, analysis, translation, and dissemination. The U.S. Army and Marine Corps combat divisions that comprised CJTF-7 had set up their own coordination centers with the local ICDC units with the primary intention of preventing fratricides during their operations. Fast made a clear distinction between "coordination" and "intelligence sharing." She wanted to sharply restrict any Iraqi access to coalition intelligence because of the suspect nature of the vetting process for newly appointed Iraqi civilian and military officials. "Vetting is not the same as a security investigation," she pointed out. In filling positions in the new regime, she predicted "We will err on the side of capacity, and we will bring in bad guys with the good."

Correspondingly, the Iraqis did not reflexively pass information on to their U.S. sponsors. The ICDC's 36th Battalion had its own intelligence service, which captured from insurgents a set of floor plans of the Republican Palace that housed the CPA, along with a cache of anesthetics. Despite regular contact with U.S. liaison officers, the intelligence staff of the 36th Battalion did not pass on the news of this discovery for ten days. When the British argued for a single intelligence coordinator for all the coalition members, Fast stood against that plan, arguing that improved intelligence sharing was the solution to integration.

Fast was a member of the CPA's intelligence steering committee to Eaton's CMATT. At the national level, she had her staff standardize several report formats in anticipation of easing the bureaucratic interaction between the new Iraqi National Intelligence Service and what Fast envisioned as the future "Iraqi Military Intelligence Service." Inside Baghdad's Green Zone, the CPA had already set aside two buildings as the headquarters for the new service: one for analysts, and one for the steering committee.

In discussing the question of the mission of the future Iraqi military intelligence service, Fast felt there was a "fundamental decision" to be made—would the service focus on internal security only or on both internal and external threats? To the general, an internal orientation was obvious, because "the police are not capable in the near term" of dealing with the insurgents. An external orientation was necessary as well, she stated, "because you've got to protect your borders." These remarks were contrary to Eaton's CMATT mission concept of training the NIA solely to be prepared to defend the country from foreign invasion but not conduct military operations against "internal threats" such as native insurgents.

Ambassador David C. Gompert, the influential CPA senior adviser for security affairs and former president of RAND Corporation's European office, held a third view. During the current emergency, he proposed that the police would provide internal security, but the Iraqi army, while not the preferred instrument of internal stability, could be used by the government against insurgents if absolutely necessary. The "internal/external" mission distinction was further blurred by a coalition debate over the role of the ICDC. In the British view, the police would not be able to maintain order without the ICDC, which would be an internal security mission. However, the U.S.-led CJTF-7 headquarters wanted to control the ICDC as a military reserve for national defense. Either arrangement would markedly affect the intelligence architecture of the ICDC if a division of functions between internal and external missions were maintained.

In Fast's estimation, obstacles to efficient intelligence operations in the U.S. task force included outdated signal intelligence modem systems and lack of strategic-level training and expertise among intelligence staff officers. She also had to contend with command and intelligence "stovepipes" from higher headquarters to units inside Iraq that disallowed her visibility of operations in her purview, and with "cultural mindsets" inside U.S. headquarters. Some of this related to organizational and service cultures, but it apparently also had to do with the aspect of American national culture that disregarded and ignored foreign cultures.

A senior coalition officer compared the CJTF-7 commanding general to a one-man executive-level patrol, who in his meetings with senior Iraqi political leaders had a unique opportunity to "reconnoiter" these key personalities. However, the officer noted the general received no cultural intelligence preparation before these encounters and, as a result, brought none back. At the lowest tactical level, American combat units searching for intelligence would close themselves off from their sources by conduct inappropriate and offensive to the Iraqi culture. Even during the Saddam regime, when secret police from the much-feared Directorate of General Intelligence knocked on doors in the middle of the night to make arrests, they waited fifteen minutes before entering to give any women in the house time to get dressed.

In CJTF-7's Red Cell, Dr. Harvey discovered that U.S. patrols were submitting reports that were not subsequently recorded by their superiors. The various watch officers in the numerous task force headquarters charged with keeping the daily logs decided individually what was logged, or not, based on their own standards of significance. As a result, only about 20 percent of attacks on U.S. forces were entered into the intelligence database, while the others disregarded as insignificant. If all the incidents had been logged, the information gathered would have enabled an early pattern analysis of insurgent activity. This trend would continue to affect later attempts to assess coalition progress.

Other senior staff officers observed an "adversarial relationship" between the CJTF-7 headquarters and its subordinate combat division staffs. Described as "command by consensus," this further impaired intelligence reporting and dissemination. As for its relations with the CPA, its political counterpart and ostensible directorate, the CJTF-7 staff only placed a single PowerPoint slide addressing CPA matters in their commanding general's daily briefings. This lone page of information was presented by a major from the Task Force's own Civil Affairs/C-9 section.

Fast acknowledged that detainee operations, an important source of intelligence, were "a real problem," knowing in January 2004 of the then-classified investigation into misconduct by U.S. soldiers at the Abu Ghraib prison facility. However, the difficulty for viable intelligence collection stemmed principally from indifferent handling and processing of the detainees, the shortage of interpreters, the lack of adequate holding facilities disallowing segregation of suspects, and the inability of the U.S. intelligence database systems to accept Arabic names. The resulting confusion over transcribing richly alphabetized Arabic into fewer English characters sometimes caused detainees to be registered under several different names—because of different spellings by different translators—as they were processed through the various levels of control. Ultimately, none of the names matched correctly with the detainees, who were then "lost" in the records system as well as in their holding facility.

The senior technical adviser to the Ministry of the Interior, Mr. Ed McVaney, suggested one part of the solution to this problem as universal issue of personal I.D. cards. According to his assessment, the UN-mandated "Oil-for-Food" ration program had all the necessary individual information in its archived database, which needed only to be verified to allow issue of cards to all Iraqi adults.

At U.S. CENTCOM's (Central Command) forward headquarters in as-Sayliyah, Qatar, Brigadier General John Custer observed similar shortcomings in coalition intelligence operations inside Iraq. Custer was the chief of intelligence, or J-2, for CENTCOM and worked to support CJTF-7. For several months after their arrival, CJTF-7 had considerable difficulty with its communications; for example, no video-teleconferencing was available. Only half of the additional staff personnel due to the headquarters on account of the continuing war had arrived. Many of those who had were transferred from other important intelligence operations in homeland defense, such as the U.S. Border Patrol and Immigration and Naturalization Service. Custer recognized that database management had to be adjusted from the force-oriented system employed during the invasion, to a more precise, individual-oriented system to counter the insurgency. The intelligence database programs then in use included "Starlight," which he thought was overly intricate and required too much operator training, ASAS (all-source analysis system) and ASAS-Light, and "Analyst's Notebook," which was more adaptable.

Custer's first priority became to "fuse" all the databases, which was a technical information–management and data processing issue. Mr. Jim Allen, head of the National Security Agency's intelligence branch, observed "Fusion is a conversation." The central problem in improving U.S. intelligence operations, Custer thought, was lack of trained personnel. Money was available, but schooled and experienced people were not. "You can't buy HUMINTers [human intelligence specialists]," he said, "and you can't buy analysts."[15] He also refocused intelligence efforts at the headquarters level on discerning "high value targets"—that is, key leaders and operators in the numerous insurgent groups in Iraq. These efforts to enhance U.S. intelligence functions and organizations underscored the need to make the same sort of improvements to the Iraqi intelligence systems, such as the creation of a common intelligence database. The disorganization of the CPA and its contentious relationship with CJTF-7 never permitted these programs to advance in a viable manner.

Summary

The U.S. Army in Iraq—a single, cohesive, internetted organization—has experienced exceeding difficulty in attempting to unify its several intelligence databases. As it was discovered once the occupation and counterinsurgency operations began, the various systems in use were not compatible, retarding collection, analysis, and dissemination of intelligence.

The CENTCOM J-2, Custer, told the National Security Agency Associate Director for Research that his "number one priority" is to fuse the U.S. intelligence databases. Some aggregation could easily be done. For the most part, however, this effort was slow and required constant general officer attention to proceed. Custer was familiar with the database and software programs such as "Analyst's Notebook," made famous for the complex network diagram it drew for the 4th Infantry Division G-2 staff of Saddam Hussein's personal associations, and "Starlight," a very intricate program requiring extensive training. These admitted problems ought to have prompted the development of a database system for the Iraqi police, military, and national government intelligence services. This did not happen.

In a counterinsurgency, population control is one of the most critical measures the government must take in order to identify insurgents and criminals fighting against the government and civic order. Population control is managed most completely through a national identity card system. In some societies, this is difficult to achieve. There may be a lack of any tradition of identity cards, or a cultural resistance to what is seen as a breach of privacy, or political opposition to a centralized system that appears to undermine the primacy and prerogatives of local or tribal control of a given community or region.

There was already a national identity card system in operation in Iraq, which had been established as a result of the sanctions imposed by the First Gulf War of 1991. The Senior Technical Adviser to the Ministry of the Interior, Mr. Ed McVaney identified several existing Iraqi databases that survived the recent war. Every Iraqi adult was issued an "Oil for Food" card, and the national-level database of this program exists today. These records were in the possession of the Senior Adviser to the Ministry of Trade, Ambassador Dick Jones, and his military assistant, Colonel Tracy Wright.

The Senior Adviser for Security Affairs, Ambassador David C. Gompert personally stated "The first awareness and the first response to security problems will come from the police." In the British-led MND-SE sector headquartered in Basra, the division Provost Marshal Lt. Col. Jeremy Green was convinced that "intelligence-led policing" is the key to suppression of both the insurgency and the organized crime.

Eaton said that in his effort to form a NIA he considered development of military intelligence functions to be a low priority because of his limited resources. He felt that the sensors and related collection equipment necessary to replicate a U.S.-style capability would not be available for three to five years and that his own priority was to create viable combat arms battalions before adding other specialized units or capabilities. In the meantime, he has relegated the training of each new battalion's staff intelligence officer to the Jordanian Army.

Trust is the most important element in "fusing" intelligence—each component of the intelligence community must freely offer up its share of information. Given the history and culture of the Iraqi intelligence community, it is unrealistic to expect that fusing will readily occur if there is no common database in place. The old Iraqi intelligence system consisted of five independent secret agencies, deliberately separated to prevent the superiority of any one or combination of agencies over another, which might then threaten Saddam's rule. As has been seen in the former Soviet Union and Eastern Europe, after the collapse of a totalitarian regime, organized crime syndicates become active during the lapse of public order.

When LTG Gerald Templer took over the British effort in Malaya in 1951 to bring the violent insurgency there to heel, he announced in his first meeting with his staff that "This is an intelligence war." This outlook influenced all the efforts that followed, and led to the effective destruction of the terrorist organizations bent on seizing power. It may well have been useful for the coalition military and political leadership in Iraq to have taken the same approach. Clearly, the actions they did take, and failed to take in the realm of human and technical intelligence, did not aid the suppression of the insurgency at its weakest and most vulnerable stage—in the first year of the occupation, 2003–04.

CHAPTER 5

CREATING THE IRAQI SECURITY FORCES

William C. Thomas

It would be easy to assume the U.S. military learned a valuable lesson from the lack of effective post-conflict planning for Iraq. That, unfortunately, is not the case. While coalition forces in Iraq operated under an overarching "campaign plan" created by MNF-I (Multinational Force–Iraq), it only provided general guidance. The blanks needed to be filled in by subordinate units. One of those units, MNSTC-I (Multinational Security Transition Command–Iraq), failed to develop a plan early on, and this mistake affected the development of security forces through 2006.

MNSTC-I had a mission most would consider important: organizing, training, and equipping the Iraqi military and police. Not only were effective security forces essential for Iraq's counterinsurgency effort and future development, they were also the ticket home for coalition forces. By 2005, the coalition's goal was not to defeat the insurgency but instead to build indigenous security forces to the point where they can gain and maintain stability so foreign militaries can withdraw. It would seem obvious that MNSTC-I would develop a plan that could provide a roadmap toward the desired end state while also being adaptable for changing conditions. The command instead seemed to be describing goals without a COA (course of action) to reach them, ignoring potential problems, and hoping for the best. While optimism is important, this hope should not take the place of a coordinated plan. The lack of planning led to a hodgepodge of ISF (Iraqi security forces) whose structure depended more on the personalities of Iraqi leaders than on integrated efforts with the coalition. At the same time, there was a lack of common focus among the MNSTC-I staff because the commander's vision was not communicated downward.

A plan on the shelf does not guarantee victory, of course, but that is not its purpose. A plan is a starting point, providing guidance to the command and suggesting a path to success. The plan itself is less important than the planning process, in which assumptions are made and challenged, questions are asked and realities determined, and difficult choices are made between competing priorities. It is this process that brings together the various staff elements, that communicates the leader's vision to that staff, and that forces the staff to consider what might go wrong. In the case of Iraq, this process should include Iraqi representation as well, which was sorely lacking. The failure to make decisions about the future often allowed the passage of time to be the deciding factor, resulting in options being overcome by events before they could be explored. This study explores what should have happened, compares it with what actually happened, and suggests reasons why it happened the way it did. The report is based in large measure on the author's experience as a planning officer in MNSTC-I's Plans and Policy section from October 2004 to February 2005. It becomes apparent that the development of the ISF was hampered by a lack of planning, threatening the overall coalition mission and the security of Iraq.

Background

Following the invasion of Iraq and overthrow of the Saddam Hussein regime in 2003, the American administrator in Iraq ordered the dissolution of all Iraqi security–related ministries and their forces.[1] What apparently seemed like a good idea at the time has in retrospect been derided as a poor decision, as suggested by former Speaker of the House Newt Gingrich who said, "[t]he mistake in Iraq was not keeping the Iraqi regular army intact to assume the responsibility of policing in June 2003."[2] When the security forces were disbanded there was no immediate plan for replacing them.

It was not until August 2003 that the CPA (Coalition Provisional Authority) issued an order for the creation of a new Army.[3] The following month saw an order issued to create the ICDC (Iraqi Civil Defense Corps), a "temporary institution" that was to "complement operations conducted by Coalition military forces in Iraq."[4] The development of these security organizations, along with the new MoD (Ministry of Defense) and MoI (Ministry of Interior), would be affected by CPA Order 1, which had restricted senior Ba'ath Party members— including many who worked within the top three levels of leadership at the former ministries—from serving in the new government.[5] The original plan was to have an Office of Security Transition, led by a military officer but residing in the U.S. Embassy, oversee the development of the new security forces.[6]

In 2004, the emerging insurgency could not be ignored, and major changes to the structure of Iraqi military and police forces were implemented. For example, the ICDC, the "temporary" organization created late in 2003, was transferred to the MoD in April 2004.[7] More attention was given to reconstituting the police forces, which would typically be a State Department function but which, owing to the situation in Iraq, would now be overseen by the military.[8]

With the expansion of training requirements, a new organizational structure was created. U.S. Central Command was given responsibility for developing the security forces.[9] MNSTC-I took over the functions of the Office of Security Transition and became a subordinate command to MNF-I, which oversaw all coalition military forces in Iraq. In this capacity it joined MNC-I (Multinational Corps–Iraq), which conducted active military operations throughout Iraq. MNSTC-I's new commanding general, LTG (Lieutenant General) David Petraeus, reported to Baghdad in May 2004 and organized his new command to address the expanding needs of the Iraqi military and police.

At the same time as this new organization was created, responsibility for developing the civilian leaders and bureaucrats in the MoD and MoI rested with the IRMO (Iraq Reconstruction Management Office). This was the U.S. State Department–run organization designed to establish the various Iraqi ministries and assist in the development of a bureaucracy and leadership for carrying out ministry functions.[10] In addition to working with the Ministry of Oil, Ministry of Youth and Sport, and others, there were also teams assigned to MoD and MoI.

What Should Have Happened?

American military doctrine outlines how forces should operate but can be adapted as appropriate for a situation. The individual services have their own doctrine that takes advantage of their specialized capabilities, and this is complemented by joint doctrine that addresses how to bring forces together in pursuit of an objective. One explanation often suggested for the poor state of affairs in Iraq is the lack of U.S. doctrine for counterinsurgency operations. While this was true in 2004 and 2005, the United States did have doctrine for how to plan military operations in general. This joint doctrine for planning provides forces with a guide to developing a plan for a military campaign.

Campaign planning is critical because it outlines how forces will be employed to achieve a strategic objective and provides guidance to lower echelon commanders for developing and carrying out operations. Joint doctrine notes that

> Campaign planning is a primary means by which combatant commanders arrange for strategic unity of effort and through which they guide the planning of joint operations in their theater. It communicates the commander's purpose, requirements, objectives, and concept to subordinate components, as well as to supporting commands and Services, so that they may make necessary preparations.[11]

Following this guidance, MNF-I would develop a campaign plan that identified how its various elements would work together to achieve success in Iraq and that would provide information to subordinate commands, including MNSTC-I, for the development of their own plans.

One argument that was made against having MNSTC-I develop a campaign plan is that it was up to MNF-I to plan the overall Iraqi campaign, with MNSTC-I playing a subordinate role and merely contributing to the MNF-I campaign objectives. However, as noted in joint doctrine,

> Subordinate JFCs [joint force commanders] may develop subordinate campaign plans or operation plans that accomplish (or contribute to the accomplishment of) theater strategic objectives. Thus, *subordinate unified commands typically develop campaign plans to accomplish assigned missions.* [italics added] Also, JTFs [joint task forces] can develop and execute campaign plans if missions require military operations of substantial size, complexity, and duration and cannot be accomplished within the framework of a single major joint operation.[12]

Whether MNSTC-I was considered a subordinate unified command with a broadly defined mission under MNF-I or a joint task force with a more limited mission, it was still within its purview to develop some sort of plan—whether called a "campaign plan," an "operation plan," or some other name—to conduct operations that supported MNF-I's objectives.

Military headquarters have a section dedicated to planning. On a joint staff this is typically a function of the J-5 section, which goes by names such as "Plans and Policy," "Future Plans," or something along those lines.[13] The actual structure of the staff and the responsibilities of each section are ultimately determined by the commander that the staff supports, but the use of "the 5" as a planning group is typical. It provides a central point for planning responsibilities within the staff and draws on expertise and inputs from other staff sections as needed.

Once the process is complete the command's campaign plan should include at least the following elements:

- guidance from higher headquarters, including a description of the desired end state;
- the command's own desired end state that supports the strategic campaign objectives;
- a set of realistic assumptions that include an assessment of the current situation and the constraints that will be faced as the operation moves forward;
- a set of COAs that allow progress from the current status to the desired end state;
- assessment criteria for those COAs so that progress can be monitored and actions can be adjusted as necessary;
- clearly defined relationships, horizontal as well as vertical, with higher commands, subordinate units, and other organizations working toward the same overall goals.[14]

This allows a command to see where they are and where they want to be, identify how they will get there in cooperation with others and within realistic limits, and monitor how they are doing along the way. With these general guidelines in mind, it is possible to examine MNSTC-I and see how the process should have gone and what they should have developed in 2004.

First, MNSTC-I needed strategic guidance from MNF-I regarding the desired end state, limitations on COAs, and clearly defined relationships between not only military units but also the State Department and other agencies. This would come in the form of the MNF-I Campaign Plan, which was the responsibility of MNF-I/SPA (MNF-I Strategy, Plans, and Assessment), their version of the J-5. Ideally, MNSTC-I would participate in the development of the MNF-I Campaign Plan so there would be no surprises later. With this guidance from the commander of MNF-I, the commanding general of MNSTC-I would communicate his own goals to his J-5 staff. Perhaps the most important part of this "commander's guidance" is his view of the command's mission and the goals it must achieve to help MNF-I achieve its desired end state.

MNSTC-I J-5 would then conduct a "mission analysis," perhaps the most important part of which would involve identifying questions that needed answering before COAs could be developed. This would help identify the assumptions that provide a baseline for the planning effort and would suggest constraints within which planning must occur. One assumption, for example, might be that Iraqi forces will need to return home once a month with their pay because there is no central banking system allowing them to deposit their pay at one place and have their family withdraw it for their use elsewhere.[15] Other important assumptions, dealing with such issues as Iraqi culture and the nature of the insurgent threat, could also be highlighted during this process. This is also the phase in which other agencies and their missions could be identified so that potential overlaps and important relationships can be incorporated into the plan.

A key element of the mission analysis is a description of the ultimate Iraqi force structure. This should include not only the numbers of forces but also the types of missions they should be able to conduct and the skills they need to complete those missions. The force structure should include combat, combat support, and combat service support capabilities, just as American forces do. Cooperation with the Iraqi government at this point is critical because ultimately it is the Iraqis who will control these forces, so they should have some say in how these forces are designed. Formal Iraqi agreement at this point would encourage their cooperation in the development of forces and discourage any ad hoc changes to the force structure if the coalition leadership is able to point to an agreement and hold the Iraqis to it.

With the end state in mind, the current state understood, and the constraints clearly defined, J-5 could then move forward and develop multiple COAs designed to get from the current Point A to the desired Point B. These COAs would include such elements as an explanation of basic and advanced training, a timeline for force development, a basing structure that includes not only training facilities but also the operational bases to which forces will transition, a means of vetting former officers and soldiers who wish to join, a desired flow of incoming equipment for training and operational purposes, procedures for recruiting and paying Iraqi personnel, and a method for transitioning from coalition control over training and operations to Iraqi control.

Included with these COAs should be some method of assessing their progress so that problems can be identified and adjustments made during their implementation. The U.S. military uses METLs (Mission Essential Task Lists) to identify the tasks a unit should be able to accomplish. Commanders use METLs to set standards of performance and develop training strategies to achieve that level of performance.[16]

Once the possible COAs are developed they would go to the Commanding General for selection. The actual implementation would be the responsibility of the J-3 (Operations), J-4 (Logistics), and other staff sections, as well as subordinate commands, including the CMATT (Coalition Military Assistance Training Team), the CPATT (Coalition Police Advisory Training Team), and the Joint Headquarters Advisory Support Team.[17] J-5 would be in a position to provide an objective assessment of progress and recommend adjustments over time, while also maintaining a close relationship with the MoD and MoI.

Though J-5 would typically be responsible for planning, that does not mean they would operate in a vacuum. Other staff sections need to be involved so they can differentiate between the possible and impossible in their areas of expertise and also keep their sections apprised of what tasks are coming up. Other agencies, such as IRMO, MNF-I/SPA, and MNC-I, should also participate so they can provide insight from their unique perspectives. Managing all of this participation so that it does not get out of control and bog down the process takes strong leadership from the J-5, but this participation is essential for minimizing problems later.

U.S. doctrine clearly outlines how planning should take place across the range of military operations. Much of this doctrine is based on lessons learned from past experience and so should not be discarded lightly. Military doctrine examines how resources should be employed in an ideal environment. Since most environments are not ideal, the application of military doctrine needs to be tailored to a specific scenario. History, too, is a useful teacher, but again the lessons from the past must be viewed in the context of a current situation. In the case of the development of Iraqi forces, doctrine and history were ignored rather than misapplied. MNSTC-I and other agencies cast aside existing doctrine and failed to provide effective operational planning for this critical mission, adopting instead an ad hoc approach to developing ISF. This led to serious problems in developing a proper force structure, assessing Iraqi capabilities, and transitioning security to Iraqi control.

What Actually Happened

Strategic guidance was provided by MNF-I, which published a campaign plan in 2004. When new officers arrived in MNSTC-I J-5, this was often one of the first documents they reviewed. The MNF-I plan outlined in broad terms the desired end state for Iraq and the various integrated means for getting there. It was short on details, but that is not unexpected. The MNF-I plan was designed to provide overarching guidance to the various elements carrying out the plan, such as MNSTC-I and MNC-I, and those subordinate commands and associated agencies needed to "fill in the blanks" by determining how best to accomplish the goals laid out in the MNF-I plan.

After reading through MNF-I's plan, a common question asked by new MNSTC-I planners was "where's *our* plan?" A long silence would often follow, because MNSTC-I did not have a plan for accomplishing the tasks assigned by its higher headquarters. Unlike the MNF-I campaign plan, there was no document to which MNSTC-I personnel could turn to determine what the command should be doing and what part they played in carrying that out. When asked for a plan, senior staff officers would often bring out PowerPoint presentations, but these were merely supposed to be briefings about a plan, not the plan itself. The planning process identified in joint doctrine was not carried out in MNSTC-I, and the result was that the command's activities were driven by PowerPoint briefings and desired timelines rather than by a well-thought-out roadmap that was available to those who were supposed to be carrying it out.

Though strategic guidance was provided through MNF-I's campaign plan, commander's guidance within MNSTC-I was lacking. The desired end state was numbers-based with little discussion of capabilities. The goal was simply to have an Iraqi command structure in place and a certain number of people in each security force, leading to the forces being "manned, trained, and equipped" at 100 percent, with no explanation of what capabilities those forces should have.

For example, in the Iraqi Army, the force structure of combat battalions did not take into account combat support and combat service support capabilities. A military needs more than "trigger pullers." Some specialties essential in a counterinsurgency—such as military police and EOD (explosive ordnance demolition)—were delayed much longer than they should have been. Development of EOD capability did not begin until a 29 November 2004 agreement was reached between Iraq and MNSTC-I.[18] A J-5 staff officer spent the next two months identifying possible sites for the school and determining his requirements for trainers. Though the training program eventually opened and began creating EOD companies, it was months before the need for this capability was even identified, a need which likely would have been identified earlier had a dedicated planning process taken place. Other combat support functions were also developed later, seemingly as afterthoughts.

Similar to not having a well-defined "Point B," MNSTC-I was also unclear on "Point A," the starting status. Throughout the staff, including in J-5, there was little understanding of Iraqi culture and the role that security forces would play in it. For instance, one of the accepted fundamentals of counterinsurgency is the importance of the police, but given that the police had been the tool of a dictator for many years, it would have been worth asking if the population's perception of the police would allow that force to be effective.[19] One director of J-5, a British Royal Marine, said in November 2004 that perhaps the British had overstated the importance of the police when they came to Iraq based largely on their past experiences in Malaya and Northern Ireland.[20]

In addition to understanding the culture, it was important to recognize the effect of the current state of affairs in Iraq, such as the lack of a banking system. As a result of the unexpected absence of Iraqi trainees once a month to take their pay home, the training schedules established by MNSTC-I were disrupted very quickly. A more unfortunate effect was felt with the deaths of forty-nine soldiers in October 2004 who were headed home on leave; no one had identified an appropriate set of force protection procedures for these troops, thus leaving them vulnerable to insurgent attacks.[21] Had questions been asked early on, some of these conditions might have been better addressed.

Ask an MNSTC-I staff member, "what are your courses of action," and you would likely get a blank stare. Though training programs were started and a logistics pipeline was established, these were not done as part of a coordinated plan but instead met needs as they were identified. The problem with this, of course, is that it is very easy to go down an unnecessary path, wasting time that could have been better spent if the effort had been put into identifying requirements. The ad hoc nature of the effort led to inconsistent training as regular Army forces were trained by a U.S. Army division assigned to MNSTC-I, Iraqi National Guard forces were trained by coalition forces assigned to MNC-I, and police forces were trained at a variety of facilities, including one in Jordan. The lack of a coordinated set of COAs designed to get from the current state to the desired end state led to military and other personnel simply doing what they felt was appropriate, and while their initiative is commendable, the result was a mix of training that might, or might not, yield the desired ISF.

By not creating and following a series of COAs, it was very difficult for MNSTC-I to prioritize resources. In response to a question, the deputy director of the J-5 section said "we don't need priorities as long as we have all the resources we need."[22] However, some problems emerged with the disbursement of equipment, while others arose over the establishment of operational bases. This second point had a particularly negative impact on training: if operational bases were not

ready to receive troops, those forces that had completed training had to remain at
their training base, which blocked the next group of trainees from entering.

One of the most relied upon documents in MNSTC-I was a timeline referred
to as "the sand chart." The multicolored chart showed anticipated levels of
development for the various security forces at different points in time. The goals
identified in the sand chart were based on numbers, not on capability. When
asked for "the plan," this is the document MNSTC-I planners would often refer
to. The sand chart, of course, was not a plan but merely a statement of desire; it
identified times by which MNSTC-I hoped to have forces ready but did not
explain how they were to reach that point. This affected not only MNSTC-I's
ability to perform its mission but also its ability to work with the Iraqi
government and other agencies.

The only real assessment criteria employed were numerical goals. There were
no METLs used to evaluate forces' capabilities, merely a measurement of how
many forces had been recruited, how many had completed training, how much
of their equipment they had received, and whether or not they had a command
structure above them. This final point was the key to determining if units were
capable of independent operations, could lead operations with coalition support,
could support coalition operations, or were incapable of operations. When
MNSTC-I offered a monthly assessment to the MNF-I commander, it could
provide the numbers, but the question of whether Iraqi units were capable
of operations was largely a "best guess." A Department of Defense Inspector
General's report on police training found that "the emphasis on numbers overshadows the attention that should be given to the qualitative performance of those
trained."[23]

Any plan for developing ISF needed to be done in coordination with the
Iraqi ministries of Defense and Interior. This would have allowed MNSTC-I to
coordinate its activities closely with the Iraqis and also give the Iraqis more
"ownership" of the development process, while also helping to lock them into a
defined force structure. As it was, without an agreed-upon plan, the Iraqi ministries had a tendency to create new forces at will. In October 2004, for instance,
the anticipated size of the Highway Patrol was tripled from 1,900 to 6,000, a fact
that J-5 planners learned from MNSTC-I's weekly newsletter.[24] In late 2004, the
MoD created the Muthana Brigade, which was not a part of the Army structure
anticipated by MNSTC-I, and in early 2005, it repeated that by creating the
Defenders of Baghdad.[25] Who were these groups? Were they going to be rolled
into the existing Army structure? Were they special units created for unique
needs? Were they sectarian militias suddenly put into uniforms and equipped by
the coalition? It was unclear. Petraeus spoke in February 2005 about "executing
the plan for the Iraqi Security Forces that everyone agreed on," but in fact there
was no written agreement to which the coalition and the Iraqis could be held.[26]
The lack of a common plan made it easier for the Iraqis to create units where none

were anticipated and then request resources to equip these units. This had the potential to slow the development of those units that were already expected to be built as their resources were diverted.

Adjustments happened on the part of the coalition as well. In late 2004, a new model for advisory teams was developed that included Military Assistance Teams, Police Assistance Teams, Special Police Assistance Teams, and Border Assistance Teams that would be embedded with ISF units.[27] This concept was developed without coordination with the Iraqis up to the point where coalition forces were being identified to fill out these teams. When finally presented with the idea, the Minister of Defense agreed to it but the Minister of Interior declined to participate, finally agreeing to an "experimental" application of the concept with a few police stations in Baghdad. A complete, well-thought-out planning process should have included the Iraqis early on rather than presenting them with a *fait accompli.*

The lack of a clear plan also led to a confusing relationship with IRMO. The relationship between the IRMO teams, which were responsible for developing the civilian officials in MoD and MoI, and MNSTC-I, which was responsible for developing the forces, was never clear. The management of potential overlap seemed dependent upon the personalities of the team members and MNSTC-I staff and with the turnover of personnel in both organizations that created a situation that could change without warning. The development of the ministries and their forces needed to be aligned, yet there was no agreed-upon plan between the two responsible agencies.

This is not to say that there was no strategic thinking within MNSTC-I, but it was concentrated in the three-person CAG (Commander's Action Group) rather than in J-5, and that thinking was not widely disseminated throughout the command. The CAG was an extremely capable group—it included officers who were Rhodes Scholars and others who held Ph.D.s—but it was somewhat removed from the rest of the headquarters. While a commander can organize his staff in the way he sees best, keeping his strategic thinkers so close to him kept them somewhat isolated from the rest of the staff. Had the J-5 been the center of strategic planning—as U.S. doctrine suggests it should be—it would have been easier to incorporate the entire staff into the planning process.

The bottom line is that the United States ignored its own doctrine when setting out to create the ISF. It failed to identify desired capabilities for the security forces and instead relied upon numbers of "manned, trained, and equipped" troops, a situation oddly reminiscent of the "body count" mentality and Robert McNamara's "Whiz Kids" in the Vietnam War. The problem did not go unnoticed. In December 2004, the commanding general told the new chief of the J-5 section to "get out of the weeds" and think long term, but as spring and summer approached, the section failed to move beyond the initial stages of developing a plan. Staff officers in J-5 raised their concerns but were rebuffed by their deputy section chief who was "not convinced that the benefit of having a plan outweighs the cost of creating one."[28] The insurgents, however, did not wait around, and they continued to maintain the initiative.

The effects of this lack of planning revealed themselves over time as Iraqi forces developed in fits and starts through 2005. Changing U.S. goals—from defeating the insurgency to developing an Iraqi force that could defeat the insurgency—further confused the training effort.[29] It is one thing to adapt an existing plan; it is far more difficult to change course when there is no plan to adapt. Without a plan, it was difficult to prioritize resources or keep the MNSTC-I staff and training personnel on a common path.

One result of the unclear strategic goals was that the development of military forces was emphasized at the expense of the police. MNSTC-I had one subordinate command focused on the military and a second focused on police forces. Within the headquarters staff, however, far greater emphasis was given to the military. For example, within the J-5 section in early 2005, only one of the fourteen staff officers worked on police issues while a second worked on the MoI's Border Patrol; all of the other officers focused on military matters. A further impediment to cooperation was that CPATT was located in a different compound from MNSTC-I headquarters, whereas CMATT was located down the hall from J-5. The phone and e-mail systems between MNSTC-I, the U.S. Embassy, and CPATT had some compatibility problems, making it even more difficult to work together. A lack of clear guidance in the form of a plan for force development led MNSTC-I's planning section to largely ignore the development of this important asset.

Finally, the lack of effective planning provided a poor example for Iraqi military and police personnel. As coalition forces attempted to create professional military and police forces, one thing the Iraqis should have learned was the importance of seizing the initiative by planning rather than simply responding to changing situations. As long as Iraqi forces merely react to insurgents rather than taking a proactive stance against them they are unlikely to succeed. Unfortunately, the lesson they learned from the coalition may have been to proceed in an ad hoc fashion.

Hindsight is often derided because later reviewers have the advantage of seeing pitfalls that were not obvious at the time, and as a result it might be easy to dismiss criticism of MNSTC-I's effort. The point here, however, is that those pitfalls should have been apparent had planning taken place. Even if that planning did not occur before the start of training operations, many of these problems were clearly identified by staff officers, yet the planning efforts that should have followed did not happen. While it may be easy to say "we should have known, but we didn't," it is harder to say "we did know, and we did nothing." Perhaps an understanding of why planning was lacking during the training operation can lead to steps to avoid that problem in the future.

Why Did It Happen?

Perhaps one reason why planning was lacking was that U.S. military officers remain unfamiliar with counterinsurgency requirements. There is, however, a vast library of counterinsurgency history that outlines many of the fundamentals and the lessons learned when training indigenous forces. Some of this history is American, such as Heinie Aderholt's emphasis on civic action early in Vietnam discussed in *Air Commando One* and Edward Landsdale's experiences during the Philippine insurrection chronicled in *In the Midst of Wars*.[30] The United States has faced military force development and counterinsurgency before, and through its successes and failures, all well documented, there were lessons to be learned. Many of these lessons were unacknowledged by the officers on the ground in Iraq. Few Americans in MNSTC-I seemed to be aware of the U.S. role in countering insurgency in the Philippines in the 1950s, and while military personnel are of course familiar with the Vietnam War, sound bites and rhetoric are more common knowledge than the lessons about the development of another nation's military.

It is not surprising that many officers are unfamiliar with the literature on past attempts at security force development. Not everyone has the opportunity for graduate study where this might be required reading, and even those who attend staff schools and war colleges often get merely an introduction to such topics rather than an in-depth education. However, these lessons from the past have informed military doctrine and this is the sort of material with which military officers should be familiar. Beyond the doctrine for planning, there exists joint doctrine for foreign internal defense—the training of indigenous forces for internal security—and U.S. Army doctrine for stability and security operations, all of which provide a robust knowledge base for the campaign MNSTC-I faces. Other military guidance exists beyond traditional doctrine manuals that would have supported the planning effort. The Marine Corps' *Small Wars Manual* dedicates an entire chapter to developing security forces in occupied countries, and though it was written in the first half of the twentieth century, its lessons could provide a starting point for modern planning efforts, but only if it is actually read.[31]

One reason for the continued lack of planning might be simple bureaucratic inertia. Once having started down a path, the focus might have been on continuing rather than pausing long enough to determine if it was the correct path, or if it might have taken a turn somewhere along the line. There was also an oft-stated view that different agencies should stay "in their lane" rather than crossing over into another agency's responsibilities. This seemed to inhibit communication between organizations that needed to work together, such as MNSTC-I and IRMO or the J-5 staff and CPATT.

There appeared to be a degree of unwillingness on the part of many senior staff to raise questions to commanders or be the bearers of potentially bad news. Though not confined to MNSTC-I, such unwillingness was particularly harmful in a mission where the measurement of progress is essential and a requirement to shift course must be identified. One retired Army general officer noted in 1997 that "[a]n idea long enunciated by many respected senior Army leaders – disagreement is not disloyalty – has not permeated the fabric of the institution."[32] Such problems are not new; a 1970 U.S. Army War College study found the Army's culture during the Vietnam War included

> persistent and rather ubiquitous overtones of: selfish behavior that places personal success ahead of the good of the Service; looking upward to please superiors rather than looking downward to fulfill the legitimate needs of subordinates...[and] incomplete communication between junior and seniors that leave the senior uninformed.[33]

The 1970 study found that "a basic cause appears to be the striving for personal success."[34] Was such an atmosphere recreated in the war in Iraq? Were staff officers unwilling to suggest a new approach because they did not want to challenge current thinking? That would be highly unfortunate if true.

Finally, MNSTC-I might have viewed the "organize, train, and equip" mission in Iraq as being similar to the development of forces at home. After all, the U.S. Army does not have a "campaign plan" for organizing, training, and equipping its own forces. The difference, of course, is that the United States is not trying to get its own forces from Point A to Point B but is merely maintaining the status quo with minor adjustments along the way. In Iraq, however, there is no status quo to maintain. MNSTC-I was working toward a goal, at which point the emphasis can transition from creation of something new to maintenance of a status quo. In 2004, the mission of training Iraqis was not at all comparable to training American forces at home.

What Next?

In case the political guidance was not clear before, it should have been once the United States published its *National Strategy for Victory in Iraq* in December 2005. Some lessons apparently still had not been learned, however, as the MNSTC-I commanding general did not see the new strategy until it was released to the press.[35] This suggests that the command might have had little input into that strategy, which would be unfortunate as they were in the best position to outline the then-current status of the Iraqi forces and what might be possible rather than what might be wished for.

In late May 2005, a staff officer from J-5 indicated that a rough draft of a mission analysis had been written.[36] This was at least the third attempt at developing a mission analysis since January 2005, but it was a step in the right direction. Anthony Cordesman noted in late 2005 that, while a plan did not appear to be in place in the spring, MNSTC-I reported that such a plan was currently available.[37] Whether this was actually a written document that emerged from a dedicated planning process or merely another PowerPoint briefing put together by J-5 is unclear.

Assessments of Iraqi capabilities have apparently not improved. According to Cordesman, the MoI and CPATT started using quality assessments in May 2005.[38] The MNF-I commander said in September 2005, however, that "when we were assessing these guys, you're assessing manning, you're assessing training, you're assessing leadership, you're assessing equipment."[39] The standards appeared to be no different than what was used earlier in the year. This leads one to question the usefulness of such statements as "more than 80 [Iraqi battalions] are fighting side-by-side with Coalition forces and more than 40 others are taking the lead in the fight."[40] If the only measures of ability are the number of troops recruited and trained, the number that have basic equipment, and the existence of divisional headquarters to oversee battalions below them, then that provides little insight into the actual abilities of the Iraqi forces.

One positive change was the merging of the IRMO missions for the MoD and MoI into MNSTC-I's responsibilities. Soon after arriving as the new commanding general of MNSTC-I, LTG Martin Dempsey announced the development of the ministerial infrastructure would be aligned with the development of the forces as the IRMO teams for MoI and MoD would fall under MNSTC-I.[41] This enhanced the establishment of civilian control over the military and police and allowed MNSTC-I a better view of what was going on in the ministries so intervention can be applied where needed.

LTG Dempsey's assumption of command in late 2005 may have allowed MNSTC-I to shift course. Maybe a new commander was needed, not because Petraeus was not up to the job but because inertia had set in and a new vision was needed. It would have been hard to find a better commander for MNSTC-I's early days than Petraeus; in addition to his Ph.D. in international relations that helps provide him with a strategic view, his experiences as a division commander during the invasion of Iraq gave him the operational insight needed to interact effectively with the emerging Iraqi leadership. One problem that he might have faced, however, is that having been appointed to the MNSTC-I command by the president, he may have been under pressure to produce quantifiable results quickly, particularly since the president was running for reelection later that year.[42] Numbers indicating "manned, trained, and equipped" forces are the easiest measure to provide, and once headed down that path, it might have been difficult to change course. A new commander, who did not have to operate in the same spotlight as Petraeus did, might have been in a better position to make changes without making waves.

There are some options the United States should consider for conducting similar operations in the future. As doctrine already suggests, a commander should have a centralized planning section that leverages the expertise of the entire headquarters staff. Some means of assessing progress—qualitatively, not just quantitatively—is an important element of such a planning office. Commanders should consider developing a training program for new staff officers and creating a recommended reading list for personnel facing deployment to the staff. Finally, over the long term, the United States should work to enhance its understanding of counterinsurgency and lower-intensity conflicts through training, doctrine, and professional military education.

Examples of these options exist in some form. In Iraq, the MNF-I/SPA office encompassed long-range strategy, operational planning, and assessment of progress, suggesting a structure that their subordinate commands could use as well. The Army established a counterinsurgency training program for officers heading to Iraq and is encouraging senior officers to read *Learning to Eat Soup With a Knife,* an examination of lessons from past counterinsurgencies written by Lieutenant Colonel John Nagl.[43] For the longer term, the Army and Marine Corps jointly published a new doctrine for counterinsurgency in December 2006.[44] However Iraq turns out, the lessons of this conflict need to be identified and incorporated into the future transformation of the U.S. military.

Success in Iraq depended on establishing an effective security force that can create an environment in which political systems can be developed and economic reconstruction can occur. As the "linchpin" mission, it is unconscionable that there was no plan for developing the ISF during at least the first year of MNSTC-I's existence. This affected the immediate coalition mission as well as the long-term status of Iraq and the region. Future U.S. conflicts may well be similar in nature, requiring effective planning rather than ad hoc programs. U.S. military forces need to be prepared to plan for emerging types of missions in order to be successful.

When Petraeus assumed command in 2004, he was jumping onto a fast-moving train that had left the station a year before. MNSTC-I needed to slow that train down just enough so it could see what lay ahead. The command needed a mission analysis that defined its tasks based on guidance from above and on the realities they faced. They needed to clearly identify the desired end state of the ISF and explore realistic COAs based on the experience they gained over time. This process should have included all of the staff sections so the entire command understood the commander's vision and could pursue that common goal. Equally important, the Iraqi ministries of Defense and Interior needed to be involved so that common agreement could be reached and the ad hoc creation of units could be avoided.

MNSTC-I's planning staff grew during 2004 and 2005, but its officers were not typically shaping the future and instead were primarily engaged in reporting about the present. They churned out PowerPoint presentations by the dozen, but the briefings had nothing underpinning them; the slides took the place of a plan. Simply starting training and hoping it works is not a COA that will lead to success. The development efforts that continue in Iraq may still allow coalition forces to come home, but with a far different country left behind than was originally hoped for.

CHAPTER 6

THE PRIMACY OF POLITICS: THE FIRST ELECTION

Thomas S. Mowle

By summer of 2004, the war in Iraq had become one of counterinsurgency. The invasion was over, successfully, and peacekeeping was over, unsuccessfully: there was no peace to keep. In this environment, strategy required the right inter-action between all four lines of operation, political, communication, security, and economics. With a campaign plan in hand, the MNF-I (Multinational Force–Iraq) reviewed its strategy, identifying politics as the critical path to success. While successful conclusion of the democratic process would not ensure success, it was the only path that created the possibility of success. With the focus on politics came a de-emphasis on early demobilization of the militias linked to Kurd and Shia Arab political parties. MNF-I worked to assess the implications of differ-ent electoral outcomes, keeping in mind above all the need for those elections to be seen as legitimate by all groups in Iraq. Finally, it tried to find a way to engage with the Sunni Arab leadership, efforts that were almost completely unsuccessful in the short term: here, immediate security needs took priority over long-term political gain. This trade-off reminds us that while politics may define the critical effort, military imperatives often drive operations in a different path.

Strategic Review

American joint doctrine identifies four main instruments of national power: DIME (diplomatic, informational, military, and economic). These instruments interact and interrelate with each other in efforts to successfully use national power. The DIME became the foundation for the campaign plan, which trans-lated its concepts into ones more specific to Iraq. The diplomatic instrument became the political line of operations, focusing on political developments within Iraq rather than on actual diplomacy. The informational instrument of power became the communicating line of operation, focusing on Iraqi opinion and attitudes rather than on the control and use of specific information. The military instrument of power became the security line of operation, focusing on the development of Iraqi capabilities against the insurgency rather than on specific MNF-I military activities. Only the economic instrument of power was brought over nearly intact to become the economic line of operation, focusing on the state of Iraq's economy and reconstruction.[1]

In its summer 2004 form, the campaign plan described these different tracks and identified some of the key milestones along each. It did not, however, prioritize among them. As written, one could not be sure whether the reopening of a major irrigation canal was more important to the overall effort than the writing of a new constitution for Iraq. In September 2004, MNF-I began a strategic review to identify the decisive points and decision points that would lead to different end states. It would link these points together, identifying the critical path to acceptable end states. The review focused on the year from the current time to August 2005, during which the Iraqis were scheduled to for the first time form a government of their own choosing and write their own constitution.

The postelection strategic review, as it came to be known, included representation from throughout the Republican Palace. The military components provided representation from strategy, planning, intelligence, political–military–economics, and civil–military affairs. The Embassy was represented by personnel from its political, political–military, and economic divisions. The review also included inputs from the IRMO (Iraq Reconstruction Management Office) and other government agencies.

The first step in the review was to identify the major decisive points anticipated—or hoped for—along each line of operation. The army understands a decisive point as "a point, if retained, that provides a commander with a marked advantage over his opponent. Decisive points are usually geographic in nature but could include other physical elements, such as enemy formations, command posts, and communications nodes." The army also defines it as "a time or location where enemy weakness is positioned that allows overwhelming combat power to be generated against it. It could be an enemy weakness to be exploited or a time when the combat potential of the enemy force is degraded."[2] These definitions display a distinct geographic bias, one mostly inappropriate to a counterinsurgency, and they also create a commensurate bias for taking military action.[3] Throughout the war, this bias would emerge in the belief that decisive military action in one of a set of key cities—such as Samarra or Fallujah—or against specific insurgent refuges in mosques or along the border would result in meaningful progress toward the campaign goals.

The strategic review mostly discarded this bias—except for including the physical security of Baghdad as the capital. Instead, it followed joint campaign doctrine, which extended "decisive point" to mean "a geographic place, specific key event, critical system, or function that allows commanders to gain a marked advantage over an enemy and greatly influence the outcome of an attack."[4] Thus the review looked at the broader notion of events or accomplishments that would degrade the insurgency's combat potential. The insurgency's center of gravity, "those characteristics, capabilities, or localities from which a military force derives its freedom of action, physical strength, or will to fight,"[5] was understood to be its support among the population relative to the support the population gave to the Iraqi government. Since this could not be attacked directly, an indirect approach was needed, one in which military action might not be the primary effort.[6] If the insurgency lost its support among the population, MNF-I and the Iraqi forces would have a marked advantage over the insurgency, even if overwhelming combat power would not turn out to be the best way to exploit that advantage.

The campaign plan identified some decisive points, but the strategic review did not limit itself to those factors. It developed more through interviews with experts in each area and general brainstorming. The strategic review then iteratively analyzed these decisive points—what events would have to occur before each one, and what events could follow the successful or unsuccessful realization of each decisive point. Through this process, additional points were identified, resulting in several dozen candidate points linked by complex lines of causality. These points were also linked to likely end states—what would be the consequences of different outcomes, and would they be acceptable? It quickly became clear that there was only one route to the desired end state, and this passed through the scheduled elections to the formation of a competent, representative government in Iraq.

While the decisive points and the lines connecting them passed back and forth among the lines of operation, it also became clear that the political line of operation drove the others. This was by no means expected. While the insurgent's center of gravity was in a sense political, it really belonged on the "communicating" line of operation—the degree to which Iraqis felt their government was legitimate. Were elections enough to make that happen, or were economic progress and physical security as important? If they were all important, how did the factors relate to each other? Part of the answer came from the situation on the ground when the review was taking place.

By September 2004, Iraqi sovereignty had been handed to an IIG (Iraqi Interim Government). As its name suggests, this government was a caretaker, serving until elections for a TNA (Transitional National Assembly), which would occur no later than January 2005. These elections were the legacy of Grand Ayatollah Ali al-Sistani, senior cleric of the Najaf *marja'iyyah* and the Object of Emulation for most Iraqi Shia Arabs. From the earliest days of the American occupation, he advocated direct national elections for Iraqi institutions, a stance that combined the ideological appeal of pure democracy with the partisan knowledge that the Shia Arabs comprised a majority of the Iraqi population.[7]

Initially, the Americans planned to have Iraqis draft a constitution before electing a sovereign government. On 15 November 2003, the Americans proposed transferring sovereignty on 30 June 2004 to a government selected indirectly via a series of regional caucuses. This government would rule under a TAL (Transitional Administrative Law) until a constitutional assembly elected in March 2005 completed its work. This constitution, written independently from the transitional government, would be submitted to a referendum in August 2005, with elections for a constitutional government following.[8]

Al-Sistani rejected this approach as undemocratic;[9] his rejection was congruent with Iraqi suspicion that such a system would be rigged by the occupying powers and the GC (Governing Council) they had created. Al-Sistani opposed the GC from the beginning, declining even to recommend names for the GC in June 2003.[10] He also issued a religious decree, a *fatwa,* which called for elections because "there is no guarantee that the [U.S.-backed] council would create a constitution conforming with the greater interests of the Iraqi people."[11] Direct national elections had drawbacks, however. In the absence of a constitution that ensured minority rights, they could empower a tyranny of the Shia Arab majority; they also would be a complex undertaking amid violence. Caucuses of local and regional leaders would be easier to secure and would do more to ensure that all groups in Iraq were represented.

While L. Paul Bremer and his CPA (Coalition Provisional Authority), supported by the GC, stood firm with their plan for several weeks, it became clear that no system rejected by al-Sistani would be accepted as legitimate by the Shia Arabs and that any protracted conflict with the Grand Ayatollah would be catastrophic. He signaled his power through large mid-January street demonstrations in Basra and Baghdad,[12] and his opposition was joined by Ahmed Chalabi of the INC (Iraqi National Congress) and Abdul Aziz al-Hakim of the SCIRI (Supreme Council for the Islamic Revolution in Iraq).[13]

On 13 February 2004, UN (United Nations) envoy Lakhdar Brahimi convinced al-Sistani to accept a new plan, which included direct elections no later than the end of January 2005. Al-Sistani conceded that it would be too difficult to conduct such an election before the planned transfer of sovereignty.[14] Instead, after Iraqi sovereignty was restored on 28 June 2004, power went to an IIG.[15] The IIG would govern until an ITG (Iraqi Transitional Government) was formed after National Assembly elections, to be held no later than 31 January 2005.[16] Formation of the ITG would initiate a second phase of Iraqi governance, which would end with the formation of a government under the Constitution written by that assembly and ratified in a national referendum.[17] United Nations Security Council Resolution 1546 (8 June 2004) endorsed this process without reference to the TAL.[18]

The IIG was chosen by a National Conference of several hundred Iraqi leaders. Scheduled for July, the National Conference was delayed until 16 August in an only partly successful attempt to encourage more Sunni Arab participation. The GC assembled a single list of 100 members (including all of the GC itself), which was pushed through the conference without organized opposition. Shia Arab Iyad Allawi of the INA (Iraqi National Accord) served as prime minister, and Sunni Arab Ghazi al-Yawr was the president; both were considered political moderates with potential appeal to both Arab groups.[19] The twenty Iraqi government ministries were distributed among different groups; Sunni Arab and Kurds each received between 20 and 25 percent of the thirty-two leadership positions, somewhat in excess of their apparent proportion of the population.[20] The new government was broadly representative of Iraqi groups, but it remained established in many Iraqi minds as a continuation of a puppet regime installed by the Americans. They did not consider it legitimate.

If progress toward legitimacy had stalled, the other lines of operation were even worse. The security situation had deteriorated throughout 2004, punctuated by an abortive invasion of Sunni Arab Fallujah in April 2004, simultaneous uprisings throughout southern Iraq by Moqtada al-Sadr's Mahdi Army, and another tortuous standoff with the Mahdi Army in Najaf in August. While the people of Najaf wanted al-Sadr expelled from the Imam Ali Shrine, a prime pilgrimage site for Shia Arabs worldwide, they also did not want the shrine damaged. The IIG was divided over how to act, and consonant with Iraqi sovereignty MNF-I waited for clear direction for each stage of the operation. Similar divisions between MNF-I and the Iraqi government beset the deteriorating situation in Fallujah, which had been turned over to the Sunni Arab First Fallujah Brigade in a deal that ended the April MNF-I assault. The First Fallujah Brigade had promised to maintain security in the city, but by September it had become a safe haven for insurgents; this example left MNF-I wary of future accommodations with local groups. The confrontation in Najaf ended rather suddenly when al-Sistani returned to Iraq from the United Kingdom, where he had been receiving medical care, and led a march to the shrine from nearby Kufa. al-Sadr and his militia vanished, but soon resumed their fighting, now in the Sadr City district of northeast Baghdad.[21]

The economic situation was equally poor. The distribution of funds allocated by Congress had been very slow, and security costs consumed more and more of these projects. As of July 2004—the tenth month of the fiscal year—only $31 million of the $1.748 billion allocated to democracy, human rights, and justice had actually been spent. Less than 2 percent.[22] In terms of overall aid, only $458 million of the $18.4 billion allocated to the CPA had been spent; or 2.5 percent. This is better than it sounds, since the UN and World Bank estimated, conservatively, that $56 billion would be needed for reconstruction in Iraq—the American contribution was only a third of this.[23] Because of looting after the invasion, much of the development money had gone to rebuilding rather than new projects, trying to simply restore the country to its condition under

Saddam. The insurgents could destroy electric lines and oil pipelines more easily than they could be defended, since the utilities were in many areas alongside major highways for easy access. Iraqis had to deal with long gas lines while sitting atop some of the largest oil reserves in the world, and electric power was intermittent and low throughout much of the country. Saddam had placed a high priority on ensuring Baghdad had reliable electric power, so the deprivations there were felt more deeply than in parts of the country that had had little utility service before the invasion. MNF-I also faced high expectations from the Iraqi people, who retained a belief that the United States ought to be capable of anything.

The problems were spelled out in a State Department survey of Iraqi urban areas released in mid-September.[24] About a quarter of the residents of Baghdad, Basra, Najaf, and Karbala thought the infrastructure problems were the most important problems facing the country, with another quarter focusing on unemployment and other economic issues. Residents of all cities polled, except those of Najaf, disapproved of the IIG's handling of the fighting in Sadr City and Anbar province (Fallujah and Ramadi). Most Iraqis had not heard very much about the national assembly selected at the national conference in August; about a third said "None" was their most trusted leader.

All lines of operation were in trouble in September 2004. The strategic review asserted that improvements in legitimacy were not going to happen until after elections had occurred. It was very unlikely that any security operations or economic outlay could have much effect on Iraqi support for the government in the time left before the elections. Delaying the elections would probably not help, since going back on our promise of elections would be likely to increase Iraqi cynicism toward MNF-I and increase their support for the insurgency—not to mention the possible devastating reaction among the Shia Arabs, who were mostly following al-Sistani's advice to be calm and let the democratic process win them power. There was no reason to believe that the insurgency would suddenly collapse in the face of increased MNF-I action, despite an unexpected success in Samarra, given the insurgents' interest in disrupting political progress. That same insurgency was the major obstacle to economic development, since increasing proportions of the funds spent would go to private security contractors. In any case, there was little time left for projects to have much impact.

The one exception to the focus on politics was the city of Baghdad. The capital held a quarter of all Iraqis, and violence and shortages there held a symbolic value even beyond the immediate effects. It seemed possible that al-Sadr could be defeated or at least be persuaded to give up the violent struggle and join the political process. If this could happen quickly, it might be possible to engage in intensive economic development there. Progress there would be the most bang for the buck, going beyond even the residents of Sadr City. Since the district was home to people from throughout southern Iraq, they would be likely to tell their families about the improvements and give them hope for their own future.

One problem that had become apparent was that Iraqis took no pleasure from hearing about economic development that did not touch their lives directly. Their innate skepticism was reinforced by having lived for decades under Saddam's propaganda. They simply were not going to believe what the government told them. But they might believe family members in Baghdad.

On 9 October, MNF-I and al-Sadr's Mahdi Army reached a peace agreement. For several weeks, the forces had been fighting each other in Sadr City. Despite the misgivings of many in the coalition, the deal included a limited weapons buy-back. In return for the money, al-Sadr would stop opposing neighborhood patrols by ISF (Iraqi security forces) and MNF-I. The buyback resulted in a large number of weapons being purchased, although no one believed it had been com-prehensive. Nevertheless, the agreement achieved its primary goal: peace in Sadr City. Once the streets were cleared of explosives, economic development projects began to have a real effect in the area, and the neighborhood became as safe an area for the coalition as any in Baghdad. This economic progress was probably not nearly as important for the overall campaign as al-Sadr's transformation from political opponent to participant. The primary effect of the agreement was to give al-Sadr a way to join the political process without losing too much face. His candidates did well in both of the 2005 elections.

Al-Sadr's was not the only militia of concern to MNF-I. In early June, the CPA had signed a series of memos that were supposed to begin a process of transition and reconciliation for militia groups that had fought against Saddam Hussein.[25] There were nine such militias, but the only large ones were two factions of Kurd *peshmerga* and the Badr Corps, which had been trained and equipped in Iran and was associated with the Shia Arab SCIRI party.[26] These militias were supposed to give the CPA and Iraqi government a list of their membership and register their membership. In return, militia members were going to be given the opportunity to join an Iraqi security force, to retire as if they had been a member of the Iraqi armed forces, or to enter a vocational and educational program. This program was supposed to be nearly complete by the end of 2004, even though the CPA's own strategy suggested a minimum of five years would be necessary.[27]

The militias project collapsed very quickly. The Iraqi government lacked the unity or interest to push the process, since many of the militias were supportive of different government factions. The Iraqi government did not trust members of the armed groups; the Minister of Defense said he did not want to employ any "Islamists," which eliminated many militia members from that option. The Iraqi government was also skeptical of claims of retirement eligibility. Likewise, the militia leaders did not trust the government and refused to turn over either their weapons or their membership lists, provisions that had not been part of the agreement they had signed. They also did not find vocational and educational programs very attractive, since even where such programs existed the Iraqi economy offered little hope for the future. The Kurd *peshmerga,* on the other hand, simply was transformed into a security force for the Kurdistan Regional Government.[28]

The coalition had two choices. It could try to force the issue and to disband the militias. This approach had its advocates among Iraqis and Americans, but it seemed unwise to provoke these mostly quiet groups into a new front in the war, and risk breakdown within the IIG. Its other choice was to wait and reexamine the strategy. A decade of UN experience indicated that armed militias could not be peacefully disarmed until a political settlement was reached.[29] This point had also been made in the CPA's original strategy.[30] This second option was followed—like so much else, the fate of militias would have to wait until after the elections.[31]

If the elections were seen as legitimate, and if they yielded a competent government, a virtuous cycle of improving conditions could result. The details of that government could have different effects, as will be discussed in a later section. Nevertheless, the elections in themselves would win over some skeptics, since the future ITG would for the first time in Iraqi history truly be one of the people's own choosing. This, and improving capabilities among ISF, could start to reduce the insurgency. The new government might also win increased financial support from other countries, supplementing American outlays which were beginning to become more efficient. The combination of progress in economics and security would add effectiveness as a reason to find the ITG legitimate, leading to support for the constitution that would be written by August 2005 and a reduced need for ethnic militias. The constitution, and the elections that were to follow in December 2005, would reinforce this process, yielding a democratic Iraq at peace with itself and its neighbors. This result was not determined—there were many possible choices along the way that could lead to very undesirable results—but there was no other path that held out the possibility of success.

Focusing on the Elections

With the strategic review complete, attention shifted to analyzing the upcoming elections. No one had the slightest idea what would happen after the elections; most Americans had very little understanding of proportional representation or parliamentary government. Thus the first step was to understand the elections law and the political landscape in Iraq. The National Assembly elections were designed to balance speed, simplicity, and equitable representation of Iraqi groups. Rather than having individual candidates run for specific seats, as in American and British elections, voters would select a political "list," a party ("entity" in the election law) or coalition of parties running together. The ballot would not name the candidates, only the list. The candidates on the lists would be selected by their party or in negotiations among several parties, or a politician could run as an individual.

Each list would be granted seats in the 275-member Assembly in proportion to its share of the national vote.[32] In most countries, either there is an artificial threshold that must be crossed for a list to win seats (for example 5 percent in Germany) or the parliament is small enough that the "natural" threshold excludes very small parties. Iraqi election law did not provide for an artificial threshold for representation in the TNA. Thus election to the TNA required receipt of only 1/275 (0.36 percent) of the national vote, or about 29,000 votes.[33] This lack of a threshold, unusual for proportional systems, especially for such a large assembly, ensured the most accurate representation of Iraqi voting preferences. It also risked promoting the election of candidates with minimal appeal—extremists as well as those with only isolated support. Electoral law required that a nonindividual electoral list include at least twelve names, at least four of whom would be women;[34] in principle this would filter out extremists (especially those most opposed to women's participation in politics), but assembling twelve like-minded individuals is not a difficult task. With political registration easy—it only required 500 signatures[35]—213 political entities registered: 49 single-person entities and 164 multi-person parties.[36] The task of anticipating who would "win" the election—and the added task of forecasting who would be the next prime minister of Iraq—was complex.

With the rules of the electoral game in hand, the next step was to identify the players. Here the State Department was particularly helpful. Their political section was not in the business of forecasting the future (which is why MNF-I was left with this rather nonmilitary task), but it had excellent information on identifying the major actors. These were grouped along two dimensions. The first dimension was which subcultural group the party was identified with: Kurds, Shia Arabs, Sunni Arabs, Turkomen, or Christian; this was an easy determination. The second dimension was labeled informally as "moderate" or "liberal/secular" and "other." This was a tougher call, because there are gradations of support for democratic principles among the parties, and few Iraqis would want to be called "secular" in the Western sense. Furthermore, the parties labeled as "other" did not necessarily have much in common politically. Explicitly religious parties were assigned to this group on the grounds that they were more likely to push for principles of Islamic law that would seem counter to democratic notions of equal rights, though Shia Arab and Sunni Arab religious parties supported very different notions of Islamic law. The "other" group also included parties associated with aspects of the insurgency, and Chalabi's INC, who after having his party offices raided in May 2004 had moved close to Moqtada al-Sadr and Iran.

The dimensional breakdown would help identify potential coalitions of parties. In a parliamentary system, parties often group themselves together into an alliance to run as a single list on the ballot. This allows them to pool their resources and supporters, and carry a greater weight in parliament after the election. Such electoral alliances do not always hold together after the election, but sometimes they do. The second type of coalition occurs after the election. Unless one election list dominated the election, several lists would need to join forces to form a ruling coalition in order to elect the Presidency Council, select a Prime Minister, and fill the cabinet ministries.

The moderate parties included all the major non-Arab parties. The two major Kurd parties were the KDP (Kurdistan Democratic Party) and the PUK (Patriotic Union of Kurdistan). These two parties mostly controlled Kurdistan; the largest of several minor Kurd parties was the KIU (Kurdistan Islamic Union). The largest party among the Christian minorities was the ADM (Assyrian Democratic Movement); the largest among the Turkomen minority was the ITF (Iraqi Turkomen Front). Moderate, clearly pro-democratic Iraqi Arab parties included the Independent Democratic Gathering and the Iraqis Grouping, both mostly including Sunni Arabs, and the INA and ICP (Iraqi Communist Party), both mostly including Shia Arabs.

Less moderate parties were found among both Shia and Sunni Arabs. In addition to the INC, the religious Shia Arabs had three factions of the Da'wa party, the OMS (Office of Muqtada al-Sadr), and the largest single Arab party, the SCIRI. The most important Sunni Arab party was the IIP (Iraqi Islamic Party). The Sunni Arab MUC (Muslim Ulema Council) had also set up a party called the United National Movement, and rumors persisted of a reconstituted Ba'ath movement, known simply as The Party. Many of these "other" parties would go on to embrace the democratic process, but they had clear differences with the "moderate" Arab parties.

The first analysis of the election outcome, in October 2004, required some estimate of the relative population in each subcultural group. Unfortunately, in the absence of a census, there was no valid estimate, only a range. The best recent data available was a late September national poll conducted by the IRI (International Republican Institute), in which 19 percent of respondents were Kurds, 2 percent Turkomen, 20 percent Sunni Arab, and 59 percent Shia Arab. This was in the general range of estimates provided by other groups, including the Central Intelligence Agency, although the absence of any Christians from the poll was surprising.[37] It seemed likely that the Sunni Arabs would participate in the election in a lower proportion than other groups, since their areas were the most violent and the MUC was considering calling a boycott—in that same IRI poll, only 73 percent of Sunni Arabs said they planned to vote, compared to 89 percent of other groups. Based on this, it appeared that 15 percent of the votes would be cast by Sunni Arabs, 20 percent by Kurds, 60 percent by Shia Arabs, and 5 percent by other minorities. The proportion of the vote that would come from each of the subcultures was one of the major unknowns in the analysis.

The other major variable was the distribution of votes among the different kinds of party in each subculture. Based on the electoral system, and expectations that normal campaigning would occur, one could (erroneously) anticipate that 20 percent of the vote among each group would go to minor, local, or tribal parties. As it turned out, several factors led to the largest electoral lists receiving the lion's share of the vote: coalitions formed among the Kurd parties and the more religious al-Sistani–endorsed Shia Arab parties, and violence effectively precluded campaigning. We expected that the two Kurd parties would get the rest of the Kurd vote and would ally with each other either before or after the election—the single important goal held by Kurds, maintaining their autonomy, was shared by both parties (and all other Kurds for that matter). In total, fifty-five seats would be held by Kurds. We anticipated that some Turkomen and Christians would vote their subculture, but that most (80 percent) would support one of the moderate Arab parties, recognizing that they were too small to be influential on their own. Thus three seats would go to the ITF and ADM.

Among the Shia Arabs, polling data suggested that about half of their vote would go to the two major religious parties, SCIRI and the Da'wa factions, both of which had participated in the GC setup by the CPA. For simplicity, we grouped these together, expecting them to win eighty-three seats. About 10 percent would go to more radical groups, such as Muqtada al-Sadr and his new ally, Chalabi, leaving those groups with seventeen seats. The remaining Shia Arab votes, about 20 percent, would go to the centrist moderate parties. One major unknown variable in this was whether or not al-Sistani would endorse a party or advance his own list of candidates. If he did, this would concentrate the Shia Arab vote around his preferred candidates and away from the others.

Finally, the Sunni Arabs lacked a party that seemed large enough to command much loyalty by itself. We estimated that a bit under a third of their total vote would go to moderate parties, and the rest to the IIP, neo-Ba'athists, and minor parties. The Sunni Arab parties would end up with twenty-nine seats in the parliament. Taking votes from all groups together, this estimate suggested that the moderate Arab parties would end up with fifty-six seats in the parliament after the elections.

After the elections, the parliament would need to assemble and elect a three-member Presidency Council. The Presidency Council would formally nominate a Prime Minister and Cabinet to the Assembly, which would then need to confirm its choice by a simple majority vote. Since the Presidency Council required two-thirds support in the National Assembly, our task was to identify different ways the parties could align themselves after the election and then identify the consequences of each outcome for Iraqi politics and MNF-I's efforts. Three basic coalitions seemed most likely, based on what we knew then: a National Coalition including all three major subcultures, similar to the IIG already in place; a partnership of Kurds and all varieties of religious Shia Arabs; and a government fully dominated by the Shia Arabs.

The National Coalition seemed at the time to be the most likely result. It would include the parties already part of the IIG—Allawi's INA, the communists, the SCIRI and Da'wa among the Shia Arabs, and perhaps even Chalabi's INC; the IIP, the IDG, and some tribal leaders like incumbent President Ghazi al-Yawr among the Sunni Arabs; the PUK and KDP for the Kurds, and a few representatives of other minorities. This government would be the most pro-Western and non-Islamist that could be chosen, and it would have a lot of continuity with its predecessor. This was important because a postelection shake-up of major government ministries could delay development of ISF and Iraq's ability to use economic assistance. Since this government would exclude his supporters, al-Sadr's Mahdi Army might return to violence. This government would not include the more radical Sunni Arabs, but the inclusion of some respected Sunni Arab leaders could be expected to gradually erode Sunni Arabs' support for the insurgency. The government would prefer a centralized Iraq, while maintaining Kurd autonomy, and have great difficulty resolving the status of Kirkuk, which the Kurds claimed as their historic capital. It would tend to oppose the continued presence of party militias. It would promote a constitution generally in line with liberal values and would generally support having coalition forces remain in Iraq.

The Kurd–Religious Shia Arab partnership would become more likely if the religious Shia Arab parties—everything from Da'wa to al-Sadr—gained in their share of the vote with respect to the more moderate parties. Two conditions would make this more likely—al-Sistani's endorsement of religious parties over moderate ones, and a lower turnout among the Sunni Arabs. This government would be able to exclude Sunni Arabs and moderate parties like Allawi's INA and the Communists. It would thus lead to general change in the government ministries, delaying their ability to act effectively. This government would include al-Sadr, so MNF-I could anticipate calm throughout the Shia Arab areas but an increased level of support among Sunni Arabs for the insurgency. This government would support a federal structure for Iraq, including allowing different regions to interpret Islamic law as they preferred, regional control of oil revenue; it would be open to a transfer of Kirkuk to Kurd control. It would be likely to accommodate militias by associating them with the government. While this government would be unlikely to demand withdrawal of coalition forces, it would be likely to press for a timetable that would remove the force sometime in 2006.

The least likely outcome was a government fully dominated by the Shia Arabs. This was only possible if both the Sunni Arab and the Kurd votes were depressed—some Kurds expressed fears that winter conditions could deprive them of their historic opportunity. Even then, the vast differences among Shia

Arabs from Allawi to al-Sadr made this coalition unlikely. If it formed, however, the consequences would be disastrous. The Kurds would be likely to secede from Iraq, relying on their *peshmerga* and perhaps MNF-I to protect them. The secession would not be peaceful, since they would try to take Kirkuk and parts of Ninewa province from Mosul east with them. Violence would skyrocket among the Sunni Arabs in response to their exclusion and the Kurd secession. Beset by policy differences and violence, this government would be unlikely to survive. Conditions for MNF-I would become very difficult with Baghdad on the front lines of a civil war.

Setting the final scenario aside, the other possibilities both had their advantages. The amount of insurgency in Iraq came to be seen as fixed; the difference would be whether it would be concentrated in one area, the so-called Sunni Triangle west of lines from Mosul to Baqubah and from Baqubah through Baghdad, or spread throughout the country. The national coalition would be a better fit with the United States, with its members supportive of democratic values and maintaining continuity with the past. But that advantage had its down side: the current government had very little legitimacy among Iraqis, so its continuance in office, especially with Allawi continuing as Prime Minister, would be used to argue that the election had been a sham. In a Kurd–religious Shia Arab partnership, on the other hand, the prime minister would probably be a religious Shia Arab, most likely Ibrahim al-Ja'afari, the Shia Arab who was most acceptable to other subcultures. Al-Ja'afari, a medical doctor, also had substantial religious credentials; his opposition to Saddam Hussein was deeply rooted, and his opposition to early American plans for delaying democratic elections gave him credibility. al-Ja'afari would probably not have been the ideal candidate from an American perspective—but for that reason, his selection would be seen as evidence that the election had been legitimate.

At first, Iraqi political leaders tried to recreate the national list used at the August National Conference. In October and early November 2004, proposals were floated that would have created a single list including the seven major parties of the IIG—the KDP, PUK, SCIRI, Da'wa, INA, INC, and IIP. After rounds of informal discussion, the parties met at Lake Dohuk in Iraqi Kurdistan in November but could not reach an agreement. This effort was doomed from the start, since it would have been very difficult for such a diverse group of parties to agree on the proportion allocated to each party and their rankings, especially with the added requirement that every third seat be allocated to a woman.

This failure was good for democracy, because the resulting national list would have been widely perceived as an attempt to fix the election results. The resulting government would have had great difficulty winning legitimacy among those dissatisfied with the status quo. The formation of an "incumbents" list would also have increased the vote for more illiberal parties excluded from the list, since such parties would be the only opposition. This hypothetical list probably would not have reduced the calls for a boycott from the Sunni Arab MUC, since the clerics would have labeled it as a continuation of the regime installed by the Americans; Sunni Arab turnout may have been higher if the IIP had been on this list but the legitimacy of the ITG would have been profoundly weakened.

In the absence of a national list, the Kurds and Shia Arabs turned to the formation of identity lists.[38] The PUK and KDP, while continuing to compete in elections for the Kurdistan Regional Assembly, agreed to form a combined list, the KA (Kurdistan Alliance). This list included representatives of other Kurdistan parties, most notably the KIU, the ANP, and the Chaldean Democratic Union Party. This turn of events closely followed expectations.

More surprisingly, al-Sistani guided the Shia Arabs to form a single list. The appeal of joining the UIA (United Iraqi Alliance) list blessed by al-Sistani—and the fear of being excluded from such a list—led the major religiously oriented Shia Arab parties to agree to accept a lesser number of seats on a list primarily composed of independent candidates. This list included the SCIRI, Da'wa, INC, representatives of Moqtada al-Sadr, and Islamic Fayli Grouping of Shia Kurds, along with many smaller parties. Development of such a truly broad-based "Sistani party" made a national coalition more unlikely, since it would depress the share of votes for more moderate parties, and it would make it impossible to include parties like Da'wa without al-Sadr as well.

Several cross-communal lists competed for the more liberal elements of the Arab population. Interim Prime Minister Allawi, a Shia Arab, formed the Iraqi list, which included Sunni Arab Planning Minister Mahdi al-Hafidh and Electricity Minister Ayham al-Samera'i. Interim President al-Yawr, a Sunni Arab, formed the Iraqis List, which included IIG members such as Shia Arab Defense Minister Hazim al-Sha'lan and Industry Minister Hachim al-Hassani. Hassani had been a member of the IIP but left the party when it asked him to resign as a protest against the November assault on Fallujah.[39] Other "moderate" parties included the People's Union/ICP, the Constitutional Monarchy Movement of al-Sharif Ali Bin al-Hussein, and the Assembly of Independent Democrats led by Adnan Pachachi.

The Sunni Arabs, and their one major party, the IIP, will be saved for the next section, because at this point MNF-I's political efforts focused on two points. One was the importance that the election be seen as fair—which meant keeping American hands away from it. Trying to influence the election would be foolish. It would be unlikely to be kept secret, but more importantly, there would not be much to gain. The United States could work with either the National Coalition or the Kurd–religious Shia Arab partnership, especially since al-Sistani was emphasizing the importance of not shutting Sunni Arabs completely out of government even if they did poorly in the election. Fairness meant ensuring a level playing field for all candidates. In practice, this meant trying to engage with the Sunni Arabs, so they would vote. This strategy failed. Even though it was self-defeating, the Sunni Arabs boycotted, with an election turnout of under 10 percent—much lower than imagined possible.

The Sunni Arab Boycott

A strategy for engaging the Sunni Arabs was developed through November 2004, futilely trying to keep pace with events on the ground. The strategy began from the premise that MNF-I's number one priority should be a legitimate election. Only such an election could begin to separate the insurgents from their center of gravity, leading to progress across other lines of operation and successful completion of the mission. If the Sunni Arabs did not vote, they might be excluded from the government and might support the insurgency more strongly, and the MNF-I mission would be more likely to fail. The strategy was simple. First, convince the Sunni Arabs that it would be safe to vote and run for office by reducing MNF-I's level of activity, especially in population centers and around important cultural sites, and by encouraging the MUC to back off its boycott threat by addressing some of their demands. Second, remind the Sunni Arabs that their grievances, whatever they are, will be addressed more thoroughly if they are in the government rather than outside it—there would be no postponement of the election and no makeup seats given to them. Third, make it clear that MNF-I and the United States encouraged the inclusion of all subcultures in the transitional government and in the constitutional committee and that the constitution should protect the rights of minorities like the Sunni Arabs.

While this strategy was never fully implemented, successful engagement with the Sunni Arabs may have been impossible under any circumstances. Unlike the other subcultures, they did not have a few leaders that could clearly speak for the rest. This may have been partly caused by their privileged position—as a group—under Saddam Hussein. The Shia Arabs and Kurds developed their leaders through rebellion. Some Sunni Arabs also resisted the Ba'ath regime—most notably the IIP—or at least spoke out against it from exile like Adnan Pachachi. Most, however, accepted the benefits that came with being part of the ruling subculture; Sunni Arabs in other countries were not particularly free either, and to be an Iraqi until the 1990s was to be better off than most. The structure of Sunni Islam may have also contributed to the pluralism among that subculture. Shia Islam is relatively hierarchal in its religious leadership, culminating in the Najaf *marja'iyyah* and al-Sistani. Most Shia, lay and clerics, would listen to these religious figures and be persuaded by them. Sunni Islam is more democratic in a sense—anyone can preach, using the Koran as a guide, so they have less religious leadership. MNF-I accumulated a list of hundreds of possibly influential Sunni Arabs but could not determine which ones had real clout.

Whatever the cause, the Sunni Arabs were disorganized, and they knew it themselves. In fact, on 26 November, several political parties met at Pachachi's home, calling for a six-month election delay to improve security and revisions to the election plan. Attendees included most Sunni Arab parties, including the IIP which had been wavering in its support for the election over the previous few days.[40] More surprisingly, some Kurds also called for a delay, saying that winter storms could make it impossible to vote in Kurdistan and that the political situation in Kirkuk need to be resolved.[41] Pachachi's motive in hosting the meeting may have reflected his party's lack of support; unlike the Kurd, Shia Arab, and other centrist parties, he would continue to advocate postponement up to a few weeks before the election.[42] Shia Arab political parties protested this idea,[43] and Abdul Hussein al-Hindawi, chair of the IECI (Independent Electoral Commission of Iraq), declined to even consider it. As Deputy Prime Minister Barhim Saleh and al-Yawr both noted, there was no legal provision for delaying the election past 31 January.[44] Allawi's party said it was there merely to observe, and the IIP temporarily agreed to continue to support the elections. Other proposals were made over the ensuing weeks, including having an election staggered by province over a period of weeks or holding voting open for several days. All were rejected or, more accurately, not even considered by the IECI. Such a move would have opened the door to discarding other sections of the TAL.

Beyond these political parties, the main Sunni Arab organization was the MUC, a loose coalition of clerics led by Harith al-Dari of the Umm al-Qasr (Mother of all Battles) mosque in western Baghdad. The MUC advocated resistance to the American occupation but also proposed negotiations with the Iraqi government. Its ties to the insurgency, and the IIP, were always unclear. They seemed to vary from mosque to mosque and spokesman to spokesman. For much of fall 2004, the IIP was a counterweight to the MUC's repeated calls for a boycott—the MUC had insisted since February that elections held under occupation were illegitimate,[45] while the IIP argued that Sunni Arab exclusion would be self-defeating. The MUC's goals included expedited disposition of mostly Sunni Arab detainees,[46] withdrawal of American forces from central cities, transfer of the election to the UN from the IECI, and a timetable for withdrawal.[47] Some of these demands were out of the question (it was far too late to change the election rules), but others were interesting, especially the question of a withdrawal timetable.

The notion of announcing a withdrawal timetable in fall 2004 was intriguing because no other single measure held out the promise of winning Iraqis, especially Sunni Arabs, away from support for the insurgency. While the most violent insurgents were fighting in part for a return of a regime similar to Saddam Hussein, and others for the incompatible goal of a medieval Islamic empire, many Iraqis seemed motivated simply by the desire to get the Americans out. They worried that the United States was there to stay. President George W. Bush would signal his resolve to Americans by promising "we will stay there until the job is done."[48] This made Iraqis nervous that the job might never be done to American satisfaction. They did not pay attention to his next words: "And then we'll leave."

A withdrawal timetable was attractive for other reasons. One was the possibility that the United States might be asked to leave by the next government. Indeed, after the election, al-Hakim of the SCIRI laughed at the notion of permanent American bases in Iraq, saying "No one in Iraq desires the establishment of permanent foreign bases on our land. The UNSC resolutions are clear: it will be up to the elected Iraqi government, when the time comes, to give those forces a specific departure date. As soon as possible."[49] al-Dari of the MUC asked for a two-year withdrawal schedule, or March 2007.[50] In mid-June 2005, nearly one-third of the TNA members called for coalition withdrawal.[51] If we were going to be asked to leave, it would be better to preempt this, perhaps announcing the plan after a major victory, just as Abraham Lincoln waited until after Antietam to announce the Emancipation Proclamation. The announcement might also build support for the IIG under Allawi, increasing the chances that a future government of Iraq would be broad-based.

Nevertheless, there were powerful arguments against announcing a withdrawal timetable.[52] It could be interpreted by Iraqis as a sign that the United States was not committed to their country, leading them to abandon efforts at democracy. It could encourage Iraqis to believe that the insurgency was winning, that the Americans were on the run just like in Beirut and Mogadishu, and encourage support for the insurgency. It could be seen as negotiating with terrorists, which the United States had vowed not to do. During this entire time, it was difficult to determine the extent to which the MUC was a front for the insurgents. And announcing a withdrawal timetable would cede initiative. There was also little precedent for thinking the strategy would work. The British announcement in 1964 that it would withdraw from Aden in 1968 seemed to spur the insurgency there, and the announcement of Indian independence led to the war of partition. Only in Malaya did withdrawal correspond to a reduction in the insurgency, and this was a slow, negotiated process. Accepting the MUC's terms for withdrawal would have been a risky move—the kind of risk that wins or loses wars.

Besides the inability to come to grips with the Sunni Arab leadership and hesitance at taking daring moves like announcing a long-term withdrawal timetable, perhaps the greatest obstacle to recognizing the primacy of the political process in Iraq was that that is not what militaries do.[53] Militaries fight, they do not sit and wait, and they certainly do not just accept blows. Being under attack daily, MNF-I wanted to seek out and destroy the insurgents before they could hit the coalition. This was the job, and the insurgents' atrocities made it urgent. These included a series of car bombs against a water plant in Baghdad—with the second and third timed to kill the children and others gathered to see the aftermath of the first. These included capturing ISF and executing them while bound, stealing their uniforms so they could infiltrate checkpoints. These included the captivity and eventual execution of Margaret Hassan, the British-born head of Care International's offices in Iraq. Closer to home, these included the infiltration of suicide bombers into the Green Zone itself, into the Green Zone Cafe and the marketplace. Ceding the initiative to such people could not be done entirely, even if every raid risked creating more insurgents than were captured or killed.

This imperative to take action held for larger missions as well. As early as August, MNF-I was pondering whether or not to launch an offensive to control one of the major population centers of northern Iraq—Baghdad, Baqubah, Tikrit, Mosul, Samarra, Ramadi, or Fallujah. There were pros and cons to each option, but most strategists argued two things. One was that any offensive should be launched soon, so as to be over before Ramadan began in mid-October. One of the inequities of fighting in Iraq was that it was bad form for MNF-I to attack during the holy month, but some Sunni Arab clerics argued that it was extra-virtuous to kill Americans during that month. Ramadan would not end until mid-November, so an attack after Ramadan would run into the Iraqi political campaign season, leaving little time for Sunni Arabs to accept the action and for reconstruction to undo the damage.

The other major argument held by many strategists was that of all the options, Fallujah was the worst target. Fallujah was a small city—gaining control of other cities would create more of a safe zone for voting. Fallujah also had a reputation as an outlaw area—even Saddam Hussein, as we understood it, did not fully control the place. But Fallujah also had been the site of the aborted offensive in April. After four contract security workers were captured, killed, burned, and hung from the bridge over the Euphrates, the Marines moved in. After a few days of fighting, they had pulled out, turning the city over to local groups that promised to keep it safe. This did not last long, and by fall, Fallujah had become a safe haven for the insurgents, close by the capital on the highway from Syria and Jordan. Fallujah was remembered as a loss for MNF-I, and even if territory did not matter much in a counterinsurgency, pride was at stake. Fallujah would be recaptured, and this was on the front pages of the American papers on a daily basis. The only mystery was when.

The assault on Fallujah began on the night of 7 November, near the end of Ramadan and immediately after Bush's reelection. Tactically, it was a success. After six days, American and Iraqi forces controlled the city. Strategically, it was a disaster. With the assault hardly a surprise, insurgent leaders had left the town in the hands of fighters committed to self-sacrifice. Sunni Arab Iraq erupted in the worst violence to date. Iraqi defenses in Mosul vanished, with police stations ransacked by insurgents who took their equipment and uniforms. All the other cities of northern Arab Iraq saw an increase in violence, perhaps none more than Baghdad. Refugees from Fallujah flooded into Baghdad, bringing the battle home to Sunni Arabs there. Pro-democracy groups like the IIP were hard pressed to justify remaining part of the political process. Antidemocracy groups stepped up their intimidation, a factor we measured indirectly from opinion polling. For example, in the relatively calm Shia Arab cities of Kut and Basra, similar numbers said "it is important for Iraqis to vote" and that they "were likely to vote" (99 and 93 percent, respectively). While 92 percent in Baqubah agreed it was important to vote, only 81 percent said they were likely to; the numbers in Sunni Arab Tikrit were 78 and 67 percent.[54] An 11 percent intimidation factor. A similar gap was found in military-sponsored polls of Baghdad: between 16 September and 8 November, the percentage of Shia Arabs planning to vote held steady at 91 percent, while the numbers for Sunni Arabs dropped from 86 to 71 percent.

Hard after Fallujah, American and Iraqi forces raided the Abu Hanifa mosque in Adhamiyah, a neighborhood in north Baghdad, during Friday prayers on 19 November. Three Iraqis were killed, and nothing of great importance was found in the raid—a few guns, nothing more. Abu Hanifa was the second-most important Sunni mosque in Baghdad, though it had a greater historic claim to prominence than the newer Umm al-Qasr. Its neighborhood again erupted in violence and demanded an investigation. The Iraqi government claimed that no Iraqis were involved, just Americans in Iraqi uniforms. Between Fallujah and Abu Hanifa, any real chance at bringing Sunni Arabs into the electoral process was lost. The MUC called for a boycott, and the IIP announced on 27 December that it was withdrawing from the national election. Its position had become untenable, pressed by more-radical Sunni Arabs and with absolutely nothing to show for their strategy of participation and democracy.[55] The Sunni Arab boycott was very successful. In the election, which came off on schedule, only two seats were won by explicitly Sunni Arab parties: one for Mishan al-Jabouri's Reconciliation and Liberation Front, based in Salah ad-Din, and one for Justice Minster Malik Duhan al-Hassan's National Democratic Alliance, mostly from Baghdad.

With the Sunni Arabs boycotting and Sistani having supported a ticket, conditions were right for the Kurd–religious Shia Arab partnership. The KA won 75 seats, or 27 percent, by themselves; the al-Sistani list—the UIA—won 140 seats, or 51 percent. They could have ruled alone, but after the election, the Shia Arabs and Kurds went out of their way to find Sunni Arabs who could hold important offices, including one of the deputy Presidents, a deputy Prime Minister, Speaker of the Assembly, and Minister of Defense. Still, the lack of elected Sunni Arabs contributed to the writing of a constitution that mostly disregarded their preferences, and set up a political situation in which Sunni Arabs continue to feel disadvantaged. If the Iraqi democratic process breaks down because of Sunni Arab perception of its illegitimacy, the failure to bring Sunni Arabs and the IIP into the political process will likely be seen as a preventable tragedy greater than disbanding the Iraqi army, the blanket de-Ba'athification order, and the looting of Iraqi infrastructure.[56] If it does not break down, then we must credit the persistence of Shia Arabs in including the Sunni Arabs, and the real commitment of most Sunni Arabs to a democratic process.

Conclusions and Lessons Learned

Even though the Sunni Arabs did not participate, the Iraqi elections must still be seen as a tremendous accomplishment. While it was the IECI that kept the elections on schedule, the United States deserves credit for never encouraging a postponement, as did so many editorial pages. Only elections could begin the route to a decent peace in Iraq. There is no reason to think that delay would have improved Sunni Arab participation very much—Fallujah did not recover quickly, and further operations continued. Perhaps the only thing that might have been improved about the election scheme was to have allocated seats by province, as they would be in the 15 December 2005 elections. While there were many benefits to having a single national district, it magnified the effects of the low Sunni Arabs turnout. If delegates had been elected by province, the Sunni Arabs would still have won their share of seats. If this had been anticipated when the electoral law was being devised, a different system could have been adopted; equally, accepting the electoral law as a given, more effort could have been made to create conditions under which more Sunni Arabs would have voted.[57]

Strategic patience, waiting for events to play out, is difficult for a military organization under attack. Failure to act is more likely to be criticized than doing the wrong thing. But Fallujah and Abu Hanifa should not be seen simply as military operations that led to bad results. They also signify a deeper problem, which is the lack of empathy for the insurgents. Empathy is not surrender or acceptance, but simply a recognition of what their motives and values were. Ironically, the night before Abu Hanifa, the strategy office screened *The Fog of War*, in which former Secretary of Defense Robert McNamara notes the same lack of empathy as an American failing in the Vietnam War. On the other hand, things could have been worse. On Monday, 30 May 2005, American forces broke into the home of Mohsen Abdul-Hamid, leader of the IIP, and arrested him, outraging al-Ja'afari and President Jalal Talabani.[58] And it was not until 8 January 2006, with all the elections safely completed, that American forces raided the MUC headquarters at the Umm al-Qasr mosque—and at least this raid was on a Sunday, rather than a Friday.[59]

As a group, MNF-I never fully appreciated the impact its actions had on the Sunni Arabs. Secretary of Defense Donald Rumsfeld had wondered in October 2003 "Are we capturing, killing or deterring and dissuading more terrorists every day than the madrassas and the radical clerics are recruiting, training and deploying against us?"[60] We did not consider whether or not our own actions helped to recruit insurgents. To MNF-I, the tens of thousands of detainees in Iraq were suspects. To their families, they had disappeared. To MNF-I, anti-American clerics were dangerous. To their faithful, they were prophetic voices. We could not properly assess the value of a raid on a home or mosque unless we took the backlash into account. As long as we are conducting this kind of war, we need to begin to place more emphasis on understanding what motivates the enemy. Maybe the MUC's conditions for supporting the elections were insincere. But they were reasonable and worth engaging.

This, of course, would have been a hard choice, perhaps between bad options. But operations often involve hard choices. One such was the question of disarming militias. Engaging them early risked spreading the war, while waiting risked having them turn into death squads. The debate over announcing withdrawal timetables was another hard call. Doing it would have undermined the President's declared resolve on terrorism, but it might also have had positive results. Fallujah was a third hard call. Not attacking the city would have left a dangerous haven for the insurgency intact. Attacking it before Ramadan would have escalated the war during the American presidential election campaign, perhaps turning American opinion against the war and Bush—a consideration seen as very important by some officials in Washington and in Baghdad. Attacking it after the election, as we did, resulted in losing any element of surprise and turning the Sunni Arabs against the elections.

The final lesson is to remember that war is a political exercise as well as a military one. The political line of operation cannot be neglected; it must be considered from the beginning. One might think this job would be done by the State Department, but in Iraq at least they were not willing to do that. If State would not, then the military must. Fuller consideration of the political consequences of military decisions might have changed some of those decisions early in the war and in 2004. If the coalition had engaged with the Sunni Arabs, or even simply refrained from increasing their hostility, we might have been able to persuade them to vote in larger numbers in January 2005. With greater representation in the TNA, the Sunni Arabs would have been able to draft the Iraqi constitution with a voice equal to that of other groups, and the Iraqi constitution thus would not have been so offensive to their preferences. In addition, the Sunni Arabs would have been in a stronger position to stop the Interior Ministry from being turned over to Byan Baqir Jabr of the Badr Corps militia, a position that allowed the Shia Arabs to operate paramilitary death squads under official cover. No mosque raid, no cleansing of a small city in Anbar province, was worth the damage caused by neglect of the political goal: an election with a level playing field, producing results accepted as legitimate across the Iraqi subcultures.

CHAPTER 7

STRIKE TWO: *BUREAUCRACY DOES ITS THING* REPRISED

Nathan Freier and Donald G. Rose

In 2004–05, Robert Komer's clinical account of the American failure of structure and imagination in Vietnam—*Bureaucracy Does Its Thing*—was required reading for officers destined to serve in the strategy division of the MNF-I (Multinational Force–Iraq) headquarters.[1] Unfortunately, to many American and coalition officers who found themselves operating at the theater strategic level of the conflict, very little had changed with regard to American corporate understanding and handling of large-scale irregular conflict. As Komer suggested in 1972 about the war in Vietnam:

> We perceived the difficulties we confronted better than our responses would suggest. But a series of constraints—largely inherent in the behavior patterns of [U.S. and indigenous] institutions...made it difficult for them to gear their responses sufficiently well to those perceptions. Almost regardless of what the policy called for, these institutions tended to play out their existing institutional repertoires, and to adapt themselves only slowly to even felt needs. And there was very little top-level follow through or adequate management machinery to force them into different patterns of response. Largely, as a result, much of what we did turned out to be futile, wasted, and even irrelevant.[2]

The American leviathan could have learned but never fully implemented a number of painful political, military, and economic lessons from more than a decade of irregular conflict in Southeast Asia. More than 30 years after the massive but failed pacification and state-building effort in Vietnam, the United States in 2004–05 was again heavily engaged in an even more complex state-building exercise in Iraq.[3] The challenge and complexity of managing the reconstruction of a large, important state's political, economic, and security order under conditions of continuing violence were apparent from the moment of the authors' arrival in late 2004–early 2005. Each day brought new lessons about how to and how not to go about fundamentally reengineering and resuscitating a broken state. Clear throughout was that Iraq's march toward constitutional democracy and market economy exposed real sectarian, socio-economic, and political fault lines that had previously been tempered by force and corruption under the previous regime. These quickly became obstacles to accommodation in a politically underdeveloped Iraqi society that was struggling to adapt to revolutionary changes in its system of governance at the same time Iraqis were trying to safeguard their families and livelihoods from increasing instability.

In some ways, the cure—liberation, occupation, reconstruction, and mentored sovereignty—proved as painful as the disease of Ba'athist dictatorship. Iraq had collapsed. Now both the effects of the collapse and the coalition efforts at revolutionary state reconstruction were exposing an emerging Iraqi proto-state to disruptive forces of social disconnectedness, political dissolution, inter- and intracommunal conflict, and painful economic adjustment. By late 2004, coalition authorities and the IIG (Iraqi Interim Government) were faced with a complex set of political challenges. Shia Arabs and Kurd elites were successfully positioned to become the newly elected rulers of Iraq with the January 2005 elections. Sunni Arab nationalists, who had long identified themselves as the dominant group in Iraqi society would, whether they voted or not, see their minority status institutionalized. Thus, following the guidance from both the mosques and secular agitators, they rejected the new order and participation in it en masse. Meanwhile, in spite of the opening of a new era of political freedom, popular expectations were rising out of all proportion to the coalition or IIG's ability to meet them. Any hope of controlling the social, political, and economic disruption in Iraq rested on the agents of the coalition and their Iraqi partners managing the Iraqi population's expectations and then employing the resources at their disposal in a synchronized, integrated, and nimble fashion in order to meet them. In practice, the results were disappointing.

In late 2004 and early 2005, the authors saw the impending elections for the Iraqi National Assembly as holding both the promise of a durable political transformation and the prospect of political and social catastrophe. The coalition leadership hoped that successful elections would bring Iraq closer to becoming a free and democratic state, but that hope was tempered by the Herculean task of helping Iraq conduct free, fair, safe, and inclusive elections in the face of a growing insurgency the coalition was still trying to understand. Although generally seen as successful, the elections did not end or even reduce insurgent violence in Iraq. Nevertheless, they seemed to create more favorable political conditions that might give the United States and its coalition partners a fresh start on addressing Iraq's many challenges.

For its part, MNF-I turned its attention to those pressing politico-security issues that needed to be addressed with an elected Iraqi government: maintaining the coalition, prosecuting a counterinsurgency, continuing to reach out to Sunni

Arabs, and shaping the U.S.–Iraqi military relationship. On the political front, rather than achieving rapid progress in forming the ITG (Iraqi Transitional Government), the process initially drifted. This, in the authors' view, was in part a function of the coalition's "hands off" approach. Further, it is our view that the constraints of the Iraqi constitutional process dictated that by the time the transitional government did form, fresh politico-security crises prevented MNF-I from achieving much counterinsurgency progress in 2005.

That said, electoral success could not have been exploited because of the organizational pathologies of USG (U.S. Government) operations in Iraq. The situation in Iraq required the deft interaction of four lines of operation—political, communications, security, and economics. Equally clear, however, was that this synergy could only be achieved when there was both a unity of purpose and effort in the application of all the instruments of national and international power employed in the field. In short, if the full array of coalition power, resources, and influence had been exercised under the control of a single, effective authority, the prospects for success would have been substantially greater.[4]

The authors' fundamental insight from their experience in Iraq is that the USG is insufficiently prepared for exercises in state building at the very time that they may be among the nation's most common and strategically consequential undertakings. This underpreparedness stems from structural, intellectual, and cultural gaps in both capability and capacity within the deployed agencies of the USG. The authors' experience in Iraq indicated that, as structured and socialized, the USG is best prepared only for the most traditional twentieth-century security challenges. Our bureaucratic structures and cultures are inadequate for the task of appreciating and contending with dramatically changed strategic and operational conditions like those found in Iraq. Further, in the view of the authors, our personnel are culturally under equipped for the complexity associated with long-duration, irregular, politico-security challenges. While individually capable, they are not corporately prepared or organized for success. American institutions were deployed to Iraq colored by the experiences in the Cold War, Desert Storm, and the military interventions and peacekeeping efforts of the 1980s and 1990s—all the while blocking out some of the most relevant historical experience in the war in Vietnam and America's brief foray into small wars of empire. Iraq was none of these in 2004–05, but it was clearly closer to the latter than it was to the former.

Employing a baseball analogy, we contend that inadequate preparation for post-conflict occupation and reconstruction in Iraq and the resultant inability of the U.S.-led coalition to rapidly capitalize on its conventional military victory in the political, economic, and social dimensions constituted "strike one" against the United States and its partners. This chapter recounts the events of early–mid-2005 as newly elected Iraqi leaders struggled to form an inclusive government and a constitutional process, and MNF-I struggled to accomplish tasks just out of its reach. It ends with a strategic assessment of the problems inherent in nation-building missions, given current USG organization. In brief, this chapter argues that "strike two" came with both the coalition's inability and unwilling-ness to assert its substantial influence over the speed and effectiveness, but not necessarily the actual composition, of Iraq's postelection political arrangements.

It is fair to ask "What were Headquarters, MNF-I, the U.S. Embassy, the Iraq Reconstruction Management Office (IRMO), and all the other agencies doing while insurgent and sectarian violence grew more virulent?" The short answer is quite a bit. However, they were not all working under a unitary chain of theater strategic command and control nor were they acting within a coherent strategic design that had been internalized across and within the agencies of the coalition's deployed instruments of power. In the authors' view, to borrow from Komer, they were simply "doing their own thing," often as they always had—in spite of being thrust into a dizzying security and reconstruction challenge requiring very different organizational behaviors and structures.

Elections and Aftermath

The Independent Electoral Commission of Iraq announced tentative election results on 14 February 2005. After a three-day waiting period in which potential irregularities were reported and assessed, the Commission certified the results on 17 February. As had been widely rumored and discussed over the preceding two weeks, the primarily Shia Arab UIA (United Iraq Alliance), sponsored by Grand Ayatollah Ali al-Sistani, dominated the National Assembly with 140 seats (51 percent). Also as expected, the KA (Kurdistan Alliance) was the next most represented group with 75 seats (27 percent). The only other group with more than five seats was interim Prime Minister Iyad Allawi's Iraqi List with 40 seats (15 percent). The remaining 20 seats were divided among nine other coalitions and parties.[5] The leading groups set out to form a new government but, unexpectedly, it would take weeks of protracted negotiations for them to do so.

The process of moving from occupation to sovereign Iraqi government was guided by the March 2004 Law of Administration for the State of Iraq for the Transitional Period, or the TAL (Transitional Administrative Law).[6] The TAL, a document filled with deadlines and "no later than" dates, prescribed how the new government would be formed. Article 38 stipulated that the Presidency Council had two weeks to nominate a Prime Minister who then had one month to nominate a cabinet. Once this cabinet and Prime Minister were confirmed by the National Assembly, they could begin governing. It was this moment of gov-erning for which MNF-I was most prepared. But it did not come as quickly as expected. The TAL simply did not include a deadline for the National Assembly to elect a Presidency Council. Once elected, a series of deadlines came into effect. But without a Presidency Council, it was impossible to tell when things would occur. This flexibility, or oversight, allowed the process to drag out much longer than anyone anticipated and cost the new government and the coalition much of the psychological and emotional momentum gained in the elections.

The newly elected National Assembly did not even convene for the first time until 16 March 2005—a month after the Electoral Commission certified the election results. This initial meeting only served to disappoint. Expectations were raised in the press in mid-March that the UIA and KA had agreed that Jalal Talabani of the KA and Ibrahim al-Ja'afari of the UIA would be nominated for the presidential and prime ministerial posts, respectively. But negotiations broke down and, on the day, the parliamentarians adjourned after a brief ceremony.[7] One of the causes of the delays in forming a new government can be traced to one clause in Article 36 of the TAL. It stated that the National Assembly would elect the Presidency Council "by a two-thirds majority of the members' votes." Almost every other important decision regarding the formation of a government and ensuing legislation would be made by simple majority. So the minority parties wanted to negotiate a "package deal" before electing a Presidency Council. It was in their interest to try to reach as many agreements as possible regarding cabinet posts, constitutional principles, and government priorities before triggering the TAL process with all its deadlines. They feared that, once the Presidency Council was elected and the need for a two-thirds majority was gone, the UIA with its slim majority could dominate government proceedings.

As March dragged on without apparent progress, rumors started to fly that the UIA was reconsidering its prime ministerial nominee and perhaps even falling apart.[8] But the Shia Arab coalition held and, after some abortive attempts, the National Assembly showed that movement was possible by electing a Sunni Arab speaker, Hajim al-Hassani—interim Industry Minister and a former member of the IIP (Iraqi Islamic Party), with Shia Arab and Kurd deputies on 3 April 2005. However, before making even this modest step, the National Assembly had to overcome division and confusion within the Sunni Arab community—a consistent theme in post-Saddam Iraq.

Since there were only seventeen Sunni Arab members of the National Assembly because of the successful Sunni Arab boycott of the elections, it probably should not have been that difficult to find a candidate—but there were complicating factors. One of the obvious candidates, interim President Ghazi al-Yawir, turned down the position; he was hoping to be included in the new Presidency Council and saw the speakership as too much of a demotion. More practically, if he accepted the speakership, he would have lost the personal protection contingent he and his family enjoyed in the office of the presidency. Another candidate, Mishan al-Jabouri, was acceptable to Sunni Arabs but not to the Shia Arabs because he was a former Ba'athist and an associate of Saddam's family. Finally, those Sunni Arabs who had joined the UIA were unacceptable to their own community, being seen as Shia Arab collaborators.

A key hurdle to forming a government seemed to have been surmounted on 7 April 2005 when the three-member Presidency Council was sworn in. Talabani did become the first non-Arab president of an Arab state. His two deputies, the UIA's Adel Abd al-Mahdi, who served as interim finance minister, and interim President Ghazi al-Yawr, represented the other main ethno-religious groups of Iraq. This Presidency Council immediately nominated Islamic Dawa Party spokesman and UIA member Ibrahim al-Ja'afari to be Prime Minister.[9] The TAL clock could finally be started. Al-Ja'afari then had thirty days to nominate a cabinet for the National Assembly to consider. Given the swiftness of his own nomination, many assumed that a package deal had been agreed upon and that al-Ja'afari would make a cabinet announcement shortly. But there would be three more weeks of negotiations and horse trading before al-Ja'afari announced even an incomplete cabinet.

Beyond delays attributable to difficulties accommodating and co-opting the Sunni Arab community, it seems clear that the Kurd Alliance was also contributing to the delays. The secular, mostly Sunni Kurds were simply not comfortable with the prospect of participating in a Shia Arab Islamist government with the UIA. It was not an obvious ideological match. So for several weeks, the Kurds seemed to pursue a two-track strategy. On one hand, they negotiated at a measured pace for the best possible position in a Kurd–Shia Arab coalition government and concessions on federalism and Kurd autonomy. On the other hand, they worked on the possibility of creating an alternative coalition government. Their preferred option was a coalition including Allawi's Iraqi List with other minority parties supporting it. But the electoral math was clearly not in their favor. Even with their own votes and all other minor parties', they could only gather 135, leaving them needing 49 more to allow them to elect a Presidency Council that would nominate their preferred Prime Minister.

The Kurds' only hope for an alternative coalition lay in fracturing the UIA. This was not an outlandish proposition since the Alliance was mainly one of convenience—the main thing Alliance members had in common was the desire to benefit from al-Sistani's support. So the Kurds' deliberate negotiations over policy issues and ministerial portfolios served to create the best possible position in a Kurd–UIA government and acted as a smokescreen for attempts to break up the UIA. This best explains the longevity of the otherwise hopeless candidacy of Allawi for prime minister and the reports of dissent and potential mutiny within the UIA.[10] Only with the potential support of the Kurds and their seventy-five National Assembly seats could breakaway movements hope to succeed. In the end, of course, the UIA held firm, the Kurds participated in their less-preferred option, and the Transitional Government got off to a delayed and inauspicious beginning.

The final pieces to the puzzle were added in late April and early May 2005. Al-Ja'afari presented a partial cabinet to the National Assembly on 28 April.

Several key posts, such as the defense minister and oil minister, were not included in this initial list and had to be filled a few days later. In the final cabinet, the number of ministries roughly reflected the electoral results, with "extra" seats going to the Sunni Arab community in line with the policy of reaching out and inclusion after the boycott of the elections. Shia Arab leaders took eighteen of the thirty-six cabinet positions, Kurds filled ten seats, Sunni Arabs seven, and a Christian held one.[11] A Turkoman female was eventually nominated to fill one of the deputy prime minister positions, but the National Assembly never approved the nomination.[12] Each of the three major ethno-religious groups was represented by a deputy prime minister and each held at least one of the "major" ministries. A Kurd was Foreign Minister, a Sunni Arab ran the Defense Ministry, and the Shia Arabs held on to the Interior and Oil ministries.

Every announcement about the makeup of the cabinet was met with dismay from Sunni Arab quarters. In early April, they railed against the rumor that only four cabinet positions would go to Sunni Arabs.[13] In the last few days of April 2005 and into early May, Sunni Arab leaders lamented the low number of Sunni Arab cabinet positions, accused the Shia Arabs of negotiating in bad faith, and criticized the parliamentary process.[14] This reaction both encapsulated the main reason for long delays in forming the government and presaged the difficulties that would be encountered in the constitution-writing process. Finding acceptable and willing Sunni Arab candidates to fill allotted cabinet positions was a major challenge. Several Sunni Arab leaders were simply too close to the Saddam regime to be acceptable to the newly elected leadership. Others turned down positions for a variety of ostensible reasons but personal safety could not have been far from their minds. Further, the Sunni Arab groups were disorganized, recalcitrant, and often contradicted one another. The condition of the Sunni Arab community did not bode well for the upcoming tasks of forming a committee to write the constitution and then actually producing the document.

Looking back at the government formation process, one might wonder whether a few days or weeks here and there really made any difference. At the time, it seemed tremendously important. The delays prevented MNF-I from working with an elected, legitimate Iraqi government on essential security issues. Each day these issues were not discussed and acted upon felt like a reprieve for the insurgency. Perhaps more importantly, it compressed an already ambitious constitutional schedule laid out in the TAL. The main tasks of the National Assembly were to form a transitional government and to write a "permanent" constitution by 15 August 2005. A referendum on that document was to be held by 15 October 2005, and elections based on the new constitution by 31 December 2005. Indeed, the whole UNSCR (United Nations Security Council Resolution) 1546–approved process for Iraqi politics rested on the completion of a constitution. But owing to the delays in seating the National Assembly and forming the new government, work on that crucial document would not begin in earnest until there were less than two months to complete it. Once the National Assembly had convened in mid-March, there were no procedural barriers to forming a constitutional committee, but the political leaders were focused on government formation to the exclusion of all other topics; the constitutional effort had to wait.[15]

There were a few promising signs about the constitution writing process in early 2005. A wide range of nongovernmental and international organizations stood ready to assist the National Assembly: the National Democratic Institute, the International Republican Institute, and the American Bar Association were all prepared to provide information and expertise. In late 2004, the UN (United Nations), charged by UNSCR 1546 to assist the constitutional process, had commissioned legal and constitutional experts to draft papers and summaries regarding the various issues that would confront the constitution drafting committee, such as federalism, revenue sharing, and minority protection.[16] This material was translated into Arabic and eventually provided to the Iraqis along with example provisions from other countries' constitutions which dealt with similar circumstances. In mid-April 2005, in anticipation of government formation, the UN dispatched a constitutional support team to make preparations for the effort. Besides external support, a potentially promising internal indication was the apparent willingness of several Sunni Arab leaders and organizations to participate in the drafting process.[17]

But these promising indicators were overwhelmed by more delays. Although the National Assembly created a Constitutional Drafting Committee on 10 May 2005, just one week after confirming al-Ja'afari's Transitional Government, the Committee did not formally request UN assistance until 31 May[18] and did not begin substantive work until mid-June. The National Assembly appointed fifty-five of its own members from seven different parties to write the constitution. The UIA provided twenty-eight committee members, the KA fifteen, Allawi's Iraqi List sent eight, and one member each represented the National Rafidain List (Assyrian Christians), the Iraqi Turkomen Front, the People's Union (formerly the Communist Party), and the Patriotic Cadres and Elites (a front for Moqtada al-Sadr). However, while this group of fifty-five may have represented a cross section of the National Assembly, they included only two Sunni Arabs. This alarming underrepresentation was the result of a literal reading of the TAL, perhaps influenced by frustration with the Sunni Arab community. Article 60 stated that the "National Assembly shall write a draft of the permanent constitution of Iraq." After the Sunni Arab boycott of the January 2005 elections, there were only seventeen Sunni Arab members of the 275-seat National Assembly, and some of these were not deemed to have the requisite qualifications to participate on the drafting committee.

Given the importance of the constitutional project, the resulting protest from all sides was predictable. Sunni leaders, American leaders, and even Grand

Ayatollah Ali al-Sistani complained about the lack of Sunni Arab representation and pressured the Assembly to include more Sunni Arabs in the process.[19] However, as with government formation, the problem was who to include and how to include them. Over the preceding weeks, the Sunni Arabs had demonstrated that they would reject anyone proposed by the new government and there was no legal, objective way to establish who a real Sunni Arab representative was. Many claimed to be; few were broadly representative. It would take several more weeks of muddling through to finalize a committee.

The Drafting Committee initially proposed adding thirteen Sunni Arab representatives, although whether they would be actually on the committee or be observing members was still under discussion. In response, Sunni Arab leaders convened several conferences, thus demonstrating some capacity for organization, and responded to the proposal by demanding at least twenty-five fully empowered representatives on the Constitutional Drafting Committee.[20] The two sides reached an agreement on 16 June stipulating that the Sunni Arabs would have fifteen representatives on the committee and ten "consultants" on a separate body that would be created and include representatives from other parties. However, while this structure seemed to satisfy everybody, the identity of the representatives caused further problems.

The initial list of Sunni Arabs was rejected by the National Assembly on the grounds that it did not "correctly represent Sunni personalities, parties and regions."[21] The parties agreed on an acceptable list of names on 26 June, but this list was not immediately ratified by the National Assembly, so Sunni Arab representatives did not actually join the Drafting Committee until 13 July—a month before the 15 August deadline.[22] The committee had not been idle during the negotiations with the Sunni Arabs. Subcommittees had produced draft sections of a constitution, but these and succeeding drafts received only a negative reaction from the new Sunni Arab members. The constitutional crisis of August and September 2005 was underway. References in the draft constitution to a loose federal structure and vague wording regarding the distribution of oil revenues convinced the Sunni Arabs that the document threatened the interests of their community more than they protected them. Attempts to bring Sunni Arabs on board continued long past the TAL's 15 August 2005 deadline and resulted in several "final" drafts being presented to the National Assembly in August and September.[23] At nearly the last moment, on 12 October—just three days before the referendum on the constitution—negotiations on a further amendment to the document resulted in a Sunni Arab party, the IIP, agreeing to support the draft.[24] This change added wording to Article 137 that called for the constitution to be revisited after the December 2005 elections and "necessary amendments" made and voted on in another referendum.[25] Iraqi voters approved the constitution by a national proportion of 78 percent in favor and 21 percent rejecting (approximately the estimated proportion of Sunni Arabs in Iraq).

Article 61 of the TAL stated that the draft constitution would be rejected if a two-thirds majority voted against the constitution in any three provinces. Two Sunni Arab provinces (al-Anbar and Salah ad-Din) met the two-thirds requirement, but a third, Ninewa, fell short of the mark with 55 percent voting against the document.[26]

Like the government formation and drafting committee issues before it, the constitutional crisis again captured the full attention of both Iraqi and U.S. leaders and prevented cooperation and progress on other fronts. Unlike the previous events of 2005, however, the U.S. Ambassador, Zalmay Khalilzad, was intensely involved in the negotiations over the constitution itself. This was in stark contrast to the first half of 2005, which was noteworthy for the near absence of U.S. involvement. Khalilzad's predecessor, John Negroponte, and other U.S. Embassy officials certainly observed and reported on the negotiations surrounding the formation of the ITG,[27] but their involvement seemed to be limited to reminding the Iraqis that progress needed to be made. USG representatives were only slightly more engaged in the issue of Sunni Arab participation in drafting the constitution. Some U.S. pressure was certainly applied to include more Sunni Arabs. But the overall picture in early 2005 is one of U.S. respect—perhaps to a fault—for Iraqi sovereignty. Two sets of questions arise from this stance.

First, was too much respect given to that sovereignty? Was Iraq at that point sovereign enough to warrant a hands-off approach? One could take the position that the new Iraqi leadership learned a lot about governing and the need for compromise by wrestling with the issues during these negotiations.[28] On the other hand, expecting a group of former resistance movements to suddenly transform themselves into a functioning and unified government apparatus may have been a stretch. The authors wondered then, and still wonder, if more U.S. involvement in shepherding the process would have accelerated it and allowed more progress in reconstruction and the development of a real Iraqi governing capacity. It is also worth noting that at this critical juncture Negroponte was probably not singularly focused on the issue of ITG formation. The announcement of his nomination for the position of National Director of Intelligence was made on 17 February 2005.[29] Time-consuming, high-level discussions surely preceded and followed the nomination. It is impossible to judge whether this had an effect on his approach to U.S. involvement or whether he took the position that Iraqi sovereignty was paramount.

There seemed in late 2004 through mid-2005 an obvious tension between the military and the diplomatic corps with regard to the issue of sovereignty. The hierarchical military imbued with their "can do" attitude had shed their institutional conservatism in Iraq and had, from the authors' perspective, become avid social engineers. In this view, the United States should have exercised more paternal stewardship over Iraqi affairs until Iraqis themselves were capable of exercising the responsibilities of sovereignty on their own. Whereas, the diplomats, with long experience in discussing and contending with the world's most intractable political morasses, were the social Darwinists with respect to Iraqi politics and sovereignty. The diplomats were of the mind that strategic success in Iraq would only arrive as a result of serial Iraqi tactical failures. As of 28 June 2004, Iraq was sovereign. Thus, Iraqi political leaders would either deliver those public goods commonly associated with sovereignty or perish politically through serial failure to satisfy the demands of an increasingly mobilized and aware Iraqi electorate. We touch on the question of Iraqi sovereignty again in more detail in a later section.

A final question that arises is, if the United States and coalition were not decisively engaged in the government formation process, what were they doing? The next section discusses MNF-I activity during early 2005 and shows that while there was an understanding of what needed to be done, accomplishing those tasks was just out of MNF-I's organizational reach. While arguably the best-resourced entity in Iraq, the military headquarters was not necessarily well equipped with the appropriate functional expertise nor was it actually empowered to plan for or initiate the types of activities most likely to ensure long-term success in the theater. Within the headquarters, we understood the interrelationship of activities in the political, security, economic, and physical reconstruction realms as well as their relative impact on the success or failure of the undertaking overall. However, in the absence of mechanisms for real theater strategic planning across all of the deployed instruments of power, there was no way for the military headquarters to effect meaningful change in any area other than security. Such change would have required some mechanism for the close synchronization of all the disparate political, military, and economic actions underway across Iraq. Regardless, the military tried to plan comprehensively, if for no other reason than to establish some benchmarks in areas lying outside of its reach but essential to its success. This led to several initiatives during the period of December 2004–July 2005 that were intended to fundamentally change the dynamics of the situation and push the Iraqi experiment to some favorable resolution.

MNF-I Initiatives

Just prior to and immediately after the 30 January 2005 elections, MNF-I prepared to engage the ITG and begin working on a number of initiatives. Four are particularly noteworthy: ITG coordination, Sunni Arab engagement and the strategic cities, coalition transformation, and coalition maintenance. All four demonstrate quite clearly the futility of planning any strategic action in one realm of activity—security, economic, political, reconstruction, etc.—without reference to or indeed without accounting for conditions in all other key areas simultaneously. All four initiatives rested on the assumption that positive momentum would continue to build as a result of successful Iraqi elections and would continue to be essential to the consummation of strategic success in the theater. The idea was that any psychological blow dealt to the insurgency should be repeated; any lift in Iraqi morale should be consolidated.

ITG Coordination

A principal task for the strategy section of Headquarters, MNF-I, was pulling together recommended actions for the post–January 2005 election period and prepare Iraq for the flurry of political events that were to occur throughout the remainder of the year—drafting the new constitution, the constitutional referendum, and finally the first constitutionally mandated post-Saddam elections. This would require a fully functioning synergy among the coalition's resources. General George W. Casey, the Commanding General of MNF-I, prompted this initiative during a morning briefing in early January 2005 by asking how the staff was preparing to take advantage of a successful election. As a result, the authors' office began work on a document outlining priorities and initiatives for the postelection period. Standard procedure was for such a question to be answered by a one-page point paper. A two-page response indicated a topic of some importance. The final response to Casey's question was an eleven-page document that was eventually appended to the MNF-I Campaign Plan as a Strategic Directive. Arranged along the four lines of operation, the "Momentum Paper," as it became known, acted as an organizational memory-jogger—a list of things that needed attention. It provided the MNF-I leadership with a semi-organized conception of what the postelection period was about and what needed to be accomplished.

When an MNF-I section was not tasked with such a project, it tends not to pay too much attention to the draft as it made its way around the headquarters. But as the document grew in size and scope and Casey asked pointedly about its progress, more general officers wanted to review it. The result was that the Momentum Paper received input from most MNF-I sections as well as the U.S. Embassy and IRMO. Each section, naturally, wanted to highlight and enshrine their favorite projects and this helped the document grow until it had to be divided not just along the lines of operation but also by time period. The first section focused on the immediate issues of ensuring Iraqi government continuity during the transition period, such as providing security for incoming and outgoing officials, and ensuring government ministries kept operating and paying workers, soldiers, and the police. The latter section included a list of issues to work on with the Transitional Government, such as prosecuting a counterinsurgency campaign, developing ministry capabilities, maintaining coalition presence, and preparing for the constitutional referendum.

Sunni Arab Engagement and the Strategic Cities

Another effort initiated within the military headquarters was intended to comprehensively address the political, security, economic, and social issues plaguing Iraq's Sunni Arab heartland. This was actually more than Sunni Arab engagement. It combined the prospect of increased coalition and Iraqi security initiatives as well as more fundamental politico-social efforts such as grassroots civil society development and targeted, localized economic and governance projects. It was an outline for changing fundamentally those conditions that continued to fuel Sunni Arab rejectionism.

In the wake of what was mass Sunni Arab rejection of the political process, the intent was to initiate broad efforts across all lines of operation specifically focused on improving conditions in Iraq's Sunni Arab core (the provinces of Baghdad, Salah ad-Din, Ninewa, Diyala, and al-Anbar, as well as the Sunni Arab–dominated area south of the city of Baghdad known as North Babil). The idea was to account for Sunni Arab disaffection in strategic planning and allocate resources to address it. The objective was to change circumstances fundamentally in key Sunni Arab regions in order to provide them with increased confidence in their new and secure position in the post-Saddam political order. This increased confidence was seen as necessary to moderate that part of the active resistance and opposition that was firmly grounded in Sunni Arab nationalism and political rejectionism versus that fraction of the Sunni Arab community that was irreconcilably extremist.

A previous chapter summarized initial MNF-I efforts at engaging the Sunni Arab community. Those efforts continued in the days preceding the election and the months afterward—but they were no more successful. The authors of this chapter surmised early in their tenure in Iraq that successful *short-term* engagement was probably impossible. The Sunni Arab community's position was privileged in Saddam's Iraq, but there was little developed civil society or organization beyond the Ba'athist and state structure. In short, the state provided Sunni Arabs with their principal mechanism for political organization. Once the state collapsed, there was no organizing principle for Sunni Arab political identity other than active rejection of Iraq's Shia Arab–dominated political revolution. Further, the authors sensed that real Sunni Arab engagement would have to wait until genuine, indigenous Sunni Arab leadership stepped to the fore. Candidates that were not particularly attractive included violent resistance leaders (former Ba'athists, radical Islamists, and criminal gangs), some tribal leaders—many tainted by cooperation with Saddam—local religious leaders, and finally, returning expatriates with very little real connection to Sunni Arab populations at the grass roots level. These were unattractive options, and they also could not deliver the same type of galvanizing momentum that was gathering behind the principal Shia Arab and Kurd political parties.

The concept for mollifying Iraq's Sunni Arab population through comprehensive political, military, economic, and social intervention quickly evolved in early to mid-2005 into an effort to change circumstances favorably in Iraq's most violent or potentially violent urban centers. With the constitutional referendum and first constitutional election looming on the near strategic horizon, we determined that the voting populations in those urban areas most threatened by the insurgency and its associated terrorism, as well as by the increasing prospect of sectarian violence, would be most inclined to invest in a stable Iraqi future if their political, material, and physical security was improved and guaranteed in a number of key areas. In the end, a handful of strategic urban centers or populations were identified as critical to Iraq's political success. From a coordination perspective, this effort was mildly successful in focusing and prioritizing some efforts across lines of operation. This was a result of extensive consultation with both the broad U.S. interagency deployed in Iraq and the security ministries within the ITG. However, it was still only an initiative born within the military headquarters. It did not emanate from a hybrid structure for strategic management of the conflict that would have been best equipped to see this and like initiatives carried out across agencies deployed in Iraq.

Coalition Transformation

Coalition transformation was a topic of discussion in the months that followed the January 2005 elections. The authors and their leadership assumed that as Iraq increased its sovereign capacity and as it took on more responsibility for its internal security, a fundamental restructuring of the coalition's deployed civil and military resources—not to mention substantial change in authorities, responsibilities, and command and control—would be in order. A reasonable assumption by the authors and their leadership at the time was that the coalition's military commitment to Iraq would steadily decline as either politico-security conditions gradually improved or as Iraqis became increasingly capable of exercising control over their own security affairs. Thus, the coalition and its presence would need to change commensurate with these developments. A small team of MNF-I's politico-military strategists considered numerous structural options. The most interesting among these might have been the proposal to unify all coalition efforts under a single politico-military chain of command. In the end, all of this planning was conceptual and, though it was inherently interagency in character, it was undertaken exclusively within the military headquarters.

Coalition Maintenance

Finally, one of the authors' more unique experiences in Iraq involved attempts to maintain the coalition. Komer's words from the 1970s are instructive here as well. He argued that even though the United States has fought in coalitions in every major twentieth century conflict, we neglected peacetime preparation in favor of ad hoc responses.[30] In Iraq, this meant that a significant amount of time and resources was devoted to the mechanics of coalition maintenance rather than prosecuting the counterinsurgency. The authors spent time and effort on initiatives aimed at maintaining a coalition that had limited practical effect and only questionable political or psychological benefits.

Although more than thirty nations participated in the coalition, the number of non-U.S. troops was always small.[31] The only other nation that contributed more than 5,000 troops was the United Kingdom. Sizeable Polish, Italian, Dutch, and Romanian contingents were employed in southern Iraq alongside the British troops, but most nations sent less than 200 troops to Iraq and many put restrictions on the activities of their contingents. At the risk of offending the personnel who deployed to Iraq and especially the fine Australian, British, and Dutch officers who enriched our own section with their professionalism and expertise, it was often easier to see the coalition as more a logistical burden than a force multiplier. Its primary purpose was more political or psychological; the presence of other nations proved that the United States was not acting unilaterally in Iraq.[32] Yet, the only time the coalition was mentioned in the media was when a country decided or threatened to withdraw its troops from Iraq. So, from our perspective, the psychological effect was a negative one—the news was always that of a dwindling coalition, whether that was true or not.

Though politically important as a legitimizing mechanism, the detailed management of coalition participation was a function that might have been best left to others. Other organizations certainly participated in coalition maintenance. Central Command had a directorate devoted to it—the trailers that made up "Coalition Village" took up several acres of MacDill Air Force Base where Central Command has its headquarters. In addition, the Joint Staff, the NSC (National Security Council), and the Department of State all participated in the coalition "project." Most of the involved officers within MNF-I, the authors included, thought that the national agencies should devote their attention to encouraging international participation, and leave the employment of forces to General Casey and his staff.

In this area, as in the operation as a whole, the authors' view was that the overall problem was that there was not a natural "lead" agency exercising meaningful primacy over the whole of the effort. Komer's comments on the lack of counterinsurgency management apply just as well to coalition maintenance. The result was that the authors sat in several video-television conferences during which every participant seemed to be waiting for someone else to provide direction or priorities. Coalition maintenance was a drain on MNF-I resources and an effort that MNF-I could not shape decisively from its position in Baghdad.

The observant reader will note that key components in all of these efforts lie well outside of or tangential to the purview of a military organization and its commander. Thus, many of the tasks listed in the Momentum Paper—priorities identified to contend with Sunni Arab rejectionism and the strategic cities or options considered for the maintenance of the coalition or its presence and function in Iraq—would require action by external organizations such as IRMO, the U.S. Embassy, the State Department, or the Iraqis themselves in order to succeed. Neither Casey nor his staff could order any of these entities to do those things that the military headquarters had determined (often on its own) would be essential to more comprehensive theater success. This limitation raises obvious questions about the organization of coalition efforts in Iraq, which we will turn to in greater detail in the next section.

In sum, while Iraqi leaders struggled to form a government and embark on a constitution-writing process, the coalition military headquarters prepared to deal with a sovereign government on security-related counterinsurgency issues, coordinated with national agencies on coalition maintenance, considered the future character of the military relationship between the coalition and Iraq, and attempted to address the Sunni Arab issue. The fact that MNF-I spent a lot of time and effort on issues that it was not best postured to contend with on its own raises important questions about the organization of the U.S. effort in Iraq. The key to answering those questions, we believe, lies in structural issues beyond the control of most in the theater. They are worth exploring because, until addressed, they will continue to plague U.S. foreign and security policy. For the moment, suffice it to say that the military headquarters in Iraq—given its enormous resources—was attempting to fill the gap between the reality and the practice of theater interagency strategic planning, synchronization, and execution of whole-of-coalition efforts.

Organizational Pathologies

That American planning did not adequately account for the complete collapse of the Iraqi state is not a new revelation. That the United States never fielded an authoritative and integrated interagency mechanism for the effective employment of the instruments of American and coalition power in Iraq is perhaps not as well known. Indeed, even the 2003 RAND study *America's Role in Nation-Building: From Germany to Iraq* suggested inaccurately, "In Iraq, the United States is experimenting with a novel model that brings military and civilian efforts under one unitary command."[33] By doing so, the RAND investigators were suggesting that there was from the beginning an authoritative, integrated chain of civil–military command in Iraq that enforced discipline over the nation's diverse instruments of power then deployed in the field. This was as untrue in 2003 as it was in 2004–2005. The United States and its partners never developed the requisite capacity for assessment, planning, execution, and management necessary for the integrated employment of coalition and Iraqi resources from the national to the local level and across the political, economic, social, and security domains. In the authors' opinion, the American effort in Iraq was simply Komer reprised.

By January of 2005, the short-lived mechanism for direct rule—the CPA (Coalition Provisional Authority) and its military partner CJTF-7 (Combined Joint Task Force 7)—was a memory, and the diplomatic corps in particular had abandoned all vestiges of direct authority over the day-to-day conduct of Iraq's internal and external affairs, adhering literally and, in our view, at times counterproductively to the strictest interpretation of Iraqi sovereignty. This occurred in spite of obvious, endemic Iraqi undercapacity or, arguably, incapacity for effective home rule as evidenced by the efforts to form a government in 2005. The State Department was acting in accordance with modern American convention. Neither American culture nor mainstream international norms allowed for the physical maintenance of empire-like possessions any longer than would be absolutely necessary for the establishment of a new durable, viable, and self-sustaining indigenous political order. Komer's reflections in 1972 are instructive in this regard, "State's concept of its role in Vietnam—and that of our embassy in Saigon—were quite conventional. ... [T]hey did not often deviate from the concept of normal diplomatic dealings with a sovereign allied government, even when that government was falling apart."[34] The reality was no different in Iraq in late 2004 to mid-2005.

Thus, the coalition was caught in a sovereignty trap of its own making. The long-term success of Iraq's political transformation relied increasingly on the efforts and stamina of an indigenous political leadership who, while having an enormous stake in seeing the endeavor succeed, were not capable of exercising even a modicum of real sovereignty after years of dictatorship and a sudden collapse of all of their state institutions. Compounding the Iraqis' obvious gaps in governance capacity was the inability of United States and its partners to assemble the most effective and discriminating mechanisms for the employment of their collective power in ways that would increase the prospects for success. This was in 2004–2005 and remains today one of the key challenges in the design of the state-building experiment in Iraq. At the working level, this was at times immensely frustrating. It was like being one driver among many destined for an inevitable freeway pileup. Though ostensibly in some control of his or her own vehicle, the driver remains powerless to change events in ways to avoid a catastrophic collision involving all.

The authors believe that to the extent that the intervention in Iraq did not meet the expectations of the American population or its strategic decision makers, significant blame for the coalition's underperformance rests on the structures chosen to manage the intervention and the cultures of those institutions charged with making the endeavor a success. The American military, in spite of fifteen years of post–Cold War experience in the new world disorder, was in 2004–05 still best postured to destroy industrial age armies on the battlefields of Europe and the Middle East. And the American diplomatic service remained optimized to dialogue and not to act. The former clearly demonstrated its considerable, if not one dimensional, capability in the blitz to Baghdad, and the latter in the well-choreographed—but not particularly effective—diplomatic theater that preceded the Iraq intervention. Neither was prepared structurally or culturally for the task of managing a multiagency stability operation of tremendous complexity, under conditions of continuing violence.

Of the two errors of omission, the military's was perhaps the most glaring.[35] The Pentagon had for too long held to a strategic outlook that overemphasized large-scale conventional war against a regional opponent. It therefore focused structure, training, resourcing, and capabilities against a narrow band of traditional challenges that it was most prepared to meet though not necessarily likeliest to confront. The strategic environment had changed dramatically in the fifteen years of post–Cold War experience. This transformation demanded competencies and capabilities that the American military was hesitant to adopt at the expense of a high-tech conventional military transformation. Yet, while the United States had never handed the management of state building and counterinsurgency to its diplomats, it had to its military.[36] And, there were before 9/11, Afghanistan, and Iraq significant indications that this mission was again lurking on the strategic near-horizon.[37]

In the authors' judgment, the politico-security "team" (MNF-I and U.S. Embassy) that inherited Iraq from the CPA and CJTF-7 in 2004 was, like its predecessor, an industrial-age anachronism thrown against a complex amalgam of challenges: undergovernance, insurgency, and political instability. These challenges had plagued great powers in the past but had also been made increasingly more complex by a crush of twenty-first–century security phenomena: virtual insurgent sanctuary, 24-hour satellite news, and the challenge of networked opponents unified by common interests and ideology but not by a formal chain of command.[38] One way to describe 2004–05 Iraq might be: state collapse meets insurgency, meets foreign occupation, meets political revolution, meets massive social and economic displacement. The totality of Iraq's challenge was lost in bureaucracies rooted in convention. Iraq's problems were, as Komer suggested about Vietnam's counterinsurgency campaign, "everybody's business and nobody's."[39] Just as in Komer's Vietnam experience, the authors' Iraq experience demonstrated that the United States was ill equipped for the complexity of irregular war and simultaneous physical, political, and social reconstructions in Iraq. To describe the strategic management of the war in Iraq in late 2004 through mid-2005, it is enough to cite Komer again and suggest liberal substitution of the word Iraq for Vietnam and Iraqi government for the acronym GVN (government of Vietnam). Komer observed:

> Who was responsible for conflict management of the Vietnam War? The bureaucratic fact is that below Presidential level everybody and nobody was responsible for coping with it in the round. With relatively few exceptions, neither the U.S. Government nor the GVN set up any specialized planning or operating agencies for counterinsurgency. Nor was there much overall coordinating or supervisory machinery for pulling together disparate programs within the U.S. government and GVN or between these to allies. Instead, both governments were organized conventionally, with little room for large-scale activities that cut across traditional agency lines.[40]

George Packer raises a similar issue and at the same time invokes the ghost of Robert Komer in the epilogue of his 2005 book *The Assassin's Gate: America in Iraq*. Packer relates an encounter he had with former State Department, CPA, and NSC official Drew Erdmann and his reflections on the analogy often made between Iraq and Vietnam, as well as the relevance of Komer to American experience in both. According to Packer, while Erdmann rejects many aspects of comparisons between Iraq and Vietnam, he does see one constant—the USG and "the ongoing effort to put its civilian and military branches to work in concert, the institutional constraints that made it so hard, the halting efforts to adapt imaginatively to new kinds of war, [and] the sheer organizational difficulty of pulling off something on the scale of Iraq."[41] After 2004–05, this would continue to be the great challenge in the Republican Palace on the west bank of the Tigris River. The counterinsurgency in its broadest conception was everybody's and was nobody's.

The four broad paths—political, economic, communications, and security—outlined in the MNF-I campaign plan were actually not representative of a single coordinated USG effort, but in fact four—or more—separate and often unsynchronized efforts undertaken by various civilian and military structures. One could see them as aspirational expressions of a military establishment with most of the resources but theoretically a quarter of the responsibilities. The fact that MNF-I accounted for these in its planning should in no way indicate that they were implemented. Primary responsibilities for all of these areas of effort, with the sole exception of security, quite rightly rested outside of the control of the military commander. However, they were also essential to the success of the counterinsurgency effort overall. In the authors' experience, there simply was no integrated mechanism forcing these efforts into detailed coordination.

The sequential or separate employment of American power had served the United States well throughout the Cold War, with the obvious exception of Vietnam. Most problems centered on the American relationship with the Soviet Union and on the martial dynamics of Cold War power politics. Thus, diplomacy flavored with bellicosity or military moves tempered by the dialogue of diplomats dominated the politico-security environment. After Vietnam, when the United States sought to avoid direct involvement in irregular small wars, there simply was no incentive for the USG to engage in the type of transformation that would be necessary for direct stewardship over the comprehensive rebuilding of a large, consequential state under conditions of continuing violence.[42] Thus, the United States entered and remained in Iraq with ad hoc structures for the period of "post-conflict reconstruction" and populated those structures with people possessing the same conventional biases and pathologies that had endured since the end of the Cold War.

For example, the physical and ministerial reconstruction of Iraq was the responsibility of IRMO. In MNF-I parlance, this represented the majority of what constituted the economic line of operation. In addition, IRMO exercised considerable influence over events occurring within and across all four lines of operation but had no official responsibility to act within the strictures of the military command's campaign plan. The physical reconstruction "plan" could best be described as a project list, against which the initial allocation of $18.5 billion was applied in priority. IRMO was assisted by a veritable alphabet soup of supporting agencies—GRD (Gulf Region Division) representing the Army Corps of Engineers, PCO (Project and Contracting Office), etc. IRMO had its own chain of command, its own operations staff, and its own inexorable signposts for progress. But, in the authors' experience, it did not operate according to a common set of strategic priorities that were shared across the whole of the American effort in Iraq and intended to underwrite complementary progress on all the lines of operation.

The political reconstruction of the country was a much more difficult question. The quick answer is that responsibility for Iraq's political reconstruction belonged to Iraqis. On its face, this is both the right answer and some indication of Iraq's continuing challenges. As recounted above, by early 2005, the U.S. Embassy had retreated into the role of consultant to the nascent interim Iraqi leadership. It was the authors' experience that Iraq's sovereignty, to the Embassy, was an inviolable principle in its conversations with Iraqi authorities and a club in conversations with its other interagency and military partners. This strict adherence to the concept of Iraqi sovereignty was neither surprising nor necessarily condemnable. Iraq had been declared sovereign in June 2004 whether or not it was in fact capable of exercising the basic functions of what is normally considered a sovereign entity. Further, in spite of its under capacity, Iraq had operated under the authority of a transitional government since the CPA restored Iraqi sovereignty in June 2004.

To be fair, the Department of State was neither equipped, socialized, nor acculturated to plan and execute anything remotely as complex as the remaking of a large, complex and strategically consequential state. Though nominally given primacy over American efforts in Iraq, the authors observed no attempt on the part of the Embassy to exercise direct influence over or synchronize the efforts of all of the varied activities of the American government or those of coalition partners in Iraq. If success of the political line of operation was paramount, there was no apparent Department of State-led effort or mechanism established in 2004–05 to coordinate the supporting security, communications, and economic efforts in ways most conducive to overall success. In the crucial months up to and immediately following the transition of authority between the CPA and the IIG, the authors believe that Iraq was a sovereign political unit in name only—adrift in an internal and external great game for political primacy over the conduct of its affairs—and the great power that had set that game in motion could not break with convention long enough to help guide the course of events in the most favorable way. It was just as Komer had seen it thirty years before when he quoted from Dennis J. Duncanson's work. Duncanson observed, "Aid and advice without any formal agreement to ensure consistent policy, coordination, and guidance, which ill-wishers might have condemned as 'colonialism,' tended to harden the defects of the Diem regime rather than to correct them, and to reinforce its defeats."[43]

The military in Iraq—personified at the theater strategic level in the staff of MNF-I—was responsible for all things security, yet was perpetually trapped in the Catch-22 facing all great powers involved in a counterinsurgency. Success along the security line of operation relied on demonstrated progress in the political, social, and economic dimensions of the conflict. Yet success in those dimensions was in large measure beholden to effectively moderating violence to levels that would allow a new political, economic, and social order to grow and flourish. In short, there could be no meaningful progress and no durable peace without some detailed synchronization of the disparate political, economic, social, and security efforts in Iraq. The military recognized this and accounted for it in its planning but possessed neither the requisite levels of expertise nor the command authority to ensure that its planning for the other dimensions of the conflict translated into real comprehensive action in the theater.

For this reason, it was no accident that the British campaign in Malaya was a popular source of inspiration for strategists within the military headquarters in Baghdad, as Malaya represented the last clear victory of a great power fighting a determined and capable insurgent opponent. If Vietnam, as described by Komer, was prototypical of how great powers should not prosecute counterinsurgency and state building, then British Malaya as described by John Nagl and others was the opposite. One of the most oft-cited vignettes from British experience in Malaya was the memorandum written at the beginning of the conflict by then Chief of the Imperial General Staff, Field Marshal Sir Bernard Law Montgomery, to then Colonial Secretary, Sir Oliver Lyttelton. Montgomery wrote the following:

Dear Lyttelton,
Malaya
We must have a plan.

Secondly we must have a man.
When we have a plan and a man, we shall succeed: not otherwise.
Yours Sincerely,
Montgomery (F.M.) [44]

In Iraq, while officers within MNF-I recognized the importance of the four lines of operation and planned *conceptually* for the employment of the nation's comprehensive power along them, they only truly controlled efforts on the security line. While it can be argued that the security line was paramount in late 2004 and 2005 and that it provides a foundation for success on the others, the authors observed no extant, functioning superstructure ensuring unity, discipline, precision, and mutual support in the employment of coalition power and resources along each of the others. There were informal relationships between the various bureaucracies—U.S. Embassy, MNF-I, IRMO, etc. However, each in effect had their own "man" and their own "plan." Thus, synchronizing efforts and effecting progress on the nonmilitary lines of operation required convincing, co-opting, or cajoling other responsible agencies—not an easy task in any bureaucracy; almost impossible in a combat zone. Further, the synchronization that was achieved was most dependent on personal relationships and informal ententes but certainly not on any formal unity of command and effort. [45]

Clearly, the Iraqis must ultimately succeed themselves. Packer cites Drew Erdmann's conclusion, for example,

> The ultimate objectives can only achieved by the Iraqis. . . . We can help. But we are in a position where victory will only be achieved through the efforts of others. That's a paradoxical situation. We may have the power, but precisely because of the nature of our objectives, we can't use our power to force a specific outcome. [46]

This is consistent with a phrase from T. E. Lawrence that was popular in the MNF-I headquarters and has perhaps now become trite. Lawrence said,

> Do not try to do too much with your own hands. Better the Arabs do it tolerably than that you do it perfectly. It is their war, and you are to help them, not to win it for them. Actually, also, under the very odd conditions of Arabia, your practical work will not be as good as, perhaps, you think it is. [47]

Yet, it is, in the authors' view, clear that the coalition presence was not established, structured, or socialized to maximize its impact and underwrite long-term Iraqi success either.

Observations and Conclusions

As Iraq approached an historic period of political transformation—the drafting of a permanent constitution, a nationwide constitutional referendum, and finally, election of a permanent, democratic government, the authors departed the theater. Their experience in Iraq combined with their background as military officers, social scientists, and students of the politics of security and insecurity yielded a key personal insight that has become increasingly relevant as the conflict has subsequently developed: The USG effort in Iraq continued to be unprepared structurally and culturally for the demands of the environment in spite of almost two years of operational experience.

In the main, this insight was the product of academic training and military judgment colliding with six months of intensive in-theater study of Iraq's specific challenges and the inherent political, social, economic, ethno-religious, and security complexities the coalition and its Iraqi partners had to overcome. There simply was no standing mechanism for assessment, planning, execution, and management with authority over all of the various instruments of power employed in Iraq. And, even if one existed, the institutional biases and patholo-gies of the representative agencies would have militated against effective employ-ment of those instruments.

Context is important to illustrate this point. Therefore, a review of the policy-level conclusions emanating from Washington but originating from within the U.S. Embassy and military command in Baghdad is appropriate. It was common in the Spring/Summer of 2005 for senior political and military leaders in Washington and Iraq to argue that the Iraqi government and its coalition partners had collected a string of stunning politico-security successes between June 2004 and mid-2005. They would at the same time point out that this was accomplished in the face of relentless insurgent and terrorist resistance and that, at every turn, the insurgent/terrorist opposition in Iraq failed in its attempts to derail a nascent Iraqi democracy's political development. The President, for example, observed in a June 2005 speech:

> The terrorists—both foreign and Iraqi—failed to stop the transfer of sovereignty. They failed to break our Coalition and force a mass withdrawal by our allies. They failed to incite an Iraqi civil war. They failed to prevent free elections. They failed to stop the formation of a democratic Iraqi government that represents all of Iraq's diverse popula-tion. And they failed to stop Iraqis from signing up in large number with the police forces and the army to defend their new democracy. . ... The lesson of this experience is clear: The terrorists can kill the innocent, but they cannot stop the advance of freedom.[48]

Later, in February of 2006, Secretary of Defense Donald Rumsfeld observed similarly:

> [Iraq's insurgent/terrorist opposition] failed to stop the January elections, they failed to stop the drafting of the constitution, they failed to stop the referendum on the constitution, they failed to stop the most recent election, they failed to stop the seating of the parliament, they're going to fail to stop the seating of a new government. . ... They are on the run. . ... They have failed in almost everything they have tried thus far.[49]

Yet, while both of these statements were in the main correct on one level and while it was likely that these themes were closely coordinated with their senior diplomatic and military representatives on the ground in Iraq, these also only addressed the most visible of Iraq's politico-security developments. Their conclusions, while factually correct and signs of some progress, were also perhaps less relevant to the overall success of the endeavor than other less visible but more important developments such as real growth in Iraqi civil society at the grass roots level or the emergence of some consociational accord between Iraq's sectarian constituencies.[50] In 2005, Iraq "succeeded" politically at a national level, while it increasingly failed in these latter two areas.

The development of civil society at the grass roots level, for example, was only possible in those areas of Iraq that were safe from persistent violence and intimidation and only then because of the tradition of political mobilization already resident in the sectarian and ethnic parties of the former Shia Arab and Kurd political opposition. Thus, what civil society did emerge was from its inception poisoned by ethnic and sectarian parochialism. As for the establishment of any sort of accord between sectarian constituencies, this too was increasingly stymied by a Shia Arab–dominated political agenda and the concomitant intransigence of Iraq's Sunni Arabs. The former were eager to exercise their newfound power, while the latter faced the certainty that Iraq's new democratic political order would institutionalize their minority status in perpetuity. This combination provided fuel for the later escalation of sectarian conflict as Shia Arabs were increasingly attacked by Sunni Arab extremists attempting to foment civil war and ordinary Sunni Arabs became increasingly insecure about their personal and economic security in the shadow of a Shia Arab–dominated political authority. Thus, the much-trumpeted politico-security successes of 2005 were important but not necessarily decisive to the overall outcome—and in some cases served to increase Iraq's peril exponentially.

Clearly, increased political participation, successful elections and government formation, reconstruction project starts, and a steady increase in the number of Iraqis under arms were signs of progress. But the question remained, were these sufficient for a stable, durable, self-sustaining, and inclusive political order? And, if not, were we missing important considerations in our strategic decision making? In the authors' opinion, the answer to the former is certainly no and to the latter a resounding yes.

After all, increases in political participation and social mobilization are not necessarily indications of success. Depending on electoral outcomes, they may prove to be the opposite. In an immature polity, the sudden mobilization of a previously intransigent group, like Iraq's Sunni Arabs, may only galvanize them into a more obstructionist and extreme opposition if their mobilization is the product of their own unrealistic expectations. Electoral outcomes that fail to meet expectations, and at the same time institutionalize a constituent group's minority status, can serve to push them toward informal forms of political organization and illegitimate forms of political opposition. As Samuel Huntington observes,

> Elections to be meaningful presuppose a certain level of political organization. The problem is not to hold elections but to create organizations. In many, if not most, modernizing countries elections serve only to enhance the power of disruptive and often reactionary social forces and to tear down the structure of public authority.[51]

Likewise, the steady increase in the number of Iraqis under arms was by itself not necessarily relevant. Their motivations for joining the armed forces, the degree to which the security forces were loyal to the nation and its constitution versus ethnic or confessional identity, tribe, political party, or special interest were all vastly more important considerations. Further, the growth in capacity of the security ministries was important but only insofar as its quality, loyalty, and control were developing in ways favorable to the enterprise of secure and durable state building. It may be, for example, that the Minister of Defense or Interior and his deputies exercised effective control over their assigned forces. However, if they and their forces represented the interests of a single ethno-religious or tribal identity more than they did the Iraqi state as an institution, then real increases in security force capacity may at the same time have fundamentally increased insecurity nationwide and become a net minus for the coalition's strategic objectives in Iraq.[52]

Dogged adherence to macroindicators of progress was representative of the structural challenges and institutional biases and pathologies that hampered both deep understanding of Iraq's continuing challenges and effective responses to contend with them. Komer might suggest that some of this structural and institutional inadequacy was coded into the DNA of those American bureaucracies most responsible for generating success in Iraq. Komer argued in the introduction to *Bureaucracy Does Its Thing*, for example, that along with environmental challenges in Vietnam, the quality (or lack of quality) of the Vietnamese ally, and the decidedly incremental approach of the USG, there were other key institutional challenges that directly impacted on the ability of American and Vietnamese bureaucracies to respond to the challenges of counterinsurgency effectively. He observed:

> What must be added is how another set of real-life constraints—largely inherent in the typical behavior patterns of the GVN and U.S. institutions involved in the conflict—made it difficult for them to cope with an unfamiliar conflict environment and greatly influenced what they could and could not, or would and would not, do. Though by no means the whole answer, these institutional constraints helped render the U.S./ GVN response to an atypical insurgency conflict unduly conventional, expensive, and slow to adapt.[53]

The authors contend that it was not difficult to recognize that these structural and cultural weaknesses decisively contributed to the coalition misreading the importance of the most visible politico-security indicators at the expense of understanding the less tangible but more important foundational socio-political issues that continued to fuel Iraq's unrest. In the authors' judgment, a sea of complexity was masked by coalition attempts to reduce success or failure in Iraq to a handful of easily quantifiable measures of effectiveness and this failure was in large measure the product of the structure and culture of the coalition's deployed institutions.

In the end, the American effort appeared to demonstrate a preference for hard versus soft science in its attempts to understand the myriad challenges in Iraq. Success and failure (mostly success) were measured not according to the quality of outcomes but rather according to their quantitative aspects—how many Iraqis voted, enlisted, or were trained, etc. Doing so failed to account for the more important questions—why did these events occur in the way they did and what made them significant? Put simply, the coalition preferred to count things more than appreciate them qualitatively.

Though Iraq as of 2006 was nominally sovereign, there is still great doubt as to what extent it was exercising sovereignty in the classic sense. In mid-2005 as the authors departed the theater, the key question was whether Iraq's sovereignty was maturing quickly enough to support a durable, self-sustaining, and responsible Iraqi political order capable of defending itself after the ordered withdrawal of coalition military forces. It may be that "strike three" manifests itself as the third of three chronically incapable Iraqi governments that fail to exercise effective control over the country's political, social, economic, and security affairs, while the coalition continues to muddle through.

Could "strike two" have been converted into a base hit? It appears not—particularly if MNF-I and the U.S. Embassy continued to stand by as the Iraqi political experiment devolved into internecine squabbling and the various former resistance movements learned the art of coalition government on the job. The authors' conclusion is that "strike two" could only have been averted if the coalition fielded a very different type of team in the first place. A wholesale restructuring of the means of intervention, occupation, and reconstruction would have improved the coalition's ability both to understand the character of its challenges and to employ its power in the most responsive and effective manner. The military establishment in Iraq caught up on the classics of counterinsurgency warfare and proved that it could adapt to fundamentally changed security conditions. However, the broader effort in Iraq required a strategic approach and supporting bureaucratic structures that were functionally combined and capable of appreciating and acting on Iraq's political, economic, and security complexities in a synchronized and comprehensive manner.

CHAPTER 8

CONCLUSION: HOPING FOR A PLAN

Nathan Freier, Tomislav Z. Ruby and Thomas S. Mowle

U.S. decision makers and strategic planners failed for decades to appreciate the complex demands of regime change or restoration. Given the nation's experience in Iraq, it is likely safe to assume that until today, no U.S. warplanning has ever adequately accounted for the wholesale reconstruction of a state collapsing in the aftermath of war involving U.S. forces. The Iraq experience is hopefully a clarion call for better planning, intelligence, coordination, or in their absence, for more caution in this regard. It is highly likely that in the future, the United States will need to address another consequential state collapse. Thus, we hope that the myriad strategic lessons of Iraq are heeded.

Even today, four years into the war, serious debate about the types of structural and cultural changes necessary for future success in Iraq-like environs remains muted. When it does occur, it typically revolves around adding more structure to old and not necessarily transforming old institutions into twenty-first–century hybrids better postured to accommodate fundamentally different strategic circumstances. The Iraq experience demonstrates the difficulties that accompany disunity of purpose, command, and effort at the theater strategic level. Left by themselves, bureaucracies will "do their thing," as Robert Komer suggested thirty-four years ago. The coalition effort in Iraq remains defined by ad hoc structures separated artificially by functional boundaries. Each element of the structure—MNF-I (Multinational Force–Iraq) headquarters, the U.S. Embassy in Baghdad, Multinational Security Transition Command–Iraq, and IRMO (Iraqi Reconstruction Management Office)—attempts in its own way to accomplish its conception of right. Yet in reality, as the authors of this book conclude, each often pursues mutually exclusive—even contradictory—objectives.

The coalition effort in Iraq demanded a unified interagency structure capable of detailed strategic planning and execution at the national, regional, and theater strategic levels. It called for ground breaking synchronization of the instruments of coalition power. The reality, as the authors of this book capably describe, was and remains quite different.

For these and other reasons beyond the scope of this work, the American vision for Iraq has proven frustratingly difficult to realize in practice. This book represents the collective wisdom of a group of military professionals who struggled to work at the oft-illusive intersection of the coalition's political, security, and economic efforts to stabilize Iraq from 2003 to 2005. It is intended to provide a clinical assessment of the coalition's continued structural, institutional, and cultural underpreparedness for the complexity of the Iraqi theater and the enormous challenges associated with closing those obvious capacity and capability gaps that have impeded effective prosecution of the SSTR (stability, security, transition, and reconstruction) effort.

The substantive chapters of this book have described how American strategy in Iraq through the summer of 2005 was neither comprehensive enough in fact nor integrated effectively in practice across all of the coalition's deployed instruments of power. At the theater strategic level—where the political, security, economic, and informational lines of operation met and relied on the decisive interaction of various disparate USG (U.S. Government) players for success—campaign planning proceeded in the absence of real unity of purpose, effort, and command across the various political–military–economic initiatives necessary for a stable and self-sustaining postwar Iraq. There were competing views about conditions in Iraq and their significance. At times, military operations undermined the effective pursuit of key political objectives. Similarly, the unguided course of political events often undermined what hope existed for consociational understanding and real security for vulnerable ethno-religious constituencies that perceived growing political and physical insecurity. In the opinion of some authors, the training of Iraqi forces proceeded in the absence of focus and planning, the coalition had difficulty assessing progress, and the momentum gained through real political successes, like Iraq's first free elections, evaporated with coalition inaction.

The Iraq war did not proceed as expected. That is now indisputable. The coalition entered the period after major combat operations without a real plan for Iraq's stabilization and reconstruction. That is likewise well documented. Under these circumstances, success was left to chance and not design—to hope not calculation. Others have written about the grand strategic and political policy level; we instead provide a view from inside the Green Zone, a critical analysis of lessons identified but not necessarily learned, an honest and reasoned self-assessment of coalition thinking and decision-making processes. The inadequacy of strategic planning combined with a range of political, institutional, and cultural pressures militated against effective course corrections. In the end, we were all corporately like General Helmuth von Moltke: once the war started, we could not turn the trains around.[1]

We can learn from past decisions and speculate, counterfactually, about where the coalition might be had it made different strategic decisions at key moments or if it had both planned more comprehensively prior to the intervention and had been better prepared structurally and culturally for the demands of Iraq's environment in the period after the end of major combat operations. Further, we can also inform the course of future undertakings that mirror Iraq's enormous complexity—undertakings that are quite likely given the breadth of American global interests.

This concluding chapter identifies three common themes that run throughout this book. First, the coalition exhibited a consistent under capacity for comprehensive, cross-functional strategic planning. Structure and culture militated against success in this regard. Second, there was, in the view of the authors, a persistent under appreciation for and incomplete understanding of the political, security, and social forces fueling Iraq's continued unrest. This trend was compounded by real gaps in theater intelligence. Third, there were no formal mechanisms for coordination of the agencies responsible for achieving the coalition's goals across the four lines of operation. This theme follows directly from the first and continued to be a problem even after the effects of the first two themes began to be mitigated. The authors conclude that a failure to address each of these in a thorough, thoughtful, and comprehensive manner will undermine American success under similar conditions in the future. Quite simply, if we do not learn and internalize the right strategic lessons from Iraq, we either will fail or will succeed only after enormous unnecessary cost in future like high stakes endeavors.

Cross-Functional Strategic Planning

Policy. Strategy. Doctrine. Policy makers and senior military leaders sometimes find it hard to define and place these concepts in their proper context or understand how they interact. This is particularly true at the complicated and convoluted intersection of politics, economics, and security so often encountered in messy irregular conflicts like the Iraq war. Policy is a decision about what an entity, such as a country, wants to do. It answers the "what" question. Thus, it is an end. For example, as of 2002 it was the policy of the United States to fight the global war on terror outside of the United States by denying terrorists' safe haven abroad.[2] Strategy is the detailed course designed to achieve policy ends. It answers the "how" question. How do we blend and sequence the application of our various instruments of power to achieve our desired end states? Do we phase our national efforts—attacking specific challenges with specific instruments sequentially, or do we attack one or more challenges simultaneously—employing all of our instruments in their proper combinations comprehensively? Which instrument of power is appropriate to lead the effort at particular points in time and how do the others lend decisive support to this main effort? Once policy ends are determined, there are a variety of strategies that can be employed to achieve them. The great challenge is creating the strategy that gets you to the policy end with the least amount of risk—measured as the likelihood of "failure or prohibitive costs in pursuit of strategic objectives [and] operational objectives."[3]

But where do strategists go to help them develop their campaigns to achieve those national policies? First they look to doctrine. Doctrine is the agreed-upon, relevant best practices and principles to achieve an end. In purely military terms, doctrine is a guide that military leaders, strategists, and planners look to for guidance. Doctrine does not provide an exact formula for the type, quantity, and method of employment for specific military resources under a given set of circumstances. It does, however, tell strategists and planners that when faced with particular conditions, one should consider certain conceptual approaches for defeating challenges and establishing favorable security conditions. In this regard, it allows the planner to rationally assess alternative combinations of broad capabilities that might be necessary to achieve a given set of objectives.

Planning is the art of bringing these three concepts into a unified effort. A strategic plan is a detailed "ends-focused, ways and means-rationalized, and risk informed" strategic design that when executed and subsequently adjusted is intended to achieve specific policy ends.[4] A good campaign plan employs the strategic and operational art and doctrine to inform critical theater strategic decision making. According to *Joint Doctrine for Campaign Planning,* the "campaign plan embodies the combatant commander's strategic vision of the arrangement of related operations necessary to attain theater strategic objectives."[5] A plan also involves what joint military doctrine calls "branches and sequels."[6] Throughout a campaign plan, there will be points in time and space when different outcomes are possible—planned deviations from the preferred path that must be accounted for in detail in order to maintain momentum toward a given set of objectives. Thus, real planning encompasses a range of prospective COAs (courses of action) and their associated outcomes and accounts for a variety of foreseeable contingencies.

There is scant evidence that real, actionable cross-functional theater strategic planning of the type described above occurred prior to the coalition intervention in Iraq. Mowle's first substantive chapter describes some of the issues associated with prewar strategic planning and the period before the authors' arrival in Baghdad. The absence of a United Nations Security Council Resolution clearly authorizing the war left the military and diplomatic lanes in conflict. As illustrated by Bremer's discussion of looting after the invasion, military decisions affected the informational line—the ability to assure Iraqis that the coalition force would preserve Iraq as a functioning, unitary state. Bremer's choices with respect to the Iraqi military, Ba'ath party members, Fallujah, and Moqtada al-Sadr were difficult because they involved complex interactions between informational, diplomatic, and military considerations under the intense pressure of time and resources. Thomas' chapter continues this theme with respect to the development of Iraqi security forces. Thomas argues that a schedule of aspirational goals was substituted for a real strategic design that described how the goals would be achieved, what resources were necessary for success, and what risks were engendered by the adopted COA. Sepp elaborates further on this theme with respect to the development of intelligence about real conditions in Iraq.

In the two years following the intervention real, actionable planning occurred only within the military headquarters. Though the State Department nominally exercised primacy over all American efforts in Iraq, it was the authors' view that there was no commensurate effort by the American Foreign Service in the field to exercise primary control over the course of strategic events. Nor, for that matter, did the State Department have the resident capacity, culture, or operational acumen to exercise control had it wanted to. Thus, plans were not the product of comprehensive, integrated political, military, and economic deliberations involving "strategic planners" representing the various deployed agencies of the American and coalition governments.

MNF-I's campaign plan was a step in the right direction. However, it was only published in the summer of 2004, a full year after the coalition intervention. As described in Ruby's chapter and to a lesser extent in Mowle's second substantive chapter, the campaign plan was clearly focused on attacking Iraq's challenges comprehensively, initially identifying and defining the four lines of operation referred to throughout this book, yet it was never informed by and only incompletely coordinated with coalition agencies outside of the uniformed military. In the end, the military campaign plan—though accounting conceptually for those non-security issues likeliest to affect security conditions on the ground—did not attempt to wrestle the entire effort in the political, economic, and information realms under the control of a single authoritative coalition leader and staff.

In 2005 in particular, a great deal of detailed cross-functional analysis and planning occurred within Headquarters, MNF-I, as described in the chapter by Freier and Rose. In the absence of unified interagency mechanisms for integrated planning, execution, and command and control, however, any synergy that resulted from this planning was often either accidental or the product of close, informal relationships between working level strategists, diplomats, and aid officials. As a result, it was difficult if not impossible to maintain any effective momentum at the theater strategic level across the coalition's deployed instruments of power. At this point in the war, it was not that MNF-I did not plan, but rather that the plans were either incomplete or difficult to operationalize because of the limited influence MNF-I exercised over the other instruments of power. "Hope" in this regard was that the other coalition agencies would conform to MNF-I's strategic vision.

Insufficient Understanding of the Situation

Military planning, at any level, can only succeed if one understands the situation into which forces are being introduced. As described in several chapters in this book—both of those by Mowle, as well as those by Ruby and Sepp—the early difficulties caused by overoptimistic strategic planning were compounded by a persistent underappreciation for the political, security, and social complexity of Iraq. This yielded a less-than-ideal decision-making environment. Planning requires assumptions, but assumptions are not facts. *Joint Doctrine for Campaign Planning* states that:

> When dealing with an assumption, changes to the plan may need to be developed should the assumption prove to be incorrect. Because of their influence on planning, the fewest possible assumptions are included in a plan. A valid assumption has three characteristics: it is logical, realistic, and essential for the planning to continue. Assumptions are made for both friendly and adversary situations. The planner should assume that the adversary would use every capability at his disposal (i.e., nuclear, biological, and chemical (NBC), asymmetric approach, etc.) and operate in the most efficient manner possible. Planners should never assume an adversary has less capability than anticipated, nor assume that key friendly forces have more capability than has been demonstrated.[7]

This doctrinal guidance was not followed as thoroughly as it might have been. Prewar planning, summarized by Mowle's first substantive chapter, has been thoroughly discussed in other works and does not bear repeating here. Nevertheless, even eighteen months into the war, the coalition effort remained reliant on assumptions that were not necessarily supported by reality on the ground. The "Campaign Progress Review," conducted in the fall of 2004 by officers working for MNF-I's Deputy Chief of Staff for Strategy, Plans, and Assessments, found that seven of ten key assumptions were not supportable by what was believed to be the situation at the time.[8]

Not only did the coalition continue to rely on a number of unsupportable assumptions, but it further had great difficulty trying to assess its own success. It struggled to assess the 215 separate "effects" by which it measured progress. Furthermore, officers on the staff did not necessarily agree whether or not cumulative success in realizing key effects would or could lead to broader theater success in the first place. In Chapter 7, for example, Rose and Freier describe the tension between empiricists who relied on measurable, quantifiable signs of progress as their principal yardstick and those who saw greater qualitative nuance within empirical trends.

Effects which seem simple enough to measure are often not. Decreasing insurgent influence in the Sunni Arab population, for example, has a number of nebulous characteristics that are difficult to either quantify or qualify. Estimating the physical size of the insurgent challenge also proved frustratingly elusive. At one point in November 2004, General George Casey asked his staff how the coalition could have killed or incarcerated more insurgents to date than he was told only months before constituted the total size of the insurgency overall.[9] This one example is indicative of the scope and complexity of irregular conflict and the real challenges associated with developing a corporate capacity to understand and attack it comprehensively. Casey's question reflects the coalition's daily struggle to comprehend Iraq's complexities, socialize them within the context of coalition objectives, and act decisively across the spectrum of deployed instruments to generate the most favorable and enduring operational effects.

Sepp's chapter explains one aspect of the problem. The United States did not have adequate intelligence of its own with respect to conditions in Iraq, and it had a very difficult time developing an effective Iraqi intelligence service. As a result, it could not determine the likely consequences of arresting Moqtada al-Sadr or allowing his movement to survive and grow. Perhaps most importantly, the coalition was unable to grasp the complicated motivations of the different constituent Sunni Arab groups, as discussed in Mowle's second substantive chapter. It did not understand, for example, the links the Muslim Ulema Council, itself a very loosely organized group, had with elements of the insurgency or with pro-democratic Sunni Arab political parties like the Iraqi Islamic Party. This, in the authors' opinion, resulted in unhelpful oversimplification that had enormous strategic impact. For example, by universally labeling the violent opposition as monolithic "anti-Iraqi forces," the coalition excluded through clever semantics differences among the groups as well as the possibility that many actively opposing Iraq's new political order may consider themselves members of a quasi-popular resistance movement defending Iraq (or at a minimum Iraq's minority Sunni Arab confessional identity) from what they perceived to be a foreign-imposed political solution.[10] And thus, they may have been open to some form of political accommodation.

While part of the coalition's difficulty in understanding the full situation in Iraq stems from insufficient intelligence, the authors perceived a frustrating, corporate inability to discern the perspective of ordinary Iraqis, and that this inability hampered material progress. The insurgency-or-resistance debate involved more than academic definitions. If obstructionist Iraqis (particularly hostile Sunni Arabs) constituted a quasi-popular resistance movement, that implied that the coalition was not perceived as a legitimate and positive force for change by a politically significant segment of the Iraqi population. In spite of the best of intentions, perception is often reality. For example, coalition policies with respect to cordon and search, the security of convoys, and the detention of Iraqis could be justified from an American operational perspective, but may be viewed as excessive and arbitrary by many Iraqis. Likewise, though chronic electricity shortages in Baghdad were in part caused by increases in the availability of electronic goods as well as coalition efforts to distribute electricity more equitably nationwide (versus concentrating it in the capital as Saddam had done), Baghdad's citizens simply saw shortages as a coalition failure to deliver basic services. While one aspect of the "ground truth," as discussed by Ruby, is the actual conditions in the country, Iraqi perceptions and expectations were other aspects of "ground truth" that required active strategic management.

There is a dual tyranny of perceptions and expectations. If , as reality bore out, many Sunni Arabs would feel threatened physically, materially, and politically by the coalition's action to depose and replace Saddam Hussein, then assertively securing that population's position in a new more equitable political order was enormously important to strategic success. Failing to do so, allowing a nascent, underdeveloped representative political system maximum freedom to determine initial outcomes, assured that minority Sunni Arabs would lose both their position of privilege but more dangerously their collective sense of security. The former was essential to restoring equity and balance to Iraqi society; the latter, however, was a recipe for cultivating alternative, disruptive forms of political expression and opposition within a leaderless Sunni Arab minority.

Likewise, intervention by the coalition raised the expectations of all Iraqis—Sunni Arab, Shia Arab, and Kurd. Average Iraqis—after a reasonable period of adjustment—expected that there would be real qualitative improvements in their daily lives. It is the authors' collective judgment that consistent failure to deliver on those expectations has driven all of Iraq's consequential political constituencies toward refuge in the strength of their ethnic group or confessional identity.

In sum, the coalition did not fully understand the complex social, economic, religious, and ethnic motivations of Iraqis. One could plan in the absence of this knowledge, but one could not plan with confidence. One could not adequately assess progress in winning broad, representative, popular support for Iraq's political transformation without understanding the perceptions, expectations, and motivations of common Iraqis representing all of the diverse communities of interest. In the face of these gaps in knowledge, gaps that will likely span the breadth of future contingencies, it is best to account in planning for the most likely and most dangerous environmental conditions. At the same time, future post-collapse scenarios demand that the United States make a more concerted effort to also understand in the most comprehensive way the motivations and risk calculus of the constellation of irregular actors certain to oppose U.S.-supported political solutions. This implies an effort to understand the strategic situation from the opposition's point of view. Knowing the opposition's goals and motivations allows one to craft a more successful strategy for eroding their natural bases of support and deliberately foreclosing their strategic options and opportunities.

Insufficient Cross-Functional Command and Control over Execution

Even the best plan, grounded in a rich understanding of oneself and the opposition, still needs to be executed properly. The failure to plan and execute the SSTR effort more comprehensively—according to a sophisticated and commonly held understanding of the character of Iraq and its challenges—was an artifact of a campaign undertaken without any authoritative structures or mechanisms for effective theater strategic planning and execution across the coalition's deployed instruments of power. It was always clear that success in Iraq hinged on the nimble employment of the coalition's various capabilities in the right sequence and combination against Iraq's myriad challenges. Yet, there was no routine process or convention that enforced this discipline over the various coalition and Iraqi players. Had the political–military–economic efforts of the coalition been informed by a common vision of Iraq's circumstances, a common understanding of the minimum essential (clearly identifiable) conditions necessary for coalition success, and guided by a truly unified and integrated political–military chain of command, the course of the conflict to date might well have been different. Instead, as described especially in the chapters by Ruby and by Thomas, it was often the case that military staffs at the various levels competed with each other for bureaucratic primacy, while different agencies of the American and coalition governments appeared to fight very different wars.

By 2005, there was no one single coalition supra-organization bearing the weight of strategic planning, decision making, and risk assessment across functional areas of responsibility. For example, the commander of the MNF-I did not control the IRMO, the PCO (Project and Contracting Office), or USAID (U.S. Agency for International Development). Nor for that matter did any of these agencies exercise any authority over military matters. Any strategic initiative or shift in strategy likely occurred according to the priorities of the coalition agency exercising functional primacy over specific efforts or events. Thus, it would likely proceed without the requisite integration of the other functional players.

Hydra-like strategic management of the conflict made it very difficult to consolidate success from the tactical to the theater strategic level. While coalition and Iraqi forces might effectively clear insurgents from a strategically significant city or region and subsequently provide a secure environment for economic reconstruction and political and social institution building, that would be no guarantee that the operation or its effects would conform to the priorities or capabilities of the civilian institutions of the coalition and Iraqi governments. Likewise, deployed civilian agencies like USAID or the British Department for

International Development may have a remarkable concept for the development of responsible civil society in a key region rife with volatile ethno-sectarian fault lines. Yet, successful execution of the concept is only likely if the civil agency's idea of key regions coincides with that of the military's and both agents synchronize and resource their efforts commensurate with success. One should not conclude that coordination never occurred among the agencies. When it did, however, it was contingent upon collegial relationships between individuals, relationships that could be disrupted by routine reassignment or redeployment.

The campaign plan for the war in Iraq delineated four clear lines of operation—a political line, an informational line, a security line, and an economic line. The campaign plan stated that it was the combined product of the coalition military and diplomatic staffs as well as the IIG. However, the latter two parties were neither signatories of the plan nor were they bound to it by unified mechanisms for strategic planning and execution. So, while the plan called for the integration of four lines of operation, they were in fact parallel and did not cross, leaving what seemed for officers working on the staff a "dangerous dysfunctionality" as discussed by Graham Allison and Philip Zelikow in *Essence of Decision.*[11]

Being in separate organizations, with historically different cultures, one would not logically expect the director of IRMO to plan his reconstruction efforts to coincide with the upcoming operations conducted by MNC-I (Multinational Corps–Iraq). This is especially true because reconstruction money resided in PCO and the contracts to actually carry out that construction had to be planned well in advance with international and local contractors. Despite expending precious resources on much needed security—spending that produced no direct tangible benefits to Iraqis, progress on projects was irregular at best given continued insurgent violence.

Likewise IRMO had to plan for their own reconstruction efforts over a wide range of functional areas. It was very difficult to synchronize a deliberate reconstruction program with ongoing military operations, as military priorities shifted in response to changing threat conditions. Even if MNC-I wanted to coordinate with the other agencies, it could not be sure they could keep the timing of the operations secret. The mere buildup of contractors in certain areas could be a strong indication of pending military operations, which could undermine success of those operations before they started. This is a classic problem articulated in organizational theory.

Furthermore, the different organizational elements and their leaders exerted significant independence in doing what they thought was best for their own organization from an institutional perspective. Embassy personnel, for example, would attend MNF-I planning sessions to learn what was being planned and exchange ideas on a personal level with their MNF-I counterparts. But they could not necessarily commit their bureaucratic and institutional weight and legitimacy to planned military operations. Likewise, in advance of routine combat operations, the authors perceived a natural military reluctance to prebrief or coordinate with key agencies like the U.S. Embassy, IRMO, or PCO. MNF-I officers from various directorates would attend daily updates with these agencies in order to stay apprised of key developments. However, these formal relationships were more exercises in information gathering than they were evidence of real mechanisms for strategic coordination or synchronization.

Interagency relations were affected by a bureaucratic struggle for primacy among senior officials as well. In the fall of 2004, there were nineteen general officers, sixty-nine colonel-equivalents, and four diplomatic officials holding ambassadorial rank under one roof in the Republican Palace. With the desire by senior leaders to ensure that their subordinates carried enough weight to get results, they sometimes neglected the lessons of bureaucratic infighting as described by Allison and Zelikow.[12] Organizations felt compelled to bring in more senior leaders because of the expectation that the more senior an officer or official, the more likely he/she would be able to coordinate their positions or enforce their organization's corporate view from a position of bureaucratic strength.

In the authors' view, this can, at times, be akin to a bureaucratic arms race where the competition for staff primacy sometimes overshadows results. In this regard, there is little difference between Baghdad and Washington. The competition among organizations for bureaucratic primacy may have adversely impacted coalition success. Any strategic operation requires coordination among the four lines of operation. These lines are often linked, as was revealed in the strategic review described in Mowle's second substantive chapter, and as further elaborated upon by Freier and Rose in their chapter. In the absence of coordination, efforts along one line of operation may collide with efforts along another, such as when military operations against Sunni Arabs in late 2004 made it difficult for their leaders to accept engagement on the political–diplomatic level. Or, as described by Ruby, efforts along one line of operation may not be supported effectively by the others, such as when economic agencies were not aware that they should have projects ready to implement for reconstruction of areas recently secured. Establishment of some leader and combined staff exercising primacy over all of these competing agencies and organizations might have enabled the coalition effort to proceed more effectively.

Consequences

These three trends coalesced as 2004 drew to a close. Everyone agreed that the upcoming elections for the Transitional National Assembly were important, and proposals for postponing them were consistently rejected. No one knew who could be influential within the Sunni Arab community or what the consequences would be of accepting their conditions for participation. As described by various

contributors to this book, military actions at times seemed to undermine political
initiatives, reconstruction stagnated, and many Iraqis were leery about anything
originating from within the coalition. Iraqi military training appeared to fall
further and further behind.

In one sense, the elections were unbelievably successful. Vast numbers of Shia
Arabs and Kurds voted—and a majority of Iraqis were indeed satisfied with their
newly acquired right to make political choices. Violence was startlingly low; there
were less than fifty deaths by most estimates. The insurgents' threats of a blood-
bath did not materialize. Pessimists on the military staffs were sufficiently chided
for their skepticism—if only momentarily. However, the Sunni Arab boycott had
held. As a result, Sunni Arab interests went un- or underrepresented in the new
parliament and its constitutional deliberations. Furthermore, as described in
Mowle's second substantive chapter, the effective alliance between Kurds and
Shia Arabs paved the way for the incorporation of militia elements associated
with those two groups into the Iraqi security services. In that sense, the elections
failed. The coalition's hope was that after the election of January 2005, all Iraqi
political constituencies of consequence would feel that they had a stake in the
development of a new representative political system. As a result of their own
collective decision to boycott the elections, the Sunni Arabs ended up feeling
disenfranchised both by the election's results and by the provisions of the new
Iraqi constitution that could effectively lock them out of real political influence
and an equitable share of Iraq's enormous resource wealth. Thus, the insurgency
continued and by 2006, began tipping into what some would label a nascent
sectarian civil war.[13]

State Failure and State Building in Future American Grand Strategy

U.S. underpreparedness for the demands of regime change or restoration tran-
scends politics, presidential administrations, and bureaucratic boundaries. It is
less an indication of ideological orientation than it is evidence of congenital
underappreciation for the challenges associated with the catastrophic failure of
a large, strategically significant state no matter the cause. The authors suspect,
for example, that one would be hard pressed to find archival evidence of a plan
for the post–World War III reconstruction of Western Europe or a strategic
design for the political, economic, social, and security reconstruction of Cuba
in the aftermath of a communist collapse.

The experience in Iraq has proven that restoration of a secure, self-sustaining
order in the aftermath of state collapse – however it occurs– is labor and capital
intensive. The clear lesson in this experience is that both the employment of
the labor and the investment of the capital require coherent mechanisms for strategic management that cross functional areas of responsibility, apply resources

strategically with precision and discrimination, and finally, enforce discipline and unity of effort from the grand strategic to the tactical levels of execution. That the United States entered Iraq without concepts or mechanisms to do these effectively is now so well-documented as to defy argument. Volumes have already been devoted to the institutional, structural, and cultural gaps with regard to serious state building in Iraq.

The complete collapse of the Iraqi state is illustrative—albeit imperfectly—of the scope of a number of prospective challenges. It demonstrates the indeterminate quality and complexity of a large state reconstruction project proceeding from a standing start, under conditions of continuing violence. The continuing difficulties in Iraq expose clear American underpreparedness for the minimum demands of deliberate, holistic reconstruction of a large, important state. This has proven the case under what might be considered the most ideal circumstances for strategic planning—in Iraq, U.S. decision makers triggered the Iraqi state's collapse and thus knew with great precision the time, place, and manner of the state's impending failure.

In this regard, our challenges in Iraq may have provided the nation and national security leaders a much needed alarm. It is immaterial whether state failure or collapse arrives via externally imposed regime change, uncontrolled civil violence, or unanticipated human disaster. All collapses will demonstrate common characteristics. American strategic thought must proceed from the certainty that a strategically significant state will collapse or fail again and that any number of collapse scenarios would require the United States to invest blood and treasure on par with or greater than that currently deployed in Iraq. Further, the United States should anticipate that the stakes from a grand strategic perspective may be even higher with respect to some future collapses than they are today in Iraq. Iraq is only the most recent example of how until now the United States has had the luxury of choosing where and when to intervene to offset the worst consequences of state collapse and under what circumstances to undertake investment in the comprehensive reconstruction of a failed state and its institutions. Indeed, in most past cases, humanitarian interest trumped strategic calculation with respect to state collapse.[14]

The circumstances are much different today. One can foresee a host of adverse strategic challenges born of the weakness, failure, or complete collapse of a handful of important states. In the absence of decisive intervention, a strategically significant state's devolution into chaos could ultimately defy all but the most extraordinary efforts to bring them under control. Thus, the capacity for state building is now a grand strategic imperative. The trajectory of issues like globalization, proliferation of weapons of mass destruction, contagious extremism, uneven economic and political development, and even public health indicate that some state-building will be necessary to the physical and economic security of the United States and its most important strategic interests.[15]

At once, the U.S.-led coalition in Iraq is trying to establish a secure and durable peace, create a functioning democratic government and market economy, grow a supporting civil society, and empower a population that is both unfamiliar with political choice and socialized toward opposition or subjugation. Yet if we view Iraq as the first and not the last in a series of like-revolutionary efforts at state building and if we recognize that the challenge may grow even more complex and dangerous over time, it leads us toward substantial change in our strategic approach. We must learn from the difficulties in Iraq and be prepared to apply them more rapidly and effectively to even more complex challenges in the future. Many of the worst of these are likely to arrive with little or no strategic warning.

The American experience in Iraq has given the nation, its policy makers, and those charged with policy execution clear evidence of the burdens of great power activism. Since the terrorist attacks of September 2001, the United States has undertaken security and defense strategies that are, at their very core, as much about effecting transformational political and economic change as they are about success on the battlefield. By design, American policy now seeks fundamental change in precrisis political, economic, and social conditions to both effect durable resolution of acute security challenges and undercut the prospects of their future recurrence. Limited war aims like restoration of a stable status quo or forceful modification of an international actor's bad behavior now yield to ambitious goals requiring wholesale transformation of a crisis state or region's preexisting order. This is a reflection of the current predilections of post-9/11 American political leadership. However, it also represents concrete policy recognition of the clear strategic challenge posed by state weakness or failure.

In the authors' opinion, Iraq may be a harbinger of our most urgent future strategic challenges. When the governing institutions and economy of strategically significant states suffer catastrophic failure, whether by external design or internal destabilization, there is very little choice but for responsible and capable states to reestablish functioning, secure, and self-sustaining political, economic, and social order. Interest in state failure and collapse has been a constant in academic debate for some time. However, few have adequately framed it in its proper strategic context. In many cases, the secure maintenance of the United States' position of primary influence may rely on decisive reversal of catastrophic failure of the type experienced in Iraq that occurs in a nation whose continued stable functioning is uniquely important to the United States, its partners, and the international system.

Recent experience in both Afghanistan and Iraq raised the profile and implications of important state failure to new levels. Afghanistan was effectively an ungoverned sanctuary at the disposal of the most "irregular" of strategic challengers for the United States. It was from Afghanistan that capable nonstate competitors conceived and coordinated the most devastating attack on American soil since Pearl Harbor. As a result, American policy makers placed new emphasis on the strategic relevance of many forgotten corners of un- or undergovernance worldwide. Iraq, on the other hand, exposed U.S. decision makers to the hazards of regime removal, where the swift collapse of an established—albeit illegitimate—political order left little to no foundation for the rapid establishment of functioning and secure self-government.

In spite of current challenges in Iraq in particular, both Iraq (if only in hindsight) and Afghanistan may represent the easiest prospective cases with regard to state collapse. One can argue, for example, that Afghanistan's geographic isolation and endemic political and economic underdevelopment make imperfect or indeterminate ends there more acceptable than in many other cases. Further, more universal recognition of the terrorist challenge and its dependence on the relative sanctuary afforded by ungoverned space implies that the costs of strategic management for a challenge like that posed by Afghanistan will be easier to justify in the future. If there are future Iraqs, on the other hand, we have a responsibility to seize advantages implicit in precise knowledge of the time, place, and manner of intervention and regime removal. We must plan more thoroughly for the complexity of a regime's complete collapse if it comes at our hand.

Harder cases of even greater strategic importance lie on the horizon. Four come to mind. The first is a failed nuclear state. The trajectory of proliferation indicates this is an increasingly likely prospect, leaving the most employable instruments of catastrophic attack vulnerable to exploitation by the most irresponsible actors. A failed nuclear state would require the restoration of a secure, functioning, and self-sustaining political order and reestablishment of responsible control over the state's nuclear arsenal. The second is failure of a state that controls access to substantial strategic resources (petroleum being the most obvious) or possesses significant economic capacity and leverage—a highly developed and active market economy, for example. Left unaddressed, state failures of this variety place the integrity and health of national, regional, and global economies at substantial risk. The third category involves failure of states in close proximity to the United States that have large populations capable of uncontrolled migration. There are only a handful of candidates in this category. However, the strategic implications associated with their collapse are numerous and extremely challenging. The final category includes states that could, with a sudden internal destabilization, trigger contagious instability and civil violence in a key strategic region.[16] Here, without quick and meaningful intervention, one key failure may result in the rapid collapse into disorder of a number of other states in a manner that would be darkly reminiscent of the revolutions of 1989. None of these are necessarily mutually exclusive. Like Iraq, all would likely be marked by state building under conditions of continuing violent conflict.[17]

Prospective catalysts or sources of any of these vary substantially. They could arise as a result of sudden political upheaval, economic collapse, pandemic,

natural disaster, and inter- or intrastate war. Though triggers for failure and
the initial course of events that result will obviously color the character of
the strategic response to each, some principles defining the minimum essential
conditions necessary for restoration of secure, functioning, and self-sustaining
political and economic order are common to all. Recognition of and preparation
to establish these minimum essential conditions under the most demanding
conditions—no matter the proximate cause of state collapse—is essential to
initially defining the scope of each particular case, underwriting more durable
strategic success, and ultimately, enabling a more rapid U.S. disengagement from
functional management and trusteeship over any individual state's future course.

The Iraq experience now colors the future course of American interventions.
While there can be reasoned debate about the necessity of the intervention from
a grand strategic perspective, there can be no debate as to the degree to which
American decision makers controlled its timing, organization, resourcing, and
conduct. Future like endeavors—including the collapse of a consequential
state and requisite large-scale American investment in a restored and responsible
stability—may not be so amenable to the preferences of U.S. strategic leaders.
Future collapses may arrive with little or no strategic warning in a state whose
stable functioning is uniquely important to the United States and whose social,
political, and economic conditions are equally, if not more complex, as those
found by the coalition in Iraq.

The American Iraq experience leaves us with two unanswered questions. Will
the difficulties encountered in Iraq after major combat operations self-deter a
rapid and effectual American response to the next strategically significant crisis
of order and governance? If not, will the United States and its institutions have
internalized the lessons of Iraq so that intervention will yield decisive and durable
political, economic, and security results?

NOTES

Chapter 1

1. *National Strategy for Victory in Iraq* (Washington: GPO, November 2005), 1. This document openly stated the "desired end state" that had previously been classified.

2. Ibid., 3.

3. President George W. Bush, response at a Press Conference, August 21, 2006, http://www.whitehouse.gov/news/releases/2006/08/20060821.html.

4. John Murtha, CBS Sunday Morning, March 19, 2006, http://www.house.gov/apps/list/press/pa12_murtha/PRcbssunday.html.

5. Borzou Daragahi, "Kurdish Oil Deal Shocks Iraq's Political Leaders," *Los Angeles Times,* December 1, 2005; "Drilling Begins for Second Oil Well in Kurdistan," *Xebat,* reprinted in *Iraqi Press Monitor* 454 (15 May 2006); Steve Negus, "Iraq Faces Clash with Kurds over Oil Deals," *Financial Times,* May 23, 2006.

6. For discussion of this period, see Bob Woodward, *Plan of Attack* (New York: Simon & Schuster, 2004), 9–23; Michael R. Gordon and Bernard E. Trainor, *Cobra II: The Inside Story of the Invasion and Occupation of Iraq* (New York: Pantheon Books, 2006), 10–5; Richard Butler, *The Greatest Threat: Iraq, Weapons of Mass Destruction, and the Crisis of Global Security* (New York: Public Affairs, 2000); Graham S. Pearson, *The UNSCOM Saga: Chemical and Biological Weapons Non-Proliferation* (London: Macmillan Press, 2000); Scott Ritter, *Endgame: Solving the Iraq Problem – Once and for All* (New York: Simon & Schuster, 1999); and Philip H. Gordon and Jeremy Shapiro, *Allies at War: America, Europe, and the Crisis over Iraq* (New York: McGraw-Hill, 2004), 39–44, 94.

7. Those interested in this question could look to Gordon and Trainor, *Cobra II,* 124–30; Seymour M. Hersh, *Chain of Command* (New York: HarperCollins, 2004), 203–47; Bob Woodward, *Plan of Attack,* 194–202; Thomas E. Ricks, *Fiasco: The American Military Adventure in Iraq* (New York: Penguin, 2006) 3–114; or Michael Isikoff and David Corn, *Hubris: The Inside Story of Spin, Scandal, and the Selling of the Iraq War* (New York: Crown, 2006).

8. See Thomas S. Mowle, "Iraq's Militia Problem," *Survival* 48 (August 2006): 41–58.

9. Such books include Gordon and Trainor, *Cobra II;* Mark Etherington, *Revolt on the Tigris: The al-Sadr Uprising and the Governing of Iraq* (Ithaca, NY: Cornell University Press,

2005); and John Ballard, *Fighting for Fallujah: A New Dawn for Iraq* (Westport, CT: Praeger, 2006).

10. Two others are Larry Diamond, *Squandered Victory: The American Occupation and the Bungled Effort to Bring Democracy to Iraq* (New York: Henry Holt and Company, 2005) and L. Paul Bremer III with Malcolm McConnell, *My Year in Iraq: The Struggle to Build a Future of Hope* (New York: Simon & Schuster, 2006). Both of these cover an earlier time period.

11. Bremer, *My Year in Iraq,* and Diamond, *Squandered Victory.* See also William Langewiesche, "Welcome to the Green Zone," *Atlantic Monthly,* November 2004.

12. Even Ricks, *Fiasco,* 390–429, only lightly touches on the time period described in this book.

13. These events, and the loss of Sunni Arab support, are depicted in the film *My Country, My Country* (2006).

Chapter 2

1. President Bush and Prime Minister Tony Blair of the United Kingdom Participate in Joint Press Availability, May 25, 2006, http://www.whitehouse.gov/news/releases/2006/05/20060525-12.html.

2. Ibid.

3. Ibid.

4. The classic work is Thomas C. Schelling, *The Strategy of Conflict* (Cambridge: Harvard University Press, 1960).

5. For example, Donald Rumsfeld, Media Availability with Jay Garner, June 18, 2003, transcript at http://www.defenselink.mil/Transcripts/Transcript.aspx?TranscriptID=2758.

6. L. Paul Bremer III with Malcolm McConnell, *My Year in Iraq: The Struggle to Build a Future of Hope* (New York: Simon & Schuster, 2006).

7. U.S. Department of State, *The Future of Iraq Project: Overview,* May 12, 2003, 4–6.

8. Michael R. Gordon and Bernard E. Trainor, *Cobra II: The Inside Story of the Invasion and Occupation of Iraq* (New York: Pantheon Books, 2006), 158–9; Bob Woodward, *Plan of Attack* (New York: Simon & Schuster, 2004), 283–4; Thomas E. Ricks, *Fiasco: The American Military Adventure in Iraq* (New York: Penguin, 2006), 103–4, asserts that the order came from Vice President Dick Cheney.

9. The author's assessment, but supported by Gordon and Trainor, *Cobra II,* 159. One of the project's greatest published advocates is David L. Phillips, *Losing Iraq: Inside the Postwar Reconstruction Fiasco* (Boulder: Westview Press, 2005).

10. U.S. Department of State, *The Future of Iraq Project.* Its section on disarmament and demobilization almost completely focuses on Iraqi government forces and ignores the ethnic militias—see Tab 9: Disarmament, Demobilization, and Reintegration of Paramilitary Forces.

11. U.S. Department of State, *The Future of Iraq Project,* March 2003, 14–5.

12. Ibid., 27.

13. Ibid., 14–5, 29.

14. All three quotes from Nigel Aylwin-Foster, "Changing the Army for Counterinsurgency Operations," *Military Review,* November–December 2005, 7.

15. John Nagl, *Counterinsurgency Lessons from Malaya and Vietnam: Learning to Eat Soup with a Knife* (New York: Praeger, 2002), 217.

16. These books are referenced as the chapter goes on, but particularly useful are Gordon and Trainor, *Cobra II;* Bremer, *My Year In Iraq;* Woodward, *Plan of Attack;* Larry Diamond,

Squandered Victory: The American Occupation and the Bungled Effort to Bring Democracy to Iraq (New York: Henry Holt and Company, 2005); Ricks, *Fiasco;* Michael Isikoff and David Corn, *Hubris: The Inside Story of Spin, Scandal, and the Selling of the Iraq War* (New York: Crown, 2006); and James Fallows, *Blind Into Baghdad: America's War in Iraq* (New York: Vintage, 2006).

17. Transcript of Press Conference at http://www.whitehouse.gov/news/releases/2003/03/20030306-8.html.

18. Within the Bush Administration, Secretary of State of Colin Powell seems to have been the strongest voice in favor of a UNSCR if things went wrong—see Woodward, *Plan of Attack,* pp. 151, 75.

19. *The National Security Strategy of the United States of America* (Washington: GPO, September 2002), 15. For discussion, see John Lewis Gaddis, "A Grand Strategy of Transformation," *Foreign Policy* 133 (November–December 2002): 50–7.

20. William C. Thompson, *One Year Later: The Fiscal Impact of 9/11 on New York City* (New York: City of New York, 2002), 1.

21. *The National Security Strategy of the United States of America,* 15.

22. Dick Cheney, Speech to the Veterans of Foreign Wars 103rd National Convention, Nashville, August 26, 2002, http://www.whitehouse.gov/news/releases/2002/08/20020826.html.

23. Quotations from UNSCR 1441. For the diplomacy, see Philip H. Gordon and Jeremy Shapiro, *Allies at War: America, Europe, and the Crisis over Iraq* (New York: McGraw-Hill, 2004), 108–14.

24. Transcript of Press Conference at http://www.whitehouse.gov/news/releases/2003/03/20030306-8.html.

25. Quoted from the version printed as "'The Transatlantic Bond Is Our Guarantee of Freedom:' Declaration of Eight European Leaders in Support of United States on Iraq," *Washington Post,* January 31, 2003, http://www.washingtonpost.com/.

26. See Gordon and Shapiro, *Allies at War,* 128–36.

27. Conclusions of the Extraordinary European Council, Brussels, 17 February 2003, Council of the European Union document number 6466/03.

28. Woodward, *Plan of Attack,* 232–6, 287.

29. Gordon and Shapiro, *Allies at War,* 118–23, 141–6.

30. Woodward, *Plan of Attack,* 308–9.

31. Rumsfeld News Briefing, April 11, 2003, http://www.defenselink.mil/transcripts/2003/tr20030411-secdef0090.html.

32. See Bremer, *My Year in Iraq,* 13–9, 29–31.

33. Gordon and Trainor, *Cobra II,* 4.

34. Ibid., 28–37.

35. Ibid., 27, 53, 68; George Packer, *The Assassins' Gate* (New York: Farrar, Straus, and Giroux, 2005), 118–20.

36. General Eric Shinseki, U.S. Senate Armed Services Committee Hearing On FY 2004 Defense Authorization, February 25, 2003.

37. Donald Rumsfeld, "Secretary Rumsfeld Media Availability with Afghan President Karzai," February 27, 2003, http://www.dod.gov/transcripts/2003/t02272003_t0227ap.html.

38. Paul Wolfowitz, statement to the Committee on the Budget, House of Representatives, February 27, 2003, 8.

39. Ibid.

40. Ibid., 9.

41. Ibid.

42. Ibid., 9–10.

43. Ibid., 10.

44. Bremer, *My Year in Iraq*, 10.

45. Gordon and Trainor, *Cobra II*, 157–8.

46. Ibid., 18, 137. For more on Chalabi's projections, and their influence on American thinking, see Seymour M. Hersh, *Chain of Command* (New York: HarperCollins, 2004), 163–84; Packer, *Assassins' Gate;* and Phillips, *Losing Iraq.*

47. Gordon and Trainor, *Cobra II*, 105, 162.

48. For critique of the decision, and Bremer's justification, see Gordon and Trainor, *Cobra II*, 482–5; Packer, *Assassins' Gate*, 190–6; and Phillips, *Losing Iraq*, 143–53.

49. Bremer, *My Year in Iraq*, 54–6.

50. CPA (Coalition Provisional Authority) Order 1, "De-Ba'athification of Iraqi Society," May 16, 2003, paragraph 1.2. See Bremer, *My Year in Iraq*, 40–5 for more discussion.

51. Ibid., paragraph 1.3.

52. Ibid., paragraph 1.6.

53. CPA Order 5, "Establishment of the Iraqi De-Baathification Council," May 25, 2003, paragraph 3.2.

54. CPA Memorandum 1, "Implementation of De-Ba'athification Order No. 1," June 3, 2003, paragraph 4.1.b.

55. CPA Memorandum 7, "Delegation of Authority under De-Ba'athification Order No. 1," November 4, 2003.

56. Transitional Administrative Law, March 8, 2004, article 49.

57. CPA Order 2, "Dissolution of Entities," May 23, 2003, paragraph 3.6. For additional discussion, see Bremer, *My Year in Iraq*, 57–8.

58. CPA Order 2, paragraph 5.

59. CPA Order 22, "Creation of a New Iraqi Army," August 7, 2003, paragraphs 6.4 and 6.5.

60. CPA Order 27, "Establishment of the Facilities Protection Service," September 4, 2003; CPA Order 28, "Establishment of the Iraqi Civil Defense Corps," September 3, 2003.

61. Bremer, *My Year in Iraq*, 39.

62. Ibid., 317.

63. Ibid., 332–3; Phillips, *Losing Iraq*, 195–8; and Diamond, *Squandered Victory*, 229–35.

64. Bremer, *My Year in Iraq*, 190–202.

65. For discussion of the whole period, see Bremer, *My Year in Iraq*, 311–32; Diamond, *Squandered Victory*, 231–6; Mark Etherington, *Revolt on the Tigris: The al-Sadr Uprising and the Governing of Iraq* (Ithaca, NY: Cornell University Press, 2005), 149–93; Philips, *Losing Iraq*, 198–201; and Ricks, *Fiasco*, 321–62.

66. Bremer, *My Year in Iraq*, 381.

Chapter 3

1. Joint Publication 1-02, DoD Dictionary of Military Terms.

2. Personal correspondence by author with Strategic Planning Council member who requested his name be withheld: "I have been pinged by the Air Staff about Iraq more in the last two weeks than in the last two years. The leading questions are 'Why did the Air Force representatives on the Strategic Planning Council recommend NOT to execute

Operation Iraqi Freedom, and why didn't we convince the rest of the members that we had it right?' The bottom line is that we couldn't see an end state."

3. Jeffrey Gingras and Tomislav Ruby, "Morality in Modern Aerial Warfare," *Joint Forces Quarterly,* Summer 2000, 110.

4. Samuel Huntington, *Soldier and the State* (Cambridge: Harvard University Press, 1957) and Peter Feaver, *Armed Servants* (Cambridge: Harvard University Press, 2003), both argue that oversight of the military by national civilian leadership is the way to get the military to do what you want them to do. However, neither author conceives of civilian leadership abdicating their oversight responsibility, thus neither seriously addresses the point of what the military should do when vague guidance, conflicting guidance or no guidance at all is given with respect to objectives and end states.

5. JP 5-00.1, Joint Doctrine for Campaign Planning (Washington: CJCS, 2002), II-3.

6. Perhaps the most salient school of literature on the subject is the time inconsistency literature dealing with monetary policy and the need to delegate authority from election-minded politicians to professional bureaucrats. See Torben Iversen and David Soskice, "New Macroeconomics and Political Science," *Annual Review of Political Science* 9 (2006): 425–53; also William Bernhard, J. Laurence Broz, and William Roberts Clark, "The Political Economy of Monetary Institutions," *International Organization* 56 (Autumn 2002). For a discussion of vote maximizing by elected officials, see William Niskanen, *Bureaucracy and Representative Government* (Chicago: Atherton Aldene, 1971). For discussions of the interactions between voters and elected officials, see also Clifford Carrubba, "The Electoral Connection in European Union Politics," *Journal of Politics* 63 (February 2001); Torben Iversen, "Political Leadership and representation in Western European Democracy: A Test of Three Models of Voting," *American Journal of Political Science* 38 (1994).

7. Senior Bulgarian military representative to MNF-I; personal discussions with author.

8. Joseph P. Hoar, "A CINC's Perspective," *Joint Forces Quarterly,* Autumn 1993, 62.

9. "President Clinton Address to the Nation Regarding NATO Air Strikes Against Serbia," March 24, 1999, http://www.pub.whitehouse.gov/uri-res/I2R?urn:pdi://oma.eop.gov.us/1999/3/24/8.text.1 (accessed April 13, 2000).

10. Colonel Tom Hyde, Chief of Checkmate, HQ USAF/XOOC, personal interview by author, May 14, 2002, The Pentagon, Washington, D.C.

11. Colonel Tom Hyde, interview by author. President Bush laid out three primary objectives as recommended by military planners: Destruction of terrorist infrastructure in Afghanistan, capture of terrorist leaders, and cessation of terrorist activities in Afghanistan. However, Secretary of Defense Rumsfeld gave different objectives on the same day that President Bush briefed the United States on the war's objectives. See http://www.global security.org/military/ops/enduring-freedom.htm.

12. Walter Clark and Jeffrey Herbst, "Somalia and the Future of Humanitarian Intervention," *Foreign Affairs,* March–April 1996, 76.

13. Arjan El Fassed, "Dutch Occupation Forces to Leave Iraq Mid-March, Electronic Iraq," January 17, 2005, http://electroniciraq.net/news/1794.shtml (accessed February 11, 2006).

14. See Richard Sobel, "Portraying American Public Opinion Towards the Bosnia Crisis," *Harvard International Journal of Press/Politics,* 3 (Spring 1998); Erica Goode, "How Culture Molds Habits of Thought," *New York Times,* August 8, 2000, http://www.artsci.lsu.edu/phil/phil1/cogburn/currentcourses/1001fa01/appearanceversusreality.html and http://www.trini center.com/historicalviews/cultureandthoughts.htm. Additionally, there are recent news

reports about purposeful misreporting and altering of photographs by individual journalists to affect public perceptions of the conflict between Israel and Hizballah in Lebanon; see http://news.yahoo.com/s/nm/20060807/ts_nm/mideast_reuters_dc_3 and http://www.little greenfootballs.com/weblog/.

15. Chairman of the Joint Chiefs of Staff, Final Draft Joint Publication 3-0, Joint Operations (December 23, 2005).

16. The 1997 Iraq census covered only 15 of 18 governates. See the UN Iraqi demographic brief at http://www.un.org/News/briefings/docs/2003/iraqdemobrf.doc.htm.

17. CNN/USA Today/Gallup Poll, March 22–April 9, 2004, at http://i.a.cnn.net/cnn/2004/WORLD/meast/04/28/iraq.poll/iraq.poll.4.28.pdf (accessed February 11, 2006).

18. William Langeweisch, "Iraq's Walled City," *Atlantic Monthly,* October 2004.

19. The coalition political authorities commissioned a poll in October 2004 , the results of which were used by planners in the Strategy, Plans, and Assessments office for use in developing courses of action for security around the time of the January 2005 election. Coalition authorities were very concerned that the pollsters not be identified with foreign governments for the safety of those conducting the polls.

20. This was the same survey used by coalition planners to determine courses of action.

21. For an excellent history of the British occupation of Iraq in the 1920s, see Toby Dodge, *Inventing Iraq* (New York: Columbia University Press, 2003).

22. General Casey was briefed on a daily basis by his directorate of Strategic Communications on misreporting by regional and international media. The day the report on the selective targeting of old ladies in Fallujah was briefed in November 2004, Casey asked what if anything the coalition could do to rebut these absurd claims. The consensus among senior leadership was to do nothing to lend any credibility to the reports by responding to them.

23. For an excellent summary of the Principal–Agent model, see Richard W. Waterman, Amelia Rouse, and Robert Wright, "The Venues of Influence: A New Theory of Political Control of the Bureaucracy," *Journal of Public Administration Research and Theory* 8 (January 1998): 13–39.

24. See Matthew McCubbins, "Abdication or Delegation? Congress, the Bureaucracy and the Delegation Dilemma," *Regulation* 22 (Summer 1999).

25. See John D. Huber and Charles R. Shippan, *Deliberate Discretion* (Cambridge: Cambridge University Press, 2003).

26. For articles on the importance of aligning principal–agent motivations, see Thomas J. Barth, "Constitutional Subordinate Authority," *Administration and Society* 25 (August 1993); James Q. Wilson, *Bureaucracy* (New York: Basic Books, 1989); John Brehm and Scott Gates, "Donut Shops and Speed Traps: Evaluating Models of Supervision of Police Behavior," *American Journal of Political Science* 27 (1993): 555–81.

27. Tom Ruby, "Making Moral Targeting Decisions in War: The Importance of Principal-Agent Motivation Alignment and Constraining Doctrine," *Journal of Military Ethics* 5 (2006): 12–31.

28. Andrew Rathmell, November 2004, Baghdad. Personal interview with author.

29. Nancy A. Youssef and Patrick Kirkstra, "Deadly Blasts rattle Iraq's Green Zone," *Seattle Times,* October 15, 2004, http://seattletimes.nwsource.com/html/iraq/2002063967_iraq15.html (accessed August 12, 2006).

30. In addition to the author's personal notes, see http://www.aforadventure.com/robdispatches8.html for a short description of what happened Halloween 2004 at the Embassy pool.

Chapter 4

1. Notable examples of current criminal insurgencies are the narco-trafficking antigovernment guerrillas in Colombia (the FARC and ELN) and Peru (the *Sendero Luminoso*), and the bandit guerrillas in Nepal (the radical Maoists), who rob banks and tourists for income to support their insurrection. The ELAS guerrillas of the Greek Civil War of 1944–49 and the "Communist-Terrorists" of the Malayan Emergency of 1948–60, both had their roots in rural bandit groups. When the Salvadoran Civil War ended in 1992, United Nations observers found that almost a third of the FMLN guerrillas refused to leave the mountains and disarm—and discovered that these were actually criminal bands and gangs who would not submit to the rule of law.

2. Major General Eaton saw the formation of the post–World War II *Bundeswehr* (the new German federal army) as an example for his effort in Iraq.

3. Separately in the British zone in southern Iraq, the British Royal Marines and the Royal Navy created the IRPS (Iraqi Riverine Patrol Service) as a maritime antismuggling unit which by 2004 was judged by them to be a "success story."

4. The "Iraqi Civil Defense Corps" was a misnomer applied by U.S. staff officers to Iraqi neighborhood self-defense militias. The name caused confusion, as "civil defense" units in the Iraqi lexicon referred to fire department and public health personnel. The ICDC label was shortly dropped in favor of "Iraqi National Guard," or ING, which was later abandoned when those units were absorbed into the Iraqi Army.

5. Major General Paul Eaton's Coalition Military Assistance Training Team staff was composed of a Deputy Commanding General, who was British; his Chief of Staff, a sixty-year-old U.S. Marine Corps Reserve colonel who had served in Vietnam and was recently an airplane broker; a C-1 Personnel Officer, who was a Marine Corps lieutenant colonel; a C-2 Intelligence Officer, who was a U.S. Army Reserve lieutenant colonel; a C-3 Operations Officer, who was a colonel from the Combat Developments department at the U.S. Army Infantry School; a C-4 Logisitics Officer, who was a colonel from the same department at the U.S. Army Field Artillery School; and a C-5 Plans Officer, who was a British Royal Marine Commando colonel. The primary CMATT interlocutor with the U.S. Congress was a lieutenant colonel of the Spanish Marines.

6. According to Maj. Gen. Eaton, the Secretary of Defense had imposed funding restrictions for the CMATT. As an example, the New Iraqi Army needed $243 million for construction of new barracks for sixteen new Iraqi battalions in April 2004, but only $160 million was allowed, and of that $74 million was withheld "to protect the money for potential use elsewhere."

7. To the Iraqis, U.S. ally Turkey is considered a traditional enemy and serious threat.

8. Inspector Steve Burfitt's primary assistant at the Headquarters of the Coalition Provisional Authority in Baghdad in January 2004 was Constable Calvin Tonks, also of the U.K. Police.

9. The Canadian-designed "Niche Records Management System" can be viewed at http://www.nicherms.com.

10. In February 2004, Mr. Steve Castel was the Senior Advisor to the Iraqi Ministry of the Interior. He was esteemed by military staff officers who worked with him as "highly intelligent" and "very capable."

11. In 2004, the MND-SE (Multinational Division-Southeast) was then composed of the British 1st Armored Division headquarters, a U.K. armored brigade, an Italian brigade, a Dutch battle group, a Danish battalion, a Japanese battalion, and detachments of Norwegians,

Czechs, Icelanders, Portuguese, New Zealanders, and Lithuanians. Both British and coalition officers privately attributed the lower incidence of attacks against their soldiers to "the fact that we're not Americans," meaning the population's ire was more focused on the U.S. forces than the other nationalities' units. A more obvious factor that would account for this disparity in number of attacks was that the majority of the population in the MND-SE zone were Shia Arabs, who suffered under that Sunni-dominated Saddam regime and hence were more tolerant of the foreign troops who had ousted their oppressors—whereas the U.S. occupation zone held the deposed Sunni Arabs who bitterly resented their downfall at the hands of the Americans.

12. The Multinational Division-Southeast headquarters expected a shipment of 1,000 desktop computers from Kuwait in February 2004 for the Iraqi police forces in their zone. Each police station was to receive several. Apparently, no Iraqi police organization below national level had previously used any kind of computer for any purpose.

13. Brigadier General Fast noted she had to work "to keep the Coalition cell morale up" because they do not have the same high-level Special Compartmented Information category access as the other cells, an important distinction among intelligence personnel.

14. The staff's perspective of the viability of this organization was not unanimous. In contrast to Brigadier General Fast's assessment of the CJTF-7 intelligence fusion cell as mostly successful, another senior coalition officer described its functioning as "deplorable" and its interagency coordination as virtually nonexistent.

15. Brigadier General John Custer posited that the shortage of intelligence personnel most suited for counterinsurgency warfare could be traced back to 1998, when the U.S. Army deliberately reduced its human intelligence corps by half in favor of technical collection means.

Chapter 5

1. CPA (Coalition Provisional Authority) Order 2, May 23, 2003.

2. Newt Gingrich, "A Leaner, Meaner Military," *Washington Post,* March 4, 2006.

3. CPA Order 22, August 18, 2003.

4. CPA Order 28, September 3, 2003.

5. CPA Order 1, May 16, 2003, and CPA Order 22, section 6, paragraph 5.

6. Anthony H. Cordesman, *Iraqi Security Forces: A Strategy For Success* (Westport, CT: Praeger, 2006), 62.

7. CPA Order 73, April 22, 2004.

8. Department of Defense Inspector General, *Statement of Mr. Thomas F. Gimble, Acting Inspector General, Department of Defense, before the Subcommittee on National Security, Emerging Threats, and International Relations, House Committee on Government Reform, on "Iraq Reconstruction, Governance and Security Oversight"* (Washington, D.C.: Department of Defense, October 18, 2005), 10, http://www.dodig.osd.mil/fo/tetimony_DODIG_Iraq_Final_101805.pdf.

9. NSPD (National Security Presidential Directive) 36, *United States Government Operations in Iraq,* May 11, 2004.

10. Ibid.

11. JP (Joint Publication) 5-0, *Doctrine for Planning Joint Operations* (Washington, D.C.: Department of Defense, April 13, 1995), II-18.

12. Ibid., II-19.

13. JP 5-00.2, *Joint Task Force Planning Guidance and Procedures* (Washington, D.C.: Department of Defense, January 13, 1999), II-3. One advantage of this structure is that it is used commonly across service lines. On an Air Force staff, the A-5 is the planning office; in an Army division, it is the G-5; and so forth, making it easier for planners to identify the complementary section on another staff.

14. This general guidance for the elements of a campaign plan is drawn from "Fundamentals of Campaign Plans" in JP 5-0.

15. "Banking in Iraq: A Tricky Operation," *Economist,* June 24, 2004, http://www.econo mist.com/finance/displayStory.cfm?story_id=2792407. The article notes that "Electronic links among bank branches, let alone to the outside world, are rare" in mid-2004.

16. Field Manual 25-100, *Training the Force* (Washington, D.C.: Department of the Army, November 15, 1988), Chapter 2.

17. "MNSTC-I Information," http://www.mnstci.iraq.centcom.mil/mission.htm.

18. SGT Jared Zalbado, "Iraqis to Undergo 'Explosive Ordnance' Training," *Advisor,* December 11, 2004, http://www.mnstci.iraq.centcom.mil/docs/advisor/archive/122004/11 DecTheAdvisor.pdf.

19. See, for example, Steven Metz and Raymond Millen, *Insurgency and Counterinsurgency in the 21st Century: Reconceptualizing Threat and Response* (Carlisle Barracks, PA: U.S. Army Strategic Studies Institute, November 2004), 29. The authors argue that "Police capability has always been vital to destroy insurgent political undergrounds but is becoming even more so as insurgency mutates. Today effective, preferably multinational law enforcement support is vital to limit insurgent access to resources whether through direct criminal activity or ties to global organized crime." This presumes, however, that the police play a positive role in society.

20. Conversation with the author, November 2004.

21. Kim Sengupta, "Massacre at Baquba," *Independent (UK),* October 25, 2004.

22. MNSTC-I J-5 staff meeting, January 2005.

23. DoD IG, 9.

24. SGT Jared Zabaldo, "Iraqi Ministry of Interior Orders Highway Patrol to 6,300 Strong," *Advisor,* October 30, 2004, http://www.mnstci.iraq.centcom.mil/docs/advisor/ archive/102004/TheAdvisorOct30.pdf.

25. Greg Jaffe, "New Factor in Iraq: Irregular Brigades Fill Security Void," *Wall Street Journal,* February 16, 2005.

26. Ibid.

27. LTG John Vines, MNC-I Commanding General, interviewed on National Public Radio's *Morning Edition,* March 14, 2005, http://www.npr.org/templates/story/story.php? storyId=4533519.

28. Conversation with the author, December 2004.

29. In November 2003, Dr. Condoleeza Rice, then the National Security Advisor, spoke of the insurgents and said "We will get a handle on this security situation and resolve the problem." See "Interview of the National Security Advisor by KING-TV, Seattle, Washington," November 10, 2003, White House Office of the Press Secretary, http://www.whitehouse.gov /news/releases/2003/11/20031111-2.html. The current emphasis is on developing Iraqi forces that can "resolve the problem." See *National Strategy for Victory in Iraq* (Washington, D.C.: GPO, November 2005), 3.

30. Warren A. Trest, *Air Commando One: Heinie Aderholt and America's Secret Air Wars* (New York: Harper Collins, 2000), and Edward G. Landsdale, *In the Midst of Wars: An American's Mission to Southeast Asia* (New York: Fordham University Press, 1991).

31. U.S. Marine Corps, *Small Wars Manual* (Manhattan, KS: Sunflower University Press, 1996).

32. Walter F. Ulmer (LTG, USA, ret), "Military Leadership into the 21st Century: Another 'Bridge Too Far'?" *Parameters,* Spring 1998, 4–25.

33. U.S. Army War College, "Study on Military Professionalism," August 1970, 13.

34. Ibid., 23.

35. LTG Martin Dempsey, Commanding General, Multinational Security Transition Command-Iraq, "DoD Operational Update Briefing" (Baghdad, December 2, 2005), http://www.mnf-iraq.com/index.php?option=com_content&task=view&id=2051&Itemid=30.

36. E-mail from MNSTC-I staff officer to the author, May 12, 2005.

37. Cordesman, 336.

38. Ibid., 212.

39. General George Casey, MNF-I Commanding General, DoD Press Conference, Washington, D.C., September 30, 2005, http://www.defenselink.mil/Transcripts/Transcript.aspx?TranscriptID=2584.

40. *National Strategy for Victory in Iraq,* 20.

41. SGT Lorie Jewell, "MNSTC-I CG Addresses Troops," *Advisor,* September 24, 2005, http://www.mnstci.iraq.centcom.mil/docs/advisor/archive/092005/24SepTheAdvisor.pdf.

42. Rod Nordland, "Iraq's Repairman," *Newsweek,* July 5, 2004, 24.

43. John A. Nagl, *Learning to Eat Soup With a Knife,* 2nd ed. (Chicago: University of Chicago Press, 2005). The foreword to the new edition was written by General Peter Schoomaker, the current Chief of Staff of the U.S. Army, suggesting high-level interest in Nagl's observations.

44. The Army and Marine Corps Announce the Release of the Counterinsurgency Field Manual, U.S. Army Combined Arms Center News Release, December 15, 2006, http://usacac.army.mil/CAC/Repository/Materials/USA-USMCCOINNewsRelease.pdf.

Chapter 6

1. Joint Publication 1, *Joint Warfare of the Armed Forces of the United States,* November 14, 2000, I-5-8.

2. Army Field Manual 101-5-1, *Operational Terms and Graphics,* September 30, 1996.

3. See Pierre Lessard, "Campaign Design for Winning the War . . . and the Peace," *Parameters,* Summer 2005, 36–50.

4. JP 5-00.1, *Joint Doctrine for Campaign Planning,* January 25, 2002, GL-5.

5. FM 101-5-1.

6. JP 5-00.1, II.14

7. Most estimates at the time suggest that the Shia Arabs are 55 to 60 percent of the population, the Kurds and Sunni Arabs 15 to 20 percent each, with Turkomen, Christians, and other minorities combining for about 5 to 10 percent of the population. Election results since then have supported these assumptions.

8. Larry Diamond, "What Went Wrong in Iraq," *Foreign Affairs* 83 (September–October 2004): 44–8, and Hiwa Osman, "Questions Surround Elections," *Iraqi Crisis Report* 37 (November 28, 2003).

9. Osman, "Questions."

10. Mohammed Ali al-Hassani, "Iraqi Shias Call for Elections," *Iraqi Crisis Report* 24 (June 25, 2003).

11. Zaki Yahya, "Iraqis Call for Self-Rule," *Iraqi Crisis Report* 25 (July 2, 2003).

12. Adnan Karem and Haytham al-Husseini, "Shias Demand Free Elections," *Iraqi Crisis Report* 45 (January 22, 2004).

13. Kamal Ali, "Ballot Debate Rumbles On," *Iraqi Crisis Report* 47 (February 9, 2004).

14. Diamond, "What Went Wrong," 48–50.

15. TAL 2.B.1.

16. TAL Annex Section 1.

17. TAL 2.A, 2.B.2.

18. UNSCR 1546, paragraph 4.

19. The term "secular," sometimes used to describe Iraqi leaders who are not overtly tied to religious parties, is both inaccurate (their views on religion are congruent to those of the American religious right) and offensive to a devout Muslim. Members of the Iraqi Communist Party are among the few who would accept such a label.

20. For details on members of the IIG, see its website, http://www.iraqigovernment.org/index_en.htm.

21. MNF-I had taken to calling this area Thawra, its original name. The previous government had renamed it as Saddam City; after the war it was called Sadr City in honor of Moqtada's father, Muhammad Sadiq al-Sadr, killed in 1999 by the Ba'ath government.

22. Anthony H. Cordesman, "U.S. Policy in Iraq: A 'Realist' Approach to its Challenges and Opportunities," (Center for Strategic and International Studies, August 6, 2004), 7.

23. Ibid., 20–4.

24. Department of State Office of Research survey, September 16, 2004.

25. Coalition Provisional Authority Order 91, Regulation of Armed Forces and Militias Within Iraq, June 7, 2004.

26. Roger Howard, *Iran in Crisis? Nuclear Ambitions and the American Response* (London: Zed Books, 2004), 77–85; Mahan Abedin, "Dossier: The Supreme Council for the Islamic Revolution in Iraq (SCIRI)," *Middle East Intelligence Bulletin* 5 (October 2003).

27. Remarks of the Prime Minister of Iraq, June 7, 2004; Transition and Reintegration Strategy, May 21, 2004, 5.

28. Iraq's Transitional Administrative Law, June 2004, Article 54.

29. *Disarmament, Demobilization, and Reintegration of Ex-Combatants in a Peacekeeping Environment: Principles and Guidelines* (New York: United Nations, 2000).

30. Transition and Reintegration Strategy, 3–5.

31. A detailed discussion of the militia problem is in Thomas S. Mowle, "Iraq's Militia Problem," *Survival* 48 (2006): 41–58.

32. CPA Order 96, paragraph 3.3.

33. CPA Order 96, paragraph 3.4.

34. CPA Order 96, paragraphs 4.3 and 4.4.

35. CPA Order 97, paragraph 2.2; IECI Regulation 03/2004, amended October 25, 2004, paragraph 3.6.4.

36. List from http://www.irc-co.com/elections/en/parties.asp.

37. Survey of Iraqi Public Opinion, International Republican Institute, September 24–October 4, 2004.

38. The most concise description of the Iraqi electoral lists is "Iraqi Election: Who Ran?" BBC World, January 31, 2005, http://news.bbc.co.uk/1/hi/world/middle_east/4051977.stm. See also Max Sicherman, "Iraqi Elections: What, How, and Who," *Policy Watch 944* (The Washington Institute, January 24, 2005), http://www.washingtoninstitute.org/templateC05.php?CID=2237.

39. *Al-Nahdhah,* reprinted in *Iraqi Press Monitor* 191 (November 10, 2004).

40. SCIRI's *Al-Adala,* reprinted in *Iraqi Press Monitor* 196 (November 24, 2004) indicated IIP's support, while *Al-Mada,* reprinted in *Iraqi Press Monitor* 197 (November 25, 2004) reported that the IIP had renewed its call for postponement.

41. *Asharq al-Aswat,* reprinted in *Iraqi Press Monitor* 196 (November 24, 2004) discussed weather, while the KDP's *al-Taakhi,* reprinted in *Iraqi Press Monitor* 198 (November 26, 2004) described other reasons to postpone elections.

42. *Addustour,* reprinted in *Iraqi Press Monitor* 215 (January 10, 2005).

43. *Al-Sabah al-Jadeed,* reprinted in *Iraqi Press Monitor* 199 (November 29, 2004).

44. Ibid., 202 (December 2, 2004).

45. Ali, "Ballot Debate."

46. Dhiya Rasan, "Jailed Without Trial," *Iraqi Crisis Report* 50 (March 1, 2004). The IECI did not allow prisoners to vote since they could not get to polling centers; polling centers were not set up in the prisons. *Al-Mashriq,* reprinted in *Iraqi Press Monitor* 185 (November 2, 2004).

47. Kamran al-Karadaghi, "Sunni Election Dilemma," *Iraqi Crisis Report* 97 (January 14, 2005).

48. This sentiment was repeated many times over a long period of time. This specific quote is from remarks at the White House on 14 November 2003, taken from the United States Mission to the European Union, http://eu.usmission.gov/Categories/GlobalAffairs/Iraq/Nov1403 BushCiampi.html.

49. Patrice Claude, "'Foreign Forces Must Leave Iraq as Soon as Possible,' Declares the Head of the Shiite Alliance," *Le Monde,* March 8, 2005.

50. Patrick J. McDonnell, "Key Sunni Arab Group Predicates Its Participation on Troops' Leaving," *Los Angeles Times,* February 16, 2005; Robert F. Worth, "Sunni Leader Insists on Timetable for U.S. Withdrawal," *New York Times,* March 29, 2005; Adrian Blomfield, "Sunnis Hold First Full Talks with New Iraqi Coalition," *Telegraph,* March 29, 2005.

51 . "82 Iraqi MPs Demand Occupation Pullout," *Turkish Weekly,* June 19, 2005.

52. For a severe critique of the idea, see W. Andrew Terrill and Conrad C. Crane, "Precedents, Variables, and Options in Planning a U.S. Military Disengagement Strategy from Iraq" (Carlisle, PA: Strategic Studies Institute, October 2005).

53. For deeper discussion of the U.S. Army's balance between political and military priorities, see Nigel Aylwin-Foster, "Changing the Army for Counterinsurgency Operations," *Military Review,* November–December 2005, 2–15. For more on the attitudes of Sunni Arabs, see Carl Conetta, "Vicious Circle: The Dynamics of Occupation and Resistance in Iraq," Project on Defense Alternatives *Research Monograph #10,* May 18, 2005.

54. Department of State Office of Research poll, November 24, 2004.

55. For more insight into Sunni Arab politics during this period, see the film *My Country, My Country,* 2006.

56. See Diamond, "What Went Wrong in Iraq?"

57. For a discussion of the electoral choices made by the UN's Carina Perelli in conjunction with occupation leaders, see Steven R. Weisman, "U.S. Is Haunted by Initial Plan for Iraq Voting," *New York Times,* January 9, 2005.

58 . "Iraqi PM Orders Probe into Arrest of Sunni Leader," *Reuters,* May 30, 2005.

59 . "U.S. Troops Raid Sunni Clerics' Iraq Office," *Reuters,* January 8, 2006.

60. Widely reported, this quote is from Fox News, October 22, 2003, http://www.fox news.com/story/0,2933,100917,00.html.

Chapter 7

1. Komer's report was just one piece of mandatory preparatory counterinsurgency reading that Colonel William Hix, MNF-I's strategy chief, required sponsors to e-mail to their incoming replacements.

2. Robert W. Komer, *Bureaucracy Does Its Thing: Institutional Constraints on U.S.-GVN Performance in Vietnam,* R-967-ARPA (Santa Monica, CA: RAND, 1972), 151.

3. The complexity implied here is created by the number of competing formal and informal centers of political authority—both internal and external, the capacity or lack there of in the indigenous partner government, and the degree to which the centrifugal forces long held in check by the Ba'athist regime began renting at the fabric of Iraqi society.

4. This implies a unitary structure for political–military–economic "command and control" with a broad mandate to employ the various instruments of power in their proper sequence and combination.

5. Iraq Election Profile, IFES Election Guide, http://www.electionguide.org/election.php?ID=72 (accessed June 24, 2006).

6. See the TAL online at http://www.constitution.org/cons/iraq/TAL.html (accessed July 20, 2006).

7. Valentinas Mite, "Iraq: Assembly Holds First Session, Without Government Deal," RadioFreeEurope/RadioLiberty, March 16, 2005, http://www.rferl.org/featuresarticle/2005/3/880588FF-9AA3-4DF7-89EC-5B55F35F6E0C.html (accessed June 10, 2006).

8. Kamran al-Karadaghi, "Al-Ja'afari Premier Credentials Questioned," *Iraqi Crisis Report,* no. 118, March 23, 2005, http://www.iwpr.net/?p=icr&s=f&o=244880&apc_state=heniicr2005 (accessed June 10, 2006).

9 . "New Iraqi Leaders Take Office, Name Prime Minister," RadioFreeEurope/Radio Liberty, April 7, 2005, http://www.rferl.org/featuresarticle/2005/4/1D3B5FC5-1943-4411-B2C9-FF1A7FB09AB4.html (accessed June 15, 2006).

10. al-Karadaghi, "Al-Ja'afari Premier Credentials Questioned," (accessed June 15, 2006).

11 . Iraq: Parliament Approves Key Cabinet Posts, But Gaps Remain," RadioFreeEurope/RadioLiberty, May 9, 2005, http://www.rferl.org/featuresarticle/2005/5/BDB8A9B3-EA2C-4C47-AD51-A6028F2E00CA.html (accessed 10 June, 2006). See also http://middleeastreference.org.uk/iraqministers.html.

12. Worldwide Guide to Women in Leadership, http://www.guide2womenleaders.com/Iraq.htm (accessed June 10, 2006).

13. Kathleen Ridolfo, "Choice of Iraqi Parliament Speaker Reveals Sunni Discord," *RFE/RL Reports: Iraq Report* 8, no. 13 (April 8, 2005), http://www.rferl.org/reports/iraq-report/2005/04/13-080405.asp (accessed June 10, 2006).

14. See, for example, Valentinas Mite, "Iraq: Sunni Representation Bedevils New Government," May 4, 2005, http://www.rferl.org/featuresarticle/2005/05/6d87e270-b342-4596-8777-dfbc31610998.html (accessed June 10, 2006) and Kathleen Ridolfo, "Iraq's Transitional Cabinet Announced After Weeks of Political Wrangling," *RFE/RL Reports: Iraq Report* 8, no. 14 (May 2, 2005), http://www.rferl.org/reports/iraq-report/2005/05/14-020505.asp (accessed June 10, 2006).

15. See interview with SCIRI representative in Sharon Otterman, "Iraq: Drafting the Constitution," April 27, 2005. Originally written for Council of Foreign Relations and posted at www.cfr.org. Superseded at cfr.org and posted at http://www.kurdistanreferendum.org/viewhome.asp?Events.ID=261 (accessed August 9, 2006).

16. Interview with UNAMI staffers, U.S. Embassy, Baghdad, early February 2005.

17. See, for example, Dawood Salman, "Some Sunni Parties Regret Boycott," *Iraqi Crisis Report,* no. 113 (February 18, 2005), http://www.iwpr.net/?p=icr&s=f&o=244946& apc_state=heniicr2005 (accessed June 10, 2006) and Valentinas Mite, "Iraq: Sunnis Seek Greater Political Participation," May 23, 2005, http://www.rferl.org/features article/2005/5/0CD9D90A-01D4-490A-8827-F5FAF8FDB97A.html (accessed June 10, 2006).

18 . "Annan Announces Iraqi Request for UN Assistance on Drafting Constitution," May 31, 2005, http://www.un.org/apps/news/story.asp?NewsID=14446&Cr=Iraq&Cr1= (accessed June 12, 2006).

19. International Crisis Group, "Iraq: Don't Rush the Constitution," *Middle East Report,* no. 42 (June 8, 2005), http://www.crisisgroup.org/home/index.cfm?id=3506&l=1 (accessed June 10, 2006).

20 . "Iraq: Sunnis Want Greater Role in Drafting Constitution," RadioFreeEurope/ RadioLiberty, June 8, 2005, http://www.rferl.org/featuresarticle/2005/6/D3184419-6533-4289-8F2F-A1702C0ADA66.html (accessed June 10, 2006).

21. Constitutional Drafting Committee member Baha al-Araji quoted in Zaineb Naji's "Constitutional Process 'On Track,'" *Iraqi Crisis Report,* no. 130 (June 28, 2005), http:// www.iwpr.net/?p=icr&s=f&o=244717&apc_state=heniicr2005 (accessed June 10, 2006).

22. See Zaineb Naji, "Constitutional Process 'On Track,'" http://www.iwpr.net/? p=icr&s=f&o=244717&apc_state=heniicr2005 (accessed June 12, 2006) and "Unmaking Iraq: A Constitutional Process Gone Awry," International Crisis Group Policy Briefing, Middle East Briefing no. 19 (September 26, 2005), http://www.crisisgroup.org/home/ index.cfm?id=3703&l=1 (accessed June 12, 2006).

23 . "Unmaking Iraq: A Constitutional Process Gone Awry," http://www.crisisgroup.org/ home/index.cfm?id=3703&l=1 (accessed June 10, 2006).

24. Charles Recknagel, "Iraq: Major Sunni Arab Party Endorses Draft Constitution," RadioFreeEurope/RadioLiberty, October 12, 2005, http://www.rferl.org/featuresarticle/ 2005/10/F97D7940-CEF8-4067-9901-BB40996A4BF3.html (accessed June 10, 2006).

25. An English version of the constitution can be found at http://www.msnbc.msn.com/id/ 9719734 (accessed August 9, 2006).

26 . "Iraq Approves Constitution," RadioFreeEurope/RadioLiberty, October 26, 2005, http://www.rferl.org/featuresarticle/2005/10/8A1D15C0-1DB0-4427-ACBB-9C389F243A23.html (accessed June 10, 2006).

27. The Iraqi Transitional Government was the government that was assembled as a result of the January 2005 elections. It replaced the Interim Iraqi Government that was appointed by the CPA in June 2004 as its sovereign replacement.

28. Sovereignty, according to some, meant that the Iraqis must know failure before they could succeed. Yet this implies that learning alone was necessary. In the post-sovereignty period, Iraq's problems were both issues of experience and capacity.

29 . "President Holds Press Conference," Office of the Press Secretary, The White House, February 17, 2005, http://www.whitehouse.gov/news/releases/2005/02/20050217-2.html (accessed June 12, 2006).

30. See Robert W. Komer, *Needed: Preparation for Coalition War,* RAND P-5707 (Santa Monica, CA: RAND, 1976).

31. Lionel Beehner, "Update: The 'Coalition of the Willing' in Iraq," Council on Foreign Relations, December 5, 2005, http://www.cfr.org/publication/9340/update.html#6 (accessed June 12, 2006).

32. For a similar argument and other objections to coalition warfare, see Patricia Weitsman, "The High Price of Friendship," *New York Times,* August 31, 2006, http://www.nytimes.com/2006/08/31/opinion/31weitsman.html (accessed August 31, 2006).

33. James Dobbins and others, *America's Role In Nation-Building: From Germany to Iraq* (Santa Monica, CA: RAND, 2003), 195.

34. Komer, *Bureaucracy Does Its Thing,* 61.

35. The military attempted to correct this problem with ex post facto strategy adjustments in documents published in 2005 such as *The National Defense Strategy, DoD Directive 3000.05,* and the *Quadrennial Defense Review Report.* DoD Directive 3000.05 is the most forthright in this regard. It states, "Stability operations are a core U.S. military mission that the Department of Defense shall be prepared to conduct and support. They shall be given priority comparable to combat operations and be explicitly addressed and integrated across all DoD activities including doctrine, organizations, training, education, exercises, material, leadership, personnel, facilities, and planning. . . . Stability operations are conducted to help establish order. . . . The immediate goal often is to provide the local populace with security, restore essential services, and meet humanitarian needs. The long-term goal is to help develop indigenous capacity for securing essential services, a viable market economy, rule of law, democratic institutions, and a robust civil society." See Department of Defense Directive Number 3000.05, November 28, 2005, paragraphs 4.1 and 4.2.

36. Robert Orr observes, "The United States has undertaken nation-building efforts outside its borders for over a century. In general historical terms, there have been five eras of nation-building efforts: the era of quasi-imperialism in the Philippines and throughout the Caribbean and Central America. . .; the post-World war II occupations of Japan, Germany, Italy, and Austria, as well as virtual protectorates in the republic of Korea and the Republic of China. . .; Cold War counterinsurgency, as epitomized by U.S. efforts in Vietnam; post-Cold war "humanitarian intervention" in the 1990s; and finally, post 9-11 interventions under a shadow of global terrorism and weapons of mass destruction, as epitomized by U.S. efforts in Afghanistan and Iraq." Noteworthy is the distinctively military lead in most, if not all, of these efforts. See Robert C. Orr, "The United States as Nation Builder," in *Winning the Peace: An American Strategy for Post-Conflict Reconstruction*, ed. Robert C. Orr (Washington D.C.: Center for Strategic and International Studies, 2004), 4.

37. See, for example, United States Commission on National Security/21st Century, Road Map for National Security: Imperative for Change, The Phase III Report of the U.S. Commission on National Security/21st Century, January 31, 2001, http://www.fas.org/irp/threat/nssg.pdf; The National Intelligence Council, Global Trends 2015: A Dialogue About the Future With Non-Government Experts, December 2000, http://www.dni.gov/nic/PDF_GIF_global/globaltrend2015.pdf; and The National Intelligence Council, Global Trends 2010, November 1997, http://www.dni.gov/nic/special_globaltrends2010.html#newconcept. None of these anticipated American involvement in irregular conflicts on the scale of Iraq. All, however, anticipated that irregular intrastate conflicts would be increasingly important to U.S. national security interests and thus by implication require expanded capabilities and competencies for conflicts that were similar in character to Iraq. For example, the Road Map for National Security stated in 2001, "This commission believes the United States should maintain full capabilities of the kind it now possesses to prevail against the possible emergence of a theater-level opponent. The United States, however, must further improve its ability to deal with small to medium violent conflicts. . .as well as long-term stability operations in tense post-conflict scenarios" (p. 76). The National Intelligence Council observed in 2000, "Through 2015, internal conflicts will pose the most frequent threat to stability around the

world. . . . Many internal conflicts. . .will continue to be vicious, long-lasting and difficult to terminate" (p. 49). Finally, four years earlier, the National Intelligence Council observed, "The structure of international relations has been based primarily on relations between states, not developments within them. . . . This has been the hallmark of the international system that emerged at the end of World War II and the environment within which the United States has become the global superpower. That system is drawing to an end." The Council argues that three changes in the international system "will render traditional approaches insufficient." Two of them provide harbingers for American involvement in post-conflict Iraq: The first that most conflicts are increasingly internal in character and the second that "some states will fail to meet the basic requirements that bind citizens to their government" and thus, may require outside intervention to offset catastrophe.

38. See John Arquilla and David Ronfeldt, *The Advent of Netwar* (Santa Monica, CA: RAND, 1996). The physical insurgent conflict in Iraq fits Arquilla and Ronfeldt's definition of netwar. They define netwar as "an emerging mode of conflict (and crime) at societal levels, involving measures short of war, in which protagonists use—indeed, depend on using—network forms of organization, doctrine, strategy, and communication. These protagonists generally consist of dispersed, often small groups who agree to communicate, coordinate, and act in an internetted manner, often without precise leadership or headquarters" (p. 5). They conclude, "Today, those who want to defend against netwar will increasingly have to adopt weapons, strategies, and organizational designs like those of their adversaries. . . . For U.S. policy. . .counternetwar will require very effective interagency operations which by their nature involved network structures" (p. 82).

39. Komer, *Bureaucracy Does Its Thing*, 76.

40. Ibid., 75–76.

41. George Packer, *The Assassin's Gate: America in Iraq* (New York: Farrar, Straus, and Giroux, 2005), 443.

42. See Max Boot, *Savage Wars of Peace: Small Wars and the Rise of American Power* (New York: Basic Books, 2002). Boot observes on p. 287, "For the American armed forces, Vietnam would be the ultimate test of their ability to fight this kind of unconventional conflict. Their failure to rise to the challenge would have profound consequences for U.S. military policy in the decades to come." Boot later concludes on p. 318, "Much of the army, indeed much of the U.S. armed forces, drew a curious lesson from Vietnam. Instead of concluding that they should employ better strategy and tactics in fighting small wars, they concluded, a la Jomini, that they should avoid fighting them altogether."

43. Dennis J. Duncanson, *Government and Revolution in Vietnam* (New York: Oxford University Press, 1968), 281. Quoted in Komer, *Bureaucracy Does Its Thing*, 27.

44. John A. Nagl, *Counterinsurgency Lessons from Malaya and Vietnam: Learning to Eat Soup with a Knife* (West Port, CT: Praeger, 2002), 87.

45. In the Spring and Summer of 2005, a number of joint planning efforts—led by headquarters MNF-I—were undertaken to address specific challenges (strategic cities, Anbar Province, Provincial Support Teams initiative, etc.). In each case, there was effective working-level synchronization and comity among various agencies but this did not represent a systemic realignment of U.S. and Coalition efforts in Iraq under the control of a single, effective political–military–economic "chain of command."

46. Packer, *The Assassin's Gate*, 443.

47. T. E. Lawrence, Twenty-Seven Articles, *Arab Bulletin*, August 20, 1917, http://www.telawrence.net/telawrencenet/works/articles_essays/1917_twenty-seven_articles.htm (accessed July 20, 2006).

48. George W. Bush, *President Addresses the Nation, Discusses Iraq, War on Terror,* White House News Release, June 28, 2005, http://www.whitehouse.gov/news/releases/2005/06/print/20050628-7.html (accessed July 13, 2006).

49. Steven Donald Smith, *Rumsfeld Notes Terrorists' Failures, Gives QDR Preview,* Armed Forces Information Service, February 1, 2006, http://www.defenselink.mil/news/Feb2006/20060201_4075.html (accessed June 10, 2006).

50. See Stephen Biddle, "Seeing Baghdad, Thinking Saigon." *Foreign Affairs* 85, no. 2 (March–April 2006). Biddle argues that the instability in Iraq is largely driven by an ethno-sectarian security dilemma and thus a low-level "communal civil war" where the obvious domination of one sectarian constituency by another is fueling increased escalation in tension and violence. These conditions were increasingly apparent to the authors. In this environment, indications of macro-political and security success may mask more troubling developments at the grass roots level.

51. Samuel P. Huntington, *Political Order in Changing Societies* (New Haven, CT: Yale University Press, 1968), 7.

52. See Biddle, "Seeing Baghdad, Thinking Saigon." On this point, Biddle observes, "Sunnis are unlikely to welcome protection provided by their ethnic or sectarian rivals; to them, the defense forces look like agents of a hostile occupation.... The creation of powerful Shiite-Kurdish security forces will also reduce the chances of reaching the only serious long-term solution to the country's communal conflict: a compromise based on a constitutional deal with ironclad powersharing arrangements protecting all parties."

53. Komer, *Bureaucracy Does Its Thing,* vi.

Chapter 8

1. A classic account is that of Barbara Tuchman, *The Guns of August* (New York: Bantam, 1976), 98–102.

2. The 2002 National Security Strategy of the United States, under which the United States went to war in Iraq, stated in its introduction that the "United States and Countries cooperating with us must not allow terrorists to develop new home bases. Together, we will seek to deny them sanctuary at every turn." See the National Security Strategy on line at http://www.whitehouse.gov/nsc/nssintro.html.

3. The National Defense Strategy of the United States of America, The Department of Defense, Washington D.C., March 2005, p. 11. Prohibitive cost in this regard should not be read to narrowly account only for fiscal resources. Rather, it is intended to imply lives, money, material, political capital, relationships, etc.

4. See Nathan Freier, Primacy without a Plan?, *Parameters,* Autumn 2006, http://www.carlisle.army.mil/USAWC/PARAMETERS/06autumn/freier.htm, p. 5–14.

5. Joint Publication 5-00.1, *Joint Doctrine for Campaign Planning,* Chairman of the Joint Chiefs of Staff, Washington, D.C., 25 January 2002, p. 16.

6. See JP 5-00.1. Specifically, JP 5-00.1 observes, "Sequencing includes the determination within operations, as well as plans for branches, sequels, and operational pauses...[D]uring execution, the combatant commander should be prepared to change or adjust the sequence for accomplishing principal tasks to exploit vulnerablities (branches), adjust to tempo, or adapt to outcomes (sequels)"; p. II-16.

7. JP 5-00.1, p. 50.

8. The Campaign Progress Review was not released to the public but was briefed to General Casey in December 2004. Its results were guardedly optimistic yet hit hard on the issue of unsupportable assumptions.

9. Personal notes from one of the authors, November 2004.

10. For example, in a State Department Office of Research poll released on 24 November 2004, less than 4 percent of those polled in Baghdad or Baqubah supported attacking Iraqi police, Iraqi government workers, or members of the IIG, while at least 18 percent in both places supported not only killing Americans, but beheading them. While support for attacks on Iraqi institutions was up to 21 percent in Tikrit and Kirkuk, 30 percent in Kirkuk and a remarkable 60 percent in Tikrit supported beheading American soldiers.

11. See Graham Allison and Philip Zelikow, *Essence of Decision: Explaining the Cuban Missile Crisis,* (New York: Longman Press, 1999), especially the chapter on Model 2 "Organizational Behavior," pp. 159–60.

12. Ibid.

13. For example, Kofi Annan, Remarks at "high level meeting on Iraq," New York, 18 September 2006. This also included commentators who had supported the war early on, such as Daniel L. Byman and Kenneth M. Pollack, "What Next?" *Washington Post,* August 20, 2006, B1; Charles Krauthammer, "Iraq: A Civil War We Still Can Win," *Washington Post,* September 8, 2006, A17.

14. See John Steinbrunner, Principles of Global Security, Washington D.C.: Brookings Institution Press, 2000, pp. 133–174. In his chapter titled "Containing Civil Violence," Steinbrunner argues that states and their military institutions have until now "made a sharp distinction between organized forms of warfare conducted by legitimately established military forces and civil violence perpetrated by individuals and illicit organizations" (p. 133). Steinbrunner goes on to observe that the "dominant legacy of the Cold War on the subject of direct international intervention in civil conflict" was that such interventions (especially given U.S. and Soviet experience in Vietnam and Afghanistan, respectively) were "error(s) of policy never again to be repeated" (p. 135). This, according to Steinbunner, left the militaries, governments, and voting populations of major powers both disinclined "to become involved in problems of communal violence and not systematically poised to react to them" (p. 136). Steinbrunner concludes this has occurred at the very time that "there is some as yet unmeasured potential for the problem of communal violence to become substantially more serious...conceivably serious enough to alter the legacy of disengagement" (p. 138). The authors conclude that American experience in Iraq however may reinforce this "legacy of disengagement" at a time when doing so may be most dangerous.

15. See Nathan Freier, The High Cost of Primacy, Online/available at http://www.strategicstudiesinstitute.army.mil/pdffiles/pub682.pdf; The Strategic Studies Institute, U.S. Army War College, October 1, 2005, p. 2.

16. See Stenibrunner, 2000, p. 139–46. Steinbrunner's discussion of the "contagion hypothesis" is instructive.

17. See Robert C. Orr, Chapter 17: An American Strategy for Post-Conflict Reconstruction, in Robert C. Orr's (ed.) Winning the Peace: An American Strategy for Post-Conflict Reconstruction, Washington D.C.: The CSIS Press, 2004, pp. 290–1. Orr argues, "A structured on-going process of matching up a defined set of U.S. national interests with potentially weak and failing states is clearly required. Such an exercise would give U.S. planners a sense of the range of potential challenges that the United States is expected to face in the coming years.

INDEX

About the Editor and Contributors

Major Thomas S. Mowle is an associate professor of political science at the U.S. Air Force Academy. He received his Ph.D. from the Ohio State University. His research focuses on Iraq, trans-Atlantic relations, and foreign policy decision making. He has published *Allies at Odds?: The United States and the European Union* (Palgrave, 2004) and with David H. Sacko *The Unipolar World: An Unbalanced Future* (Palgrave, 2007). He has also published articles in *Survival, International Studies Perspectives, and Political Psychology* and chapters in books on Iraq, Bosnia, Turkish foreign policy, and U.S. arms control policy. He served in the Strategy, Plans, and Assessment Division, Headquarters Multinational Force–Iraq, Baghdad, from August to December 2004.

Larry Diamond is a senior fellow at the Hoover Institution, coeditor of the Journal of Democracy, and codirector of the International Forum for Democratic Studies of the National Endowment for Democracy. He is also a professor of political science and sociology (by courtesy) and coordinator of the Democracy Program of the Center on Democracy, Development, and the Rule of Law at Stanford University. His books include *Squandered Victory: The American Occupation and the Bungled Effort to Bring Democracy to Iraq* (2005) and *Developing Democracy: Toward Consolidation* (1999). In addition, he has edited or coedited twenty-five books on democratic development around the world, including Nigeria, Korea, Greater China, and the Middle East. He has been an advisor to many governmental and nongovernmental organizations, including the U.S. Agency for International Development, and served during the first three months of 2004 as a senior advisor to the Coalition Provisional Authority in Iraq.

Lieutenant Colonel Nathan Freier is an Army strategist and the Director of National Security Affairs at the U.S. Army War College's Strategic Studies Institute. He has served in a variety of strategy development assignments ranging from Headquarters, MNF-I, and the Strategic Plans and Policy Directorate of the Army Staff to the Office of the Undersecretary of Defense for Policy in its Strategy division.

About the Editor and Contributors

Donald "Greg" Rose retired from active duty in 2005. He now teaches history and political science at his alma mater in Bryn Athyn, Pennsylvania, where he completed a B.A. in Religion in 1983. After joining the U.S. Air Force as an intelligence officer, he completed his M.A. in National Security Affairs at the Naval Postgraduate School (1992) and his Ph.D. in Political Science at the University of Pittsburgh (2000). A Middle East specialist, he served as Chief, Asymmetric Threat Analysis Branch at the Special Operations Command Joint Intelligence Center where he worked counterterrorism and counterproliferation issues after 9/11. He also served on the faculties of the U.S. Air Force Special Operations School and the U.S. Air Force Academy in the Department of Political Science. His articles have been published in *Defense Analysis* and *Small Wars and Insurgencies.*

Lieutenant Colonel Tomislav Z. Ruby is the Vice Dean of Education and Curriculum at the Air Command and Staff College in Montgomery, Alabama. A career intelligence officer and military planner, he served as Deputy Chief of Campaign Plans for the Multinational Force–Iraq from September to December 2004. He has served in the United States, Japan, Saudi Arabia, and United Arab Emirates. He earned his B.A. in Humanities from the Air Force Academy and Ph.D. in Political Science from the University of Kentucky.

Kalev I. Sepp is an assistant professor of Defense Analysis at the Naval Postgraduate School in Monterey, California. He took his Ph.D. in American Diplomatic History from Harvard University and earned his Combat Infantryman's Badge as a brigade adviser in the Salvadoran Civil War and as a Special Forces A–Team leader in Panama. He traveled to Afghanistan to cowrite an official study of U.S. Army special operations in the expedition there. He served in Iraq on several occasions as a consultant on intelligence, counterinsurgency, and strategy. He has testified before the U.S. Congress on the training of Iraqi military units and is currently an expert member of the Baker-Hamilton Bipartisan Commission on Iraq. He also holds a M.A. in Military Art and Science from the U.S. Army Command and General Staff College.

William C. Thomas is a lieutenant colonel in the U.S. Air Force with over eighteen years of service. He holds a Ph.D. in public policy from George Mason University and earned his B.A. in economics from the University of Virginia. During 2004–05, he served with the Multinational Security Transition Command–Iraq in Baghdad in the plans and policy division. His Air Force assignments include service as an ICBM operations officer, Associate Professor of Political Science at the U.S. Air Force Academy, and Deputy Director of the Air Force Institute for National Security Studies. He is currently a Southeast Asia policy analyst at the Pentagon.